SURVIVE!

My Fight for Life
in the
High Sierras

Peter DeLeo

Simon & Schuster

New York   London   Toronto   Sydney

SIMON & SCHUSTER
Rockefeller Center
1230 Avenue of the Americas
New York, NY 10020

For information about special discounts for bulk purchases,
please contact Simon & Schuster Special Sales at
1-800-456-6798 or business@simonandschuster.com

Designed by Karolina Harris
Map copyright Jeff Ward
All photos courtesy of the author

Manufactured in the United States of America

10 9 8 7 6 5 4 3 2 1

Library of Congress Cataloging-in-Publication Data
DeLeo, Peter.
Survive! : my fight for life in the High Sierras / Peter DeLeo.
p.   cm.
1. Aircraft accidents—California—Golden Trout Wilderness. 2. Survival after
airplane accidents, shipwrecks, etc. 3. DeLeo, Peter—Travel. 4. Sierra Nevada
(Calif. and Nev.)—Description and travel. I. Title.
TL553.7D45 2005
363.12'4'0979486—dc22   2004059011
ISBN 0-7432-7006-1

Acknowledgments

The writing of this book was made possible through the help of many people. Here are a few: A big thanks to Greg Hauser and Linda Hauser for giving me the miniature cassette recorder the day after I hiked out of the Sierras and for their endless hours of support while I struggled writing the manuscript. To my loving sister, Denise, for her unwavering help to bring the three of us who were on that plane home and for her efforts in supplying material for the book. To Rocco, my brother, for his brotherly love in searching for us while we were missing and for sharing his experience while I wrote the book. Deep thanks that can never be repaid to my dad for never giving up hope while we were missing and for his positive support while writing and publishing this book.

I would also like to thank Stewart Teed, Paul Kenning, Frank DiScala, and George Rose for their support while I was healing after the crash and for reading and rereading the manuscript.

I give thanks to all the Civil Air Patrol members for risking their lives for the three of us. Also, thanks to Captain C. E. Judd of the CAP for sharing the details of his crash landing of his twin-engine Beech while searching for us.

I'd like to thank my agent, James Fitzgerald, for his excitement about the story and my editor at Simon & Schuster, Bob Bender.

For my dad, Rocco John DeLeo Sr., who has inspired me and shown me the meaning of strength and courage through his unconditional love.

In memory of Wave Hatch and Lloyd Matsumoto, my two friends and teachers of life.

To all the Civil Air Patrol members who have flown into the blue skies searching for missing airmen and never returned.

Contents

SURVIVE!

One
The Crash of Maule N5629J

November 27, 1994

J oshua Approach, Maule N5629-Juliet, over," I say.

Both of my passengers, who are wearing headphones, listen in with me. But all we hear is static.

"It's OK, Lloyd," I say. "They can't pick us up with these mountains obstructing our radio transmission. We usually make contact with them around Owens Valley."

I scan the instrument panel. The altimeter reads 12,000 feet above sea level, a safe altitude in this part of California's Sierra Nevada, even though the tallest peaks here rise to heights greater than 14,000 feet. Our airspeed is 145 mph, and our heading, as we fly toward the Inyo Mountains and Death Valley, is 020 degrees. Holding the plane straight, I adjust the elevator trim, a wheel on the floor that helps level the plane in flight, and Maule N5629-Juliet smooths out.

"Boy, it's cold up here," Lloyd mutters through chattering teeth. "But I love it," he adds with an ear-to-ear grin. It's clear by the look on his face that Lloyd Matsumoto, a fifty-seven-year-old drug and alcohol counselor for the city of Long Beach, is having the time of his life. It's his first trip and, captivated by all these awesome views, he is not sure what to photograph first, so he snaps photos at everything he sees.

Cold air is seeping into the cockpit, so I check the exterior air temperature gauge. It reads ten below zero. No wonder I feel chilled. I pull off a glove and zip up my jacket.

Also penetrating the cockpit is the deafening roar of the 235-horsepower engine and the chopping rhythm of the propeller. Fortunately, our headsets muffle most of this extraneous noise and the three of us can communicate easily through the onboard intercom system.

"Which way this time?" asks Waverly "Wave" Hatch from the seat behind me and Lloyd. Unlike Lloyd, Wave is an experienced flyer. He knows that from our present position, we can head over to Yosemite, the Mammoth Mountain Ski Area, or Owens Valley. From Mount Whitney we can fly to Lee Vining, a small airport resting at an elevation of 6802 feet, slightly north of Mammoth on the shores of Mono Lake close to the Nevada state line.

"Why don't we head east and check out Mount Whitney and then go on to Owens Valley?" I suggest.

I scan the skies for other aircraft. Not one in sight. What an extraordinary view. Although Alaska can boast the sixteen highest peaks in the United States, including the 20,320-foot Mount McKinley, California's Mount Whitney, rising to 14,494 feet, is the tallest peak in the lower forty-eight states. Discovered in 1864 by the American geologist Josiah Dwight Whitney, this towering peak rises at the eastern border of Sequoia National Park. Mount Whitney and the surrounding 13,000-foot peaks are magnets for climbers and hikers from all over the world. From the air, one can see the sides of Mount Whitney have been burnished by ancient glaciers that once flowed down to the valleys of the Kern and Owens rivers. These days no glaciers remain, but a ten-foot snow base, from recent snowstorms, now blankets the mountain.

Not more than a hundred miles from the lofty Mount Whitney is the lowest point in the Western Hemisphere, Death Valley, an area the size of Connecticut, and in the summer the hottest spot in North America. Tourists flock to be photographed alongside a sign on the desert floor that reads "BADWATER, 282 feet/66 meters below sea level." At the peak of the summer season, temperatures reach 125 degrees and more.

This remote area is brimming with wildlife. As we fly over the mountains and across the high desert floor, we can spot deer and coyote in the skag brush and in the ravines cut out of the earth by the hard rains that flood the desert floor. Mount Whitney's windswept summit is home to hardy flocks of rosy finches. When they are not looking for handouts from hikers, these tame little brown and pink birds devour the insects that have been blown up the slope from lower elevations or have become trapped in melting ice or frozen on the surface of the snowfields. More visible in and around the lakeshore are the sage grouse, palm warblers, tundra swans, hawks, owls, ducks, Western bluebirds, American pipits, and indigo buntings in an array of sizes and colors. As soon as they hear the roar of the plane over the lake, they flock together in tight formation and their movements suddenly become sharp, erratic, and ungraceful.

The Maule's reflection in Mono Lake below is calming and gives me a sense of inner peace. This is one of the true pleasures of flying. Framing the view are clouds of all shapes and sizes. I scan the instrument panel, paying special attention to our fuel consumption. With a piston-driven engine that has a carburetor instead of fuel injection, the pilot must adjust the fuel and air mixture to achieve maximum engine performance, using the Lean Mixture knob. When the knob is pulled out the fuel is reduced, making the mixture "leaner." Push the knob in and the mixture is enriched. If the flow of fuel is excessive, the engine underperforms, horsepower is reduced, and fuel is consumed unnecessarily.

The plane is equipped with three transparent doors, two up front and one in back. Most people who have flown in the Maule remember the "greenhouse" visibility these three Plexiglas doors provide. To some, the Maule is a flying glass-bottom boat.

What we see all around us is breathtaking. The majestic mountain peaks are covered with freshly fallen snow. The Spanish settlers named the Sierras for Spain's highest mountain range, the Sierra Nevada, which means "snowy range." Here and there, we can see giant sequoias rising a hundred feet or more above the white earth.

I follow the Kern River with its frozen waterfalls and gigantic pillars of ice. Every time I pass here I'm inspired again to take up ice climbing. Then, after I gaze across this staggering wilderness, so rugged and frozen, I'm glad to be flying up here at 12,000 feet where I am able to take the easy way out of this wilderness by a mere turn of the steering yoke. This section of the river is bounded by steep, rocky canyon walls. At the river's edge, huge boulders covered with snow and ice are positioned like sentinels guarding the rapids.

As I assimilate the mountainous landscape, I continually check for a place where I could turn the craft around, or ditch it should that be necessary. It would be a tough crash landing out here in this wilderness. I look for a clearing, a patch of white. Unknown to Lloyd and Wave, whenever I fly, I frequently scan for such a clearing, even though I am confident I'll never need one.

"OK, Wave," I say. "In fifteen minutes I'll switch tanks and start burning fuel from the other wing."

"We're right on schedule," says Wave.

In order to equalize the weight in the wings so that the plane will fly straight and level with little input from the controls, I have to burn off the fuel equally in each wing. This is accomplished by setting a stopwatch at one-hour marks, then switching the fuel petcock from wing to wing.

I am chilled to the bone. "These Maule heaters ain't worth shit," I shout out in frustration to no one in particular. Part of the problem is that the Maule's Plexiglas doors are not adequately sealed to prevent cold air from seeping into the cockpit. Moreover, I'm not adequately dressed for the cold. All I have on is a T-shirt, a hooded sweatshirt, a lightweight double-layer ski jacket, briefs, long johns, jeans, gym socks, and sneakers. Fortunately, I have my Gore-Tex ski gloves and sunglasses to protect my eyes from the intense sun rays. And for sentimental reasons, I have my personal Maule cap, a white baseball cap with a picture of a Maule embroidered on it.

"If you want, we can make that heater work a whole lot better," says Wave. He not only is a skilled pilot and professional aircraft mechanic, but is gifted at making and fixing anything. I yearn for the day when I can fly my Maule through cold country with the luxury of a good heater on board.

It is so cold in the cockpit that each of us exhales thick puffs of vapor with each breath. I pull up my sweatshirt hood. Within moments I feel a bit warmer. By contrast, the prop and engine love the cold. Colder air is denser, and the prop bites it better. I check the clock. It is only 10:25 a.m., an ideal time for mountain flying because the air is still dense, crisp, and cool. In just a few hours, the sun will start to warm the air and thin it out.

No matter the terrain, I always pay attention to the slightest change in atmospheric conditions. Trees swaying in the wind may be a sign of impending updrafts, downdrafts, and turbulence. The winds can grow so strong that they push the plane off course.

Being tossed around as a result of turbulence is an unpleasant experience. A small craft flying through turbulence is akin to a pebble being bounced around in a soda can. Planes have even been ripped apart and violently thrown to the ground. Wings have been torn off by wind shear, causing the plane to spiral helplessly to earth.

I also pay close attention to the color of the ground. Wherever I see a change on the terrain color, I anticipate turbulent air. This is due to the uneven heating and cooling of the earth's surfaces. Rocks, especially dark rocks and asphalt roads, absorb the heat from the sun's rays quickly, while dirt, trees, bushes, and water collect the heat more slowly. It's like when you buy a car. You may love the color black, but you know in the summer it's going to be intensely hot; a white car will reflect the heat, keeping the car cooler. Air masses rising at different rates from different types of terrain is one cause of turbulence.

"On the way back, why don't we go to Santa Barbara for dinner," Wave suggests.

"Great idea," I say and then turn to Lloyd. "You're going to love the setup in Santa Barbara."

Lloyd fiddles with his camera without comment. I can't see whether he's snapping pictures or just playing around. Finally, he asks, "What's in Santa Barbara?"

"When you fly in, a car picks you up and brings you to a restaurant that overlooks the ocean," I say. "Not only do they have great food, but while you are dining, you can watch other planes and helicopters swooping down and taking off. Then, when you're ready to leave, a car picks you up and drops you off at your plane."

Lloyd loves the idea and his excitement registers on his face. Meanwhile, Wave continues filming with his video camera and talking up a storm. As for me, I'm in heaven. I love the mountains. I love the Maule. I love the sound of its roaring engine. And then I begin thinking, Man, I can't wait to fly this thing to Alaska and then around the world.

Anticipating some turbulence, I tighten my seat belt and remind Lloyd and Wave to do so, too. The Maule is equipped with a basic seat belt—one strap goes around the waist and the other across the chest and over the shoulder, very much like an auto seat belt.

"It's real ugly down there," I say. "Not a flat spot to be found. It would be hard even for a helicopter to land."

In general, mountain crashes are fatal. Very few people have lived to talk about the horrifying experience. Many times the planes are never found. It is not uncommon for a wreck to be discovered years later by a hunter or hiker. Since the Maule is able to fly at slow airspeeds, if it were to go down, the impact speed could be reduced, giving the passengers a better chance of surviving the crash.

Unfortunately, the odds do not favor the pilot and those passengers seated up front. They usually die because they are the first to encounter the impact of a crash. The motor, instrument panel, and yoke are apt to crush them so badly that they are not recognizable. Jagged pieces of metal tear through flesh. Vital organs can be punctured. If the victim survives the impact of the crash, he may soon choke to death on his own blood. Rescue teams have made grisly discoveries: fingers, limbs, pieces of flesh in nearby trees. I have thought about what would it be like to survive a crash, pinned in the wreckage, then die as the plane goes up in flames.

Lloyd spots a beautiful peak, and he raises his camera to his eye. I'm concentrating on flying, though I hear Wave say from the back of the plane, "Higher and higher into the high Sierras." It is time for another quick scan of the panel. Suddenly, in the midst of this check—*BAMM!*

We have hit a sudden violent turbulent patch of air. The nose of the Maule is pounded down while the tail end is kicked up. We're cruising at about 145 mph. I quickly back off the throttle to reduce airspeed in an attempt to fly straight and level. Under turbulent conditions, the Maule must operate between 100 and 125 mph, or the plane may suffer severe airframe damage—a twisted fuselage or bent wings. When this happens, the controls can jam, making flying virtually impossible. The plane is being tossed about, and her wings are bowing up and down.

I press the intercom. "Hold on, boys. Lloyd, don't touch the controls."

Fortunately, we are flying at a safe altitude, so we have time to recover. Another gust of turbulence hits us, and I feel weightless in my seat, a condition called *zero gravity*. As soon as I reduce the power, the sound of the engine shifts from a raging roar, with the prop chopping hard and fast, to a quiet motionless idle. The altitude and vertical airspeed indicators show a loss of altitude. I can hear all sorts of stuff being bounced around. I control the yoke with my left hand and with my right I grab hold of the crossbars above me. I'm afraid that if my head hits the metal crossbars hard enough, I will be knocked unconscious. I'm moving the foot pedals that control the rudder, trying to get her straight and level. Airspeed now indicates 115 to 120 mph, which is fine. I quickly scan the terrain for a clearing. The mountains, cliffs, and trees, which were majestic sights just moments ago, are now images of terror, straight from hell.

Finally she becomes straight and level, and I apply power to get her climbing again. The worst seems to be over. I scan the terrain to see how best to turn the craft around. The elevation of the mountains in front of us far exceeds our present altitude. In no time we lost about 3000 feet. There are only two ways out of this mess. Either we climb up and over the mountains or we turn around. If we turn, we are apt to lose altitude and possibly reenter the turbulent patch.

A slow climb at full throttle should put us safely over the mountains, I decide. I head into a steep climb and continue straight ahead. About forty-five seconds later, flying at full throttle, I sense the craft is not climbing fast enough to clear the mountains ahead. Seeing that the manifold pressure is low, I pull the throttle knob out and push it back in quickly, hoping that maybe the carburetor was not fully open. She comes back alive, but I know she is not popping as hard as she should.

"Hold on, guys, we have a problem." There is complete silence in the cockpit. The trees on the slopes ahead appear to be increasing in size.

"Brace yourselves in case we go down," I shout through the intercom just as I spot a few white patches along the way. "The plane ain't going to climb." I am convinced that if I try to turn now, we may go straight into the trees totally out of control. Worse, the craft might stall and crash upside down. If that should happen, we're sure to die.

"Hang on, we're going down! I'm going to try and float her into the trees and scrub some speed off."

We're gliding just above the treetops now. Everything now appears as a streak of blurred images. Instinctively I know I must slow her down and stretch out the flight in order to reach a clearing that I spot just ahead. It isn't much of a clearing—perhaps large enough for a helicopter—but it's our only chance.

Wave and Lloyd are quiet. We're short of the clearing when we make our first contact with the trees. I can hear them loudly stripping off parts of the plane. I try to assess the damage as it happens so that I can countersteer the craft with the remaining controls.

"Hang on! We're not quite there!" The engine roars. I pull

back the yoke to raise the nose. The wings flare, acting like an air brake, slowing her down. I want to make the plane drop through the trees like a helicopter. I hear banging and booming as she brushes the treetops. We're moving as slowly as we can, but I'm being jostled so violently that I can't hold my hand steady enough to find the throttle in order to pull it back and cut the engine; I also can't reach the main circuit switch so that I can kill the power to prevent a fire from flying sparks. It feels like one of the ailerons and one side of the elevator have been destroyed. More parts of the craft are being ripped off. I don't want the wheels to get caught in the trees for fear that we will be yanked down and slammed to the ground.

The seconds rush past. As the Maule keeps striking the tree-tops, I imagine being impaled in my seat by a single branch penetrating the side of the plane. I wonder who's going to get it first. Wave, seated in back, is in the safest position; Lloyd and I are the most vulnerable. With the fuselage and tail of this lightweight Maule sheathed in fabric instead of aluminum, I imagine a tree limb driving through the belly of the craft and pinning my legs or waist, and then tearing my body in half as the plane dives forward.

We have no airspeed. We are about to drop like a rock, a hundred feet or so, into what appears to be a deep gorge.

Suddenly, I hear a monotone voice from over my left shoulder asking, "Am I going to die?" After a slight pause, which seems to stretch forever, a voice coming from my right answers, "No." There is a momentary silence following which I feel like I'm being lifted from the cockpit. For a split second I look down through the plane's cutaway roof and see the three of us hurtling toward death. Each of us is shrouded in dark shadows. The dense shadows in which I am cloaked brighten while those covering Wave lighten just a bit. But Lloyd remains covered in darkness.

Just managing to clear the hundred-foot sequoias, the Maule heads to its final resting place. The roar of the engine is still audible. The plane lurches, throwing me sideways despite my safety belt. I continue flying the craft, determined to wrestle it to a soft impact on the ground. It is our only chance for survival.

I grind my teeth, twist my mouth, and tell myself, Come on, you can do it. Again, as my body is being thrown about, I reach over and try to pull back the throttle. The final roar. And now the final pull of the prop.

I shout, "We're going to hit!"

Two
Escaping the Wreck

November 27

Maule N5629-Juliet, its tail protruding from the white blanket, made it to the clearing and she's now leaning on her left wing, engine, and propeller. The plane is dwarfed by the massive sequoia trees, boulders, and cliffs surrounding it. A frozen stream—runoff from snow that melted during the daylight hours—passes through the clearing. We are at about 8800 feet in a shaded area inside a large ravine. We are in California's Golden Trout Wilderness.

The only witnesses to our disaster are the wildlife that inhabit the vast rugged territory of the Sierra Nevada. There is complete silence. I'm pinned in the cockpit seat. Blood is flowing down my face, some into my eyes, from gashes on my head. I'm trying to focus my right eye. Objects seem to fade in and out and I'm seeing double images, triple images, then double images again. As I try to regain vision with my right eye, I feel like a piece of steel has been driven through my left eye and into my skull. Things again go blurry and everything is gray and meshed together.

I cough and discover I'm having trouble breathing. With each cough, I can taste a fresh warm pool of blood building up in my mouth around my tongue. I try to spit out the blood, but I'm gasping for air. As a result, I swallow some blood and some dribbles from the corner of my mouth.

As I fade in and out of consciousness a voice inside my head tells me, "Don't panic, just relax and think." I'm pinned in by the instrument panel and the steering yoke, which, as it turns out, snapped off after breaking my ribs on the right side. With the instrument panel placing severe pressure on my chest and crushing my ribs, it is virtually impossible for me to move.

That's when I realize my arms and hands are trapped below the instrument panel. The only part on my body I can move is my head and that only with extreme difficulty.

Still in a daze, I'm uncertain how long I have been fading in and out. I become aware again of the complete silence in the craft. As I attempt to focus, everything is still a blur. I try to figure out what's going on, and then I fade out again. I try to talk, but I can't form any words.

Because the craft is resting on its nose and the left wing—my wing side—I'm bearing the full weight of Lloyd, who is leaning on me from the right and pinning me against my door. Lloyd is trapped in the copilot seat. Because of his slightly thicker torso, the instrument panel is crushing him, just short of impaling his chest and puncturing his organs. At the same time, because the tail is sticking straight up, gravity is forcing the three of us to lean forward. That means I'm bearing the full weight of Wave, who is leaning on me from behind and pushing me against what's left of the instrument panel.

I break the silence with a moan of excruciating pain. Then I cough, spitting up blood. I attempt to take a deep breath and find myself gasping. With my lungs barely filled with air, I mutter, "Wave, you with me?" He does not reply.

I can now feel parts of my body that were torn by the metal. While trapped in the seat I slowly take inventory of my body. I can't see my hands or feet because they are concealed by the twisted, demolished instrument panel. I slowly pull my head up and attempt to move my hands and feet to determine whether I am paralyzed, but I fail. Totally exhausted from the effort, my head falls forward. I am convinced that it's only a matter of time before the Maule bursts into flames.

As I slump forward, I smile strangely. I recall a time when I was in love with a special girl. We spent as much time together as two people could. I can still see her walking and smiling; I'm holding her hand as she talks to me and I'm staring into her big beautiful blue eyes. Even though I yearn for her company, I thank God that she's not aboard Maule N5629-Juliet.

"Boy, I loved her."

I try to snap out of this delusion because death seems imminent.

The torturous pain causes me to shudder when breathing. Again, I break the silence with a groan of agony. My mind makes another attempt to power up, and my right eye opens slowly. Once again I try to wiggle my fingers and toes. I can move them, so I know that at least for the short term I will be able to hang in there. My spinal cord is intact and I'm not paralyzed. Then my head slumps forward very slowly, and my eye closes as I try to regain strength.

Again I mutter, "Wave, you with me?"

There's a pause and then Wave painfully replies, "Owww, owww. Yeah, I'm here."

I take a short breath and say, "Lloyd, you with me?"

Another pause and Lloyd gasps for breath. "I'll be OK."

"Wave, get us out of here. I can't move. Lloyd's pinned, too."

"Yeah yeah, give me a minute."

Time passes and yet Wave and Lloyd do not move.

"Wave, get out of the plane!" I say. "It's going to go up in flames!"

"Yeah yeah just a minute."

"Lloyd, you with me?"

Lloyd is still trying to catch his breath. "Yeah, give me a minute. I'll be OK."

But there is no movement in the cockpit. Only when I initiate the conversation do we engage. "Wave, get out of here now!" I demand.

"I can't undo my belt. I'm trying, but it's stuck."

"We don't have much time. Hurry."

Wave says, "I can't get it."

Between coughing and spitting up blood, I manage to say, "OK, you guys, try not to lean on me. I'm going to try and bust out of here."

Suddenly Wave's weight from behind is reduced. But it's very difficult for Lloyd to move because of the severity of his injuries and the angle of the craft. I gently lean my right shoulder and head into him and push slowly to the right to create a gap between us. He drifts back to the left, so I push to the right again as I say, "Hang in there, buddy. I'm going to get us out of here."

I can see Lloyd's face for the first time. He's gasping desperately for air. "I'll be OK," he says. "Give me a minute."

Lloyd's eyes are closed and the upper half of his torso is slumped over. He seems to be concentrating on breathing to stay alive. But he is bleeding from his mouth and choking on his own blood. I am unable to help him even though I want to.

My door is buried in the snow and so badly destroyed that I can't open it. Lloyd and I are pinned. Wave can't get to his belt. And Lloyd appears to have sustained the worst of the injuries. Our only chance for survival is for me to break out of the wreckage.

As I'm trying to build up the strength to make an escape attempt, I begin to smell the forest and feel the cold air on my face. Through my right eye, the only one that works, I can see the blurred vapors of my breath.

The cockpit is no longer silent. Wave is groaning in pain with each breath; and as I slowly turn my head to the right, I see Lloyd coughing and choking.

The pain seems to lessen when I close my eyes. It is so easy just to stay pinned and wait for the plane to burst into flames. I begin to think, Why fight it? It's too hard. Everything will be all right. Then another voice breaks in: "If I die, I'm gonna die trying."

The Maule's two skylights are almost directly above the pilot and copilot seats. These windows allow the pilot and copilot to spot other aircraft flying above, but I am going to use them to escape from the plane. I take a deep breath, then groan and hiss like a trapped animal. I position my head and swing it into the window in an attempt to break it out. The dull pounding pain from battering my skull against the window feels like what I imagine one would experience in trying to break through a car windshield.

I decide to be methodical. I wind up and swing my head again and again, changing the contact points on the window and my head. With each swing I seem to get stronger and more determined and fall into a slow battering rhythm.

Finally, exhausted, I stop and let out a groan. I can hear Wave groaning too, and Lloyd is still gasping. We have to get out.

Suddenly, my groaning becomes more like a raging roar as I resume slamming my head against the skylight window. I know I'm making progress because the window seems to have moved. After a few more swings I notice that there is room between my head and the window. I stop and rest because the next phase will impose severe pain.

I'm trying to inhale deeply, but what feels like broken ribs on my right side prevents me from filling up both lungs. I ask, "Lloyd, you with me? Lloyd?"

There's a long pause. "I'll be OK," he says.

"Wave, you with me?"

"Still can't get to my belt," he says weakly.

Now that I have some clearance to work with I'm ready to make a final attempt to get free. I position my feet on what's left of the control pedals and floor and begin to push with my legs. But that provokes a stab of such intense pain that I immediately stop. My left ankle is broken, I realize.

I take a deep breath to gather up my nerve. Groaning, I push toward the roof window. I'm forced to tilt my head for lack of clearance, but finally I'm able to slip my arms out from the wrecked instrument panel. I slide back down in the seat and groan in agony. My right shoulder feels broken too, and it feels like the rotator cuff is torn. No words can describe the blazing pain.

Yet, as I gasp for air I know I must keep trying. "Hang in there," I tell Lloyd and Wave, "I'm going to break out of here."

With my good leg I push, and this time, with both arms free, I gain some leverage because I can brace myself against the interior of the craft. I slam the window with my head and left shoulder, a hard shot. The window pops out.

As I poke my head, shoulders, and arms through the opening, I'm careful to avoid ripping my flesh on the exposed jagged metal. When I've wriggled half my body out of the aircraft, I stop from pure exhaustion, leaning over so that my stomach and broken ribs rest on the window frame. That produces a fierce howl of pain. I immediately transfer all the pressure off my rib cage to my broken shoulder.

I'm afraid that if I don't protect my ribs, I will puncture my lungs. At least I can use my elbow to support my weight. Finally, I am clear of the window. I slide over to the wing face first and then into the snow.

I slide headfirst, with my left arm extended into the snow. It gets into my jacket, prickling my body with cold. But I'm so tired and in so much pain that I just lie in the cold white blanket.

I know if I get wet this early on, I will be frozen solid once the sun goes down. I maneuver myself back against the Maule. I sit there gasping and groaning with a slight bend in my legs.

Moments later, I make my way to the front of the Maule to inspect the engine compartment for fire. I am struck by the harsh circumstances of our situation. To move merely a couple of feet exhausts me. I lean against the engine compartment, unable to see or smell smoke. I can hear a *tiss, tiss,* the sound of snow melting on the engine. From its steady rate I can tell the engine is still hot, but not red hot. By estimating the air temperature and the "tiss" sound I estimate that I was unconscious for about ten minutes and spent maybe another thirty minutes escaping the wreck.

The left wing is buried in the snow and appears to be lower or at an equal height to the engine. The right wing is in the air, though. That can be a potential hazard from fuel dripping down to the engine or making contact with the exhaust. As I make my way around the craft toward Lloyd's side, I sniff the air for fuel. I figure at these temperatures in another fifteen minutes the engine will be too cold to ignite a fire. I am also concerned about sparks from the main power switch. Killing the main power is the safest action to take in the event of a crash. I'm not sure if I killed the switch, but I'm not going to turn it off now. That might cause sparks and start a fire.

I reach Lloyd and call out to him. He senses my presence and again says, "I'll be OK, give me a minute." This time his speech is weaker. He is so tightly pinned in the aircraft that, in my condition, I can't extricate him by myself. I decide to help Wave first.

I make my way to the backseat door. I keep tripping on snow-covered logs and rocks. I ask Wave if he can get to his belt, and he says no. I tell him we are safe from fire, and we have time. By looking at the backseat, I can tell that it is going to be extremely difficult to reach Wave. The doors are too badly damaged for Wave to escape through them. Perhaps I can reach in through the broken glass door and unclip his belt.

It is going to take time to free Wave, so I tell him to hang on for a while. Since I will have to lie in the snow while trying to reach through the wreck to unclip him, I decide to put on extra clothes. I look in the baggage compartment, where I usually keep a pair of Sorel snow boots and ski bibs, and there they are. "OK, Wave, hang on. I'm going to take off my sneakers and get into my bibs and boots. Then I'll free you, OK?"

"Yeah, yeah. OK."

I can't use my fingers. I can't even make a fist with either hand. I have sustained at least ten deep cuts in each hand. Using my fingers like a fishhook, I drag out the plane cover first. Like a boat cover, the plane cover is wrapped around the plane's front windshield, side windows and sunroof windows to protect them from the sun. Next I spread the cover out on the snow. I reach in and hook one boot at a time, then my bibs. Standing on the cover, I try to kick my left sneaker off without untying the laces. The broken ankle shoots out bolts of pain. Scrunching my eyes closed, I slide the left sneaker off and then the right one. The bibs go on and then the boots. I try to lace them, but I can barely move my fingers. I knot the boot laces as best I can so I won't lose them.

I call to Wave with a painful stutter, "OK, here I come. When I unclip your belt you're going to fall forward, so brace yourself. I don't want you to fall into the instrument panel."

"OK."

I get on my knees and reach with my left arm into the destroyed fuselage. My face is pushed up against the outside of the craft as I reach inside for the buckle like a blind man. I find the belt at last and work my way down to the buckle. I fiddle around with it, but I can't grip anything. I grind my teeth and force my fingers to bend just enough to unhook the buckle. With one pull, the buckle unclips. Wave is free.

"How do I get out of here?" he asks.

"Go out the way I did, through the skylight."

"I can't find the way, help me!"

"OK, wait a minute. Let me go around to the other side of the plane."

"OK."

I stumble through the snow once again, but with the boots and bibs I have more confidence. I climb back on the plane and tell Wave to climb up my arm. I reach in with my left arm. Wave grabs hold of it and uses it like a guide to move through the mangled wreckage. As he gets toward the top, I tell him to be careful not to scrape the jagged metal with his head. I'm in his way, so I slide back off the plane and collapse in the snow.

Wave climbs down from the wreckage and wades through the snow. As he brushes the white powder off his jacket and pants, he tells me he's all right. He thinks he came through with only a couple of bruises. I'm lying in the snow, looking up at him. He says, "*Wow, woo,* that was something. I can't believe we survived a mountain crash."

About fifteen minutes have elapsed since I broke free from the wreck. I struggle to my feet. "Let's get Lloyd out. But before we start, please help me with something."

"What do you need?"

"Pull the steel from my left eye, OK?"

Wave tells me there's not enough light to see, so we move to a spot that is not shaded by trees. Wave removes his gloves and I tilt my head back. Wave says he can't see because of all the blood on my face. For better visibility, we wash the blood off with snow. Then Wave puts his fingers to my face and spreads what remains of my left eyelid and eyebrow.

"I don't see anything," Wave says. "Your eye may still be intact, but your eyelid is torn, and your face and head are starting to swell real bad. You've got cuts and gashes on your face and head, too."

Wave marches through the snow, leading the way to Lloyd's door. I follow in the footprints that I created earlier in the snow. When we reach Lloyd's side, I call out to him. There is no reply, but he is breathing. We try to remove the door, but I have no strength. "Man," Wave says, concerned, "he is pinned badly."

We spend about forty-five minutes trying to extricate Lloyd, without success. We pull on the door; we try to slide the seat back; we even try to break the rails on the seat. What we need is a winch to pull the smashed metal apart or a saw to cut our way through.

Since I no longer have the full use of my hands and fingers, I ask Wave to grab the emergency locator transmitter (ELT). Fortunately, Wave is familiar with the Maule, and he knows it's under the pilot's seat. As a certified airframe and power plant mechanic (A&P), Wave has worked on the Maule and has flown in it often. (In the aviation world, a person can be certified to work solely on the frame of the aircraft, or he can be certified to work only on the engine, the power plant of the aircraft. Wave holds a dual certification, hence he is a certified A&P.)

The ELT, which is the size of a large walkie-talkie, functions by setting off a signal to aircraft flying overhead and passing satellites. After the ELT's external antenna is extended, it must be manually activated in the event that it failed to automatically activate on impact.

If we are to save Lloyd, we must get help quickly. But there is a problem. When we started this flight, we had no set destination, so we did not file a flight plan. That means that two or more days might pass before anybody realizes we are missing. Common sense dictates that we immediately inventory our supplies and work out some sort of survival plan.

We search the rear of the plane to determine what survival gear is aboard. There are two large camping tarps; one side of each tarp is blue and the other side is silver. If we include the plane cover, we have three tarps. We find about twenty feet of rope and three flares. There are a lighter and a knife in the backseat. And in the flight bag we find two Maglites—a large one and a small one. Nine quarts of oil are in the baggage compartment, as are the wheel chocks, which are made of wood and rope. A black canvas tool bag holds assorted tools—vise grips, pliers, screwdrivers, wire cutters, spare spark plugs, and wire. There is a spare tube for the tail wheel and one empty plastic container.

We move to the front of the plane and begin to discuss our options. First, how long would it be before anyone wonders where we are or before it is officially determined that we are missing? Considering that it's Sunday, November 27, around 12:45, we'd be lucky if by Monday afternoon Wave's roommate or my business partner begins asking questions. But I'm a single guy who owns a software company and a part interest in another company. It would not be unusual for me not to contact my partner until late Monday afternoon or even Tuesday, possibly even Wednesday.

My father, who is staying at my house in California, might not act quickly either. Since he is handicapped and doesn't move around very well in snow and ice, he visits me every year when the cold season starts in New England. He might also wait a couple of days before he questions my absence. He might think I went on a trip and want to be respectful of my personal life.

Wave, who works as an A&P at Long Beach Airport, also has a relatively flexible schedule. Chances are that he might not be missed if he failed to show up for work for two or three days. Perhaps, if he failed to return on Sunday night, his roommate might be suspicious. I knew Lloyd lived alone. He might have notified someone about the trip early this morning. But even if he did, how would anyone know where we are? It is quite clear to Wave and me that unless the ELT works, we might be here for a long, long time.

Even if a search for us begins on Tuesday, how would anyone know our exact position? And if we get pounded with more snow, a search-and-rescue effort might be precluded or at least delayed. Here in the center of the Sierra Nevada, about forty-five miles from the closest town, storms can last for a week. At our elevation of about 9000 feet we might also be subjected to cloud cover for days, thereby preventing a rescue.

If the weather breaks and the clouds lift, they may spend time searching a hundred miles to the north of us. Likewise, if the visibility at our elevation is good but it is cloudy at 11,000 feet, the searchers would not be able to clear the mountain passes and this too would prevent them from getting to us.

If we are extremely lucky, a search team might find us and land a helicopter about fifty yards away, but chances of that are slim. Even if they knew where we were but could not fly in, it would take a few days to reach us on snowmobiles and horses, because the snowmobiles would take them only partway in. They would have to hike in the rest of the way and we would all have to hike out.

Lloyd needs medical help immediately in order to save his life, and the chance of that is slim to none. At this time of year, it gets dark in the mountains by 4:15 p.m. In a best-case scenario, we'll be able to set off the ELT, and be rescued on Monday. We both conclude that is very unlikely, and we should be prepared to survive for at least five to seven days. The big question is the weather: will Mother Nature be good to us?

Since the transmission is apt to be greatly reduced if the mountain blocks its signal, Wave and I decide that the ELT should be positioned on or near the peak. Then, at night, it should be brought back down and kept warm to conserve the batteries. The ELT uses only C batteries, and during the day the cold temperatures will steadily weaken them—at night the extreme cold will kill them.

We can make a fire. If a plane flies over, we can signal it by pouring oil on the fire and making black smoke. We can start the fire with the leftover fuel in the fuel lines and from the bottom of the tanks. We can use tarps and pieces of the craft to construct a fort. The Maule, being made of fabric, could insulate us from the ground. It does not conduct the cold as a metal plane would.

The Maule's tail is sticking almost straight up out of the snow. Since the rudder and elevator are not completely mangled and both are free and clear from any trees or rocks, we could remove these two large control surfaces with our limited tools.

Once removed, these surfaces could provide the roof, walls, and floor of a fort. The elevator, being white on top and red on the bottom, can be used for the roof with the red side facing the sky to help searching aircraft spot us. The fabric that covers the fuselage belly and top could be cut and peeled back in large sections and used in conjunction with tree branches to help insulate the fort from the wind.

The horizontal stabilizer could be pried, bent, and beaten until it snaps off. Since it has the same paint scheme as the elevator, it too could help construct the roof with its red side facing the sky. The red engine cowling is made of fiberglass and can be used for portions of the roof and sides.

There is yet another possibility: we could attempt to hike out. But if we both go, Lloyd will be left alone. Plus, if we are on the move, it will be much more difficult for a spotter plane to see us. A red plane or a fort with a red roof in the white snow is much easier to spot than a man in the dense forest.

We know that if we are going to hike out, we must decide soon. We are at peak strength now, but with each passing day, our bodies will weaken and the cold will sap our strength. Our food supply consists of a loaf of fruit bread, a jug of water, a jug of juice, and a couple of apples.

Even if we remain at the wreckage and move about in moderation, we will lose weight in a short time. Our bodies will burn calories rapidly just to maintain sufficient body temperature. If we wait a few days before hiking out, we're apt to be weaker, colder, and probably already fighting hypothermia and frostbite. This would drastically reduce our chances for a successful journey.

What about splitting up? What if one of us stays and the other attempts to hike out? Wave and I agree that this could double our chances for survival. If the ELT fails to send a signal or the mountains are too clouded in, an air search would be delayed. The man who hikes out could carry out the backup plan.

But which way would the hiker follow? Wave and I agree on a route. If the Maule is spotted, whoever remains at the wreckage could then lead the rescue team along the predetermined hiking route. Wave and I believe the best way out of the mountains is to move south and find the Kern River, and then follow the river to Johnsondale. It's a trailer park area and there could be a phone, even though many of the people who live there during the spring and summer will be gone by now. The distance is about forty-five miles as the crow flies.

I look Wave in the eye and say, "I'm sorry—"

Before I can continue he interrupts me. "This is not your fault. There was nothing you could do."

For as long as I have known Wave, he has never once interrupted me or spoken so firmly. I see only one bruise on his forehead. He's wearing the glasses he had on during the flight.

He looks at me. "If you go, can you make it?"

Understanding what Wave is asking, I pause and look down, and then I raise my head slowly. "Yes, but it's not going to happen overnight. It's a long way over difficult terrain, and the snow is deep."

"How long do you think it will take you?"

"I'm pretty badly beaten up and, like I said, Wave, the snow is deep, real deep. If I don't run into any storms, maybe a week, maybe five days."

"Wow. If you go, what do you need to take with you?"

I pause before answering. I consider the items I need by going through a mental checklist: socks, boots, bibs, jacket, gloves, sweatshirt. "I can make it with just the clothes I'm wearing."

"You sure?"

"Yes."

"OK," Wave says.

With the decision made we look at each other, but neither one of us utters a word. I walk over to Lloyd's side of the plane.

"Lloyd, Lloyd."

Lloyd moves his head a little and whispers, "I'll be OK."

I rest my hand on his shoulder. "Lloyd, I'm going for help. Hang in there, buddy." I stare at Lloyd for several moments and then I softly add, "Good-bye, buddy. Good-bye, Lloyd Matsumoto." There is no response. My heart is broken. I want to comfort him, but I am unable to. I feel helpless.

I make my way around the craft and climb partway into the Maule. I pull out the flight bag, and climb back off the left wing. I remove my wallet, which has my driver's license and $295 in cash, and place the license and money in the inner zipper pocket of my jacket. If a hunter, hiker, or fisherman finds my remains, the license will help identify me and provide closure to my family and friends.

I walk over to Wave. I feel proud to have known him. Since the very first time I met him, he has always offered advice in a calm, cool, collected manner. He asks me to repeat my route to him. I repeat, "Go south and find the Kern River and find Johnsondale. Right?"

"Yes," he says. He then restates our plan for the ELT and the oil on the fire to create black smoke, and the ways to make a better camp each day. He also says he will do whatever he can for Lloyd and will keep trying to extricate him from the wreck.

As we embrace, I look straight into his eyes and say, "Wave, if you make a mistake, you die."

Wave nods. "Yes, I know."

I give him a smile. "Take good care of my Maule hat because I'll be back for it."

He grins. "It'll be here."

Three
The Start of the Journey

November 27

I follow the stream, one step at a time. It is a struggle just to put one foot in front of the other. I constantly lose my balance as I pull one leg out of the deep snow to move it forward. I feel as if I am locked in position like a solid concrete statue. It is an enormous task to inhale and supply my left lung with air. When I make the initial check of my progress, I estimate that I have advanced a total of only forty feet.

With great effort I turn my head to the right to catch a final glimpse of Wave and the Maule. Despite all the trees, I can see the top of his head, his gray, windblown hair as he walks toward Lloyd. He appears to be trying to find a way to extricate Lloyd from the wreckage.

My stomach is tied up in knots, and I'm trembling slightly. I begin to wonder whether I can make it. I wait for a response but none is forthcoming. Then, with very little conviction, I nod my head with my eyes closed, seemingly asking for help as I say yes.

As I continue to push on, I use each tree for support. After a while it occurs to me that the snow nearest the trees is much shallower. The branches of the fir trees protect the trunks from the snow. Moving from tree to tree will prevent my feet from getting completely wet and frostbitten, especially because I'm still unable to tie my boots.

Once again, I stop to look back over my shoulder to spot the Maule. But I am so deep in the forest that the ravines, rocks, and trees prevent me from spotting her one last time. I study the footprints I've left in the snow in an attempt to narrow down the direction where the Maule rests. I see my footprints zigging and zagging from tree to tree. Of one thing I am certain. The Maule is gone. She is out of sight.

I set two objectives on this first day of hiking. The first is to try to acclimate to the pain. The other is to reach a south-facing peak. With greater sun exposure, the temperature there can be fifteen degrees warmer.

That's what I must do. It is urgent that I leave this shaded ravine and get to a south peak as soon as possible. The sun will soon set, and I have to dry my boots and clothes before dark. I begin to push myself as much as I can. With each step, my shattered left ankle drives spikes of pain up my leg. At one point I find a walking stick, but I can't use it like an ordinary crutch because, periodically, I must climb over ledges and maneuver along ridges of snow and ice.

Up to now I have moved along a stream heading south. Now I redirect my course to the southwest in order to reach a nearby ridge. If I can scale it, I may be able to escape the cold shadows and be greeted by the warm sun. I am now gasping for air repeatedly, a reminder that time is of the essence. Better to push forward without rest, I tell myself. If I can just make it to a high point on that ridge, where the sun beats down on the rocks, I will be able to dry my things on the heated rocks.

I finally reach the depths of a steep ravine and I know the climb ahead of me is going to be exhausting. The snow is well above my waist, and the trees offer little, if any, relief. If I am to conquer this challenge, I realize that I must carefully pace myself, and stay alert. I settle in a pattern. I hike a few steps with the weight of my body leaning forward and, as I reach a tree, I anchor my body onto it. From time to time, the snow slides beneath me, taking me partially down the ravine. But by moving along the tree line, each time I hit a slippery point and start skid-

Peter DeLeo's Journey

INYO NATIONAL FOREST

395

Kern River

GOLDEN TROUT WILDERNESS

INYO CO. TULARE CO.

Owens Lake

Second night: Overlooking the Kern River & waiting for the stars

Crash area

First night in the cave

Third night in the cave

Fourth night buried under the brush

Fifth night

Jordan Hot Springs

Sixth night atop the mountain

Seventh & eighth nights: Whiteout

Ninth night: The Coffin

Twelfth night: Atop Olancha Peak at 12,123 ft., overlooking the twinkling lights coming from Owens Valley

Four and a half miles across the desert to Highway 395

Thirteenth day: The eastern slope of the Sierras

Olancha Peak, elevation 12,123 ft

The boulder field

Final descent

Monache Meadows

Eleventh night: Shelter in the outhouse

Tenth night: Spotted first search plane. Buried under the brush overlooking Monache Meadows, waiting for candlelight to appear from a cabin

Monache Mountain, elevation 9,410 ft

Kern River

© 2004 Jeffrey L. Ward

0 Miles 2 4 6 8
0 Kilometers 6 8

San Francisco

NEVADA

UTAH

Area of detail

INYO CO.

TULARE CO.

Las Vegas

ARIZONA

CALIFORNIA

Pacific Ocean

Los Angeles

0 Miles 100 200
0 Kilometers 200

ding, I grab on to one of the nearby trees with my left hand. At times when I start sliding and I'm unable to grab a branch I try to entangle my body in the trees, preventing me from tumbling down the ravine. Soon I spot the first rays of sunlight peeking through the trees. But I am still far too low on the peak to take full advantage of the sun. The mountain ridge I am ascending is about 10,000 feet high. I have barely reached the 6500-foot point. Will I be able to reach the top of the mountain ridge before the sun goes down? If I try to climb higher, will the added time the climb will take still allow adequate time to dry my clothes? Or, should I start drying my clothes right here?

I decide to stay put to take advantage of the sunlight for the longest period of time. I can dry my clothes on heated rocks that are no more than 300 feet away. Once I get within arm's length of the rocks, I can feel the heat radiating from them.

I start to remove my jacket—a two-layer-construction type—the way I normally would, but that brings a blast of agonizing pain from my broken ribs and shattered shoulder. The only way I can remove the jacket is to wriggle out of it by slowly shimmying the jacket from side to side. Once it is off, I unzip and separate the two layers and drape them over the rocks.

Exhausted and barely able to stand, I sit down on some soft warm dirt and get ready to remove my boots. My right boot slides off easily. I brace myself as I get ready to ease the left boot over my shattered, swollen ankle. Streaks of pain shoot up my leg. The pain is so excruciating that I abruptly stop, roll over, and let loose with a scream that penetrates the frozen, desolate wilderness.

I pause a few moments, regaining my composure. On the second try, the pain is still so intense that I gasp and grind my teeth. Finally, the boot comes off, leaving me totally debilitated from the effort. Still panting, I remove the liners from the boots and set them on the hottest rocks to dry along with the boots.

The ski bibs slide off quickly. Those I drape over the rock with the least amount of sunlight because they will dry the fastest.

After removing my socks, jeans, and long underwear, I set them out to dry. I'm wearing a pullover sweatshirt. With a fractured right shoulder and a mass of broken ribs, removing this one garment seems to take forever. It is such an agonizing experience that I dread putting the sweatshirt back on after it dries.

I am left in my T-shirt and underwear. Even though I am cold, I remain in the shade. As a boy, I learned that the sun can be your best friend, but you must respect it. It can cause dehydration in a few short hours, especially at higher elevations. A person can probably survive thirty days without food, but will die in just one or two days from dehydration and diarrhea, which remove all the minerals and nutrients from a person's body, leaving it without fuel.

While sitting in the shade I chew on snow, trying to absorb as much water as I can. Having spent most of the day in the shadows, I don't feel dehydrated.

There are three self-examinations that I must still carry out so that I know how hard I can push myself physically. I did one on the trail, when I coughed up spittle and inspected it for blood. I have been coughing up blood the entire day. It increased for a while, then slacked off, but it was always present. Now I must urinate and inspect it for blood, but I am too frightened.

I stand up and brace myself for the worst. As I begin to pee I see that my urine is tinted red. As I continue, I try to gauge if I'll heal under natural conditions, or if I punctured an organ. I'm angry at that thought because I know there is nothing I can do. Even if I have the strength to survive, a punctured organ will drop me in a couple of days. If it is really bad, I will not live to see the morning.

I take a few deep breaths before I start to check my rectum. Then I stop. I don't want to know the answer. Instead, I decide to test my left eye. When I hold snow against it to reduce the swelling, it is extremely painful. Earlier in the day, whenever I took a break, I often placed snow on my left eye. Hiking with only one eye has been very difficult, because my depth perception is impaired. If I encounter some extreme "technical terrain," my reduced depth perception may affect my judgment.

Finally I steel myself for the last test. I use the tips of my fingers on my left hand to feel around my rectum, and I visually inspect my underwear. Unfortunately, I find signs of blood in my underwear and on my fingers. I will have to check myself a couple of times a day to monitor my condition.

I ease myself back down to rest. I turn toward the wreckage, looking for smoke. I wonder what Wave is doing. Has he positioned the ELT on the ridge and started a fire? Has he found a way to extract Lloyd from the wreckage? Is Lloyd still alive?

I think back to when I first met Lloyd Matsumoto in Long Beach during the summer of 1992. At the time I owned a successful software company called HyperSoft Integration Systems. Each afternoon I played pool at a sports bar on the beach, called Yankee Doodle's. It had about thirty full-size professional tables, each equipped with its own TV and a phone from which to order pizza, sandwiches, or beer. I don't drink and I never really ate their food, but Yankee Doodle's was a good place to practice pool.

One afternoon, while I was shooting with my friend Gary, Lloyd approached the table smiling, his stick in hand. He was careful not to disturb us. But before Gary had to leave, he introduced us, and I invited Lloyd for a game.

Lloyd looked the table over and asked, "What do you want to play?"

"Nine-ball, straight pool, eight-ball—any of these is fine with me," I said. He loved nine-ball, so nine-ball it was.

I quickly discovered that Lloyd was an artist at the game. He took his strokes with pride and precision. He held his stick firm and steady. When he shot, only his elbow and forearm moved. It was clear that I was way out of my league and headed for doom.

Lloyd worked his way around the table like a skillful surgeon, strategically sinking each ball as he lined up his next shot. He hadn't even warmed up and he was about to run the rack. Perhaps because he was of Japanese descent, after each shot he smiled humbly.

After we played awhile I told Lloyd I first started playing pool when I was a young boy but never took the game seriously. Now I was ready and eager to learn the game. We played into the night. Once he started to give me some pointers, I realized Lloyd was a person of great integrity and someone I'd be honored to have as a friend.

After several months of Lloyd's tutoring, my game improved. We played pool a couple of times a week. Around Thanksgiving, Christmas, and New Year's, when business was slow for me, we would shoot in the mornings and afternoons. When Yankee Doodle's became overcrowded and smoke-filled, we would leave. At no time did I ever see Lloyd drink or smoke. I learned that he had two sons in their twenties and was separated from his wife. He was making progress in a reconciliation with her.

Around the same time I met Lloyd I was negotiating to purchase a 50 percent interest in a firm called X-ALLOY. The company bought excess high-quality precious-metal welding rods from large aerospace companies, nuclear power plants, and scrap yards and resold them to smaller machine shops and aerospace subcontractors. I had known Kevin Doyle, the owner, since 1984 when he and I shared a house in college. As sole owner since 1991, Kevin was now looking for a partner with some capital and business experience to move the company forward. In June 1992, we shook hands and became partners. X-ALLOY's office was about three-quarters of a mile from Yankee Doodle's. So each day, during lunch, I made my rounds from the HyperSoft office to Yankee Doodle's and then to the X-ALLOY office.

Business at X-ALLOY escalated rapidly. Within six months, we computerized the company's operations and increased sales about 350 percent. With HyperSoft cruising along, too, I was delighted to welcome in New Year's 1993.

■ ■ ■

When I was in the fourth grade, my brother, Rocco, six years my senior, bought a minibike—the ultimate toy. My parents bought a second minibike to be shared by my sister, Denise, and me. Denise rode it so infrequently that essentially it became mine. Rocco and I rode our minibikes just about everywhere. When Rocco began to do things that I was too young for, I became involved in karate. For the next few years, I was totally consumed with minibikes and karate.

Whenever my minibike broke and needed repair, my dad always came to the rescue. He would take it into his shop and either weld it or make special parts for it so it would be more reliable. One day Rocco let me ride his motorcycle in the sand pits next to our house. Although I was too short to touch the ground or the foot pegs, Rocco put me on it, clicked her into second gear, and told me to let the clutch out slowly while I gave it gas.

As I twisted the throttle, he ran alongside to help balance the bike until it was moving. I then sped away, holding on to the handlebars as tightly as I could. As I continued to roll the throttle on, the force from the acceleration caused me to slide back on the seat because I couldn't grip the foot pegs. Several times I cracked the throttle so hard that I slid back on the seat and smacked my nose on the chrome gas cap. At the same time, I kicked up my legs level with the seat, which left my feet dangling out over the rear fender.

I fell in love with the power and acceleration of the motorcycle. When it came time to stop this rocket ship, I would head back to Rocco and, as I approached him, he would run alongside, trying to grab the handlebars so he could control the clutch. Sometimes I had to make a couple of passes before Rocco could get a good, safe grip and help bring me to a stop. Once I experienced the motorcycle's explosive performance, I never returned to my minibike.

As the fall of 1992 approached, my close friend Brad Hazen and I were planning a motorcycle expedition. Starting in Idaho,

Montana, or Wyoming, Brad and I planned to ride our dirt bikes through the rugged Rocky Mountains and then across the border into Canada. We would continue north about a thousand miles and follow the salmon-filled rivers, riding across endless meadows with blooming flowers. At times we planned to ride adjacent to the Canadian railroad tracks, staying on dirt roads and surfacing in small towns only when necessary. Our expedition would last about a month and would finish up in the Brooks Range in Alaska.

Because we were familiar with the types of terrain we would be traversing, we knew the enormous preparation needed to assure a successful expedition. At the end of our planning we were still unable to overcome one daunting problem: how would we get gas to fuel up our motorcycles in the middle of the wilderness?

We scrutinized detailed maps of Canada and spent hours in the library. Based on our calculations, the distances were so far that we would surely run out of gas. Of course, we could take the roads, but we had already done that. This time we wanted to ride in the wilderness and experience the Rockies to the fullest. We reviewed the problem for several weeks. Then one day the proverbial lightbulb lit up in my head. I rushed over to Brad's and announced, "We can bury the gas."

He looked at me, his head half tilted, and laughed. I explained that I could get a pilot's license, buy a bush plane, and map out our planned route with the plane first. After we selected our route, we would fly it, bury the gas, and mark it with the Global Positioning System. We would then mount a GPS to our bikes and head for the predetermined locations. This would be the coolest way to see the Rockies, Canada, and Alaska.

I'd always been fascinated by planes. When I was a boy I flew Cox model airplanes, which had a tiny gas motor up front with a prop and were controlled by holding a connecting string. The plane went around in circles so that I could only control the climb and the descent. I would start the engine, then hand the plane off to my mother, who would hold it while I ran to the controls about twenty feet away. I would shout, "Let it go." It would take off and I would fly the plane.

I bought some flying magazines, scanned the local yellow pages, and started to inquire about the steps involved in getting a pilot's license: how long it takes, where the nearest flying facilities were, the cost, and other considerations. I asked people at the airport in Long Beach about FBOs (fixed base operators), commercial enterprises that offer a number of services, including repairing, renting, and selling private planes and running charters. Many FBOs repair and maintain aircraft for flight schools. After talking to ten different ones, I decided to train at Jack's Aircraft, a facility at the west end of Long Beach Airport.

At that time Jack had three aircraft—two Cessna 152s and one Cessna 172. I met a flight instructor, then began training in March 1993. I flew a couple of times a week and spent numerous hours in ground school.

Almost every day, on my way to play pool during lunch, I visited the hangar. At the end of the day, around 4:30 or 5:00, I would usually make a second visit. One afternoon as I was getting ready to go on a flight, I walked out on the tarmac and observed somebody working on a fifteen-foot wing, set up on a workbench. He was a gray-haired, bespectacled chap who appeared to be in his late forties. I started asking him all sorts of questions about the wing he was repairing. He explained what he was doing and introduced himself as Wave Hatch.

Whenever I went to the hangar, I made a point of stopping by to chat with Wave. He took his work seriously, and it soon became clear to me that he was a gifted craftsman. On a number of occasions I spotted other A&Ps seeking Wave's approval during a project or asking for his advice or help.

Wave was always upbeat, always making jokes, and extremely generous. He also worked at McDonnell Douglas Aircraft and rode motorcycles, so we had a natural bond. He was divorced and had a seven-year-old daughter who lived with his ex-wife. As our friendship grew, I came to realize that the limited time he spent with his daughter concerned him greatly.

By June 1993, I was continuing to work with Lloyd on improving my pool game while learning all about airplanes from Wave. In anticipation of getting my pilot's license, I began looking for a plane to purchase. I narrowed my choices down to four: the Cessna 182, Cessna 180, Cessna 185, and the Maule.

The 182 had conventional landing gear, one wheel in the front and two under the belly. Although the price was within my budget, this configuration would be impractical for the backcountry bush landings that Brad and I were planning. With one wheel up front, the propeller might strike the ground on rough airstrips.

The 180 and 185 Cessnas, otherwise known as STOL tail draggers, are designed for short-field takeoff and landing. With two wheels up front and one wheel under the tail, the plane tends to angle back, creating more clearance between the prop and the ground. They can fly low and slow, and they look like old war birds.

I favored the 185 until I saw the Maule. The M-5 Maule is also an STOL tail dragger, but because it is much lighter, it has a better climb ratio. The construction reminded me of a dune buggy. The roll-cage type design of the fuselage convinced me that it could possibly withstand a controlled crash landing. Compared with the 180 or 185, the Maule has less space in the fuselage for supplies or bicycles. But in better shape and with less accumulated flight time, the plane I was considering was about $25,000 cheaper.

At the end of May I had found a 1978 M-5 Maule with about 1300 hours on it. Private airplanes are required to go through an annual inspection. The plane is rigorously checked for cracks, corrosion, cable wear, and engine performance. The aircraft must also comply with what is known as ADs (airworthy directives)— changes or updates that must be performed on the aircraft as required by a directive from the Federal Aviation Administration.

The FAA is the police of the sky. When conducting an "annual," as these inspections are known, the A&P work from a checklist and go through it line by line. Because each aircraft model generally has a different configuration, checklists vary from model to model. The aircraft owner is given a list of modifications

and repairs that must be made in order to make the aircraft airworthy again.

I purchased Maule N5629J on June 28, 1993, shortly after it
passed its annual. For a tail dragger with over 200 horsepower,
such as my Maule, the FAA requires the pilot to train and obtain
an additional pilot endorsement—a high-performance tail-wheel
endorsement. Along with a pilot license you can get additional
pilot endorsements for floats, skis, and high-performance tail
draggers.

On a Saturday in August I completed my course, passed my
check ride, and received my private pilot license. I had been training in the Maule since I bought it, and on the following Thursday
I received my high-performance tail dragger endorsement.

Wave was eager to see the plane. As soon as I introduced him
to the Maule, they became fast friends. Wave and I started flying
the Maule one or two days during the week for about an hour,
and on the weekends for about five hours. We would fly out to
the California and Arizona deserts and land on dried-up lake beds
to take pictures. We established a route through eight different
lake beds and about five dirt roads that joined them. Using these
areas for practice I continually worked on my bush landing techniques.

Wave and Lloyd had never met until this flight. Now Lloyd's life
is in Wave's hands and I am the backup plan attempting to hike
out of the Sierra wilderness. I look back again in the direction of
the Maule, but I am unable to spot any smoke. Perhaps Wave has
a small fire going solely for warmth while he waits for a plane to
fly overhead. At that point he'll create smoke.

My ski bibs and the inner part of my jacket dry relatively
quickly, so I put them back on while waiting for the rest of my
clothes to dry out. As the sun fades to the west, I keep shifting my
clothes to keep them in the sun for as long as possible.

As I put the rest of my clothes on while they are still slightly damp, I leave my boot liners out to dry until the sun fully disappears behind the mountain. The boot liners are slightly damp but the insides of the boots are still wet. When I insert the liner into the boot, the liner will absorb the moisture, perhaps freezing my feet during the night, when the temperature drops well below zero.

The time has come to search for a place to take cover for the night. The ridge, although ideal during the day when exposed to the sun, could become my burial ground if I remain here at night. I must find a place surrounded by trees that will provide me with branches and pine needles that I can use to build a nest. The trees will protect me from the winds, which at this altitude can rise to 100 mph and drastically lower the air temperature. Should it snow during the night, the trees, branches, and pine needles will insulate me from the cold wet snow. I search until darkness is almost upon me, yet I am unable to find an adequate location. I know that I shouldn't continue looking in the darkness because it is too dangerous. There are cliffs with 300- to 500-foot drop-offs. And the ledges, with melted snow on them, freeze up immediately after the sun disappears, making them extremely hazardous.

At last I spot what appears to be a cave about seventy-five feet away. I climb up to it with extreme caution, fearing that a bear or a mountain lion may be occupying it. The floor of the cave is relatively flat, and part of it is nothing more than ordinary dirt. A lingering gamy odor suggests that a large animal took shelter here within the past few days. There is snow at the exit and the back, where the snow has slid down between the rocks above.

This cave is big enough for several people to fit inside. When I am seated upright, my head is about six inches from a thin layer of ice frozen to the rock ceiling. Although the cave is extremely cold, I'm protected from the winds and it is dry. I slide my battered body from the freezing rocks over to the dirt area. It is also frozen for lack of sunlight, but the dirt floor will not drain the heat out of my body as rapidly as the rocks.

The sun has gone down, and I now wait patiently for my right eye to adjust to the pitch-black darkness. I extend my aching body across the floor. But I discover loose rocks digging into my back and sides. I sit up and try to clear away as many of these rocks as I can. Once I clear a narrow path for my body to rest I place a rock under my head as my pillow.

As I lie there in throbbing pain, I can't help but think of my father, who is alone in my house in Long Beach. Severely paralyzed on his left side and diagnosed with bulbar palsy, he now moves about with the use of a walker. Despite his walker, he has taken several serious falls, striking his head and requiring immediate medical attention. Eating and drinking can also be difficult for him, because food or liquid often become lodged in his throat, causing him to gag. When that occurs, someone must get to him quickly and perform the Heimlich maneuver. Because I don't like to leave him alone, I always make arrangements for someone to stay with him or check up on him several times a day when I travel.

I am hoping that my business partner Kevin Doyle, or his brother Rick, will stop by my house. I have a large two-car garage, half of which is filled with welding rods stored on pallets. When an order is received for the material, Kevin usually sends Rick over to fill the order, after which Rick stops by to chat with my dad. If this routine happens soon and Rick starts asking about my whereabouts, he may realize that something is amiss. Perhaps he will also conclude that my dad should not be left alone. I can only hope for the best.

It is about 5:45 p.m. I can't focus on any thoughts anymore. My body starts to tremble slowly. The rock pillow is making my neck so cold that I remove it and place my head on the frozen ground. The trembling intensifies. I utter, *"Urrrrrrr, urrrrrrr."* My body is trying to generate heat to bring my internal body temperature to a normal level. There is nothing unusual if one's body shivers under control. But my trembling is soon so completely out of control that I am nearly in a state of convulsions.

I slide the boot liners out of the boots about halfway so I can wiggle my toes freely. I have an image of myself becoming help-lessly frozen in this cave, leaving only my right eye to roll around in my skull staring at my motionless carcass. I remember telling Wave earlier, "If you make a mistake, you die." Having been lured into the cave because it was dry and level, I realize now that I may have made a fatal mistake. In only a single hour it has stolen the heat from my body. In the back of my mind, I knew that I should not have gone in.

In the winter, caves are best when there is a fire to heat the rocks or if a tarp, tent, or sleeping bag is available to insulate a person's body from the cold rocks. Otherwise, they are damp and cold, and the rocks will drain body heat. I have nothing but the damp clothes on my back and my wet boots—conditions that rapidly escalate heat loss. Yet I don't want to risk searching for a better location. My options are limited, so I decide to wait out the darkness in the cave.

My body is shaking so vigorously that my legs are kicking while my back and shoulders twist and hop a couple of inches off the ground. This condition comes on so quickly that I don't see it coming. I begin to move my toes around and flex my biceps and abdominal muscles. I start moving my arms at the same time, flexing my quads. I change my breathing to suck air through my nose and exhale through my mouth into my jacket. On each breath I can feel the warm air from my mouth heating my chest.

I begin to do all this in a very slow synchronized rhythmic mo-tion. My body begins to calm down, and when I stop, it remains lying flat on the dirt floor. I have found a solution that will pre-vent me from becoming a human Popsicle. The message of the at-tack is crystal clear: You sleep and you die. I have to tell myself that I can do this for twelve hours straight, no problem. I try to maintain the exercises. But my injuries wear me down.

I doze off, and the shivers and convulsions creep back. Some-how I awake and say, "No! You sleep and you die. Let's go, one, two, three, four. . . ." I count up to a thousand or so. I continue the reps. A few hours elapse; all the while I keep telling myself I can do this for another twelve hours. I'm trying to stay alive for the night, but I know I need to rest and conserve energy. If I have to hike all day and fight subzero conditions all night, I will burn up calories at such a rapid rate that in just a few short days I will have no reserve left.

Back at my house the phone rings several times that night. One of those calls is from my sister, Denise. Since phone calls go through a business voice-mail system, my father cannot screen them at the house. Denise leaves a message asking my dad or me to call her back. The call is never returned.

Four
Starlight, Star Bright

The temperature continues to drop. I am exhausted from fighting the cold.

I am forced to take shorter and shorter breaks. The instant I stop doing the reps, my fingertips and toes go numb. I picture frostbite slowly but surely eating me away from my toes to my feet and ankles, and on up to my knees. I envision my fingers freezing solid like icicle sticks, then turning brittle and shattering into tiny pieces of flesh and bone.

My jacket is still zipped up, overlapping my chin. I continue to inhale as deeply as I can through my nose and exhale forcefully through my mouth, trying to heat my chest cavity. I try to sustain a sense of discipline, but I feel I'm getting an insufficient amount of oxygen. With all my strength I begin to suck harder through my nose, trying to increase the oxygen supply.

I feel like I am suffocating and am desperate to remove my jacket and sweatshirt. With my left hand, I reach up and forcefully unzip my jacket so that my face is fully exposed to the bitter cold. But I am still gasping for air. I pull off my sweatshirt hood.

I sit up, with my knees slightly bent. My breathing slows to a natural rhythm. I hunch forward, my chin sinks down, and I find myself looking at the dirt floor. I nod my head very slowly while closing my right eye, saying yes over and over.

I have just experienced something beyond my understanding, perhaps some type of delusional attack caused by hypothermia. My first thought is, Discipline. I realize that if I am subjected to extreme conditions for extended periods of time, I may crack.

Discipline . . . discipline . . . discipline. Yes, that is the answer. If I can call upon my many years of strict martial arts training, perhaps I can find the willpower to remain focused. I will be forced to fight many demons—both real and imaginary.

Although annoyed at myself for having exposed my head and face to the elements, and breaking the rhythm of inhaling and exhaling that was heating my chest, I smile slightly. I am happy. I realize that to survive, I will have to cast aside my civilized, domesticated ways. I will have to tap into my animal instincts that lie dormant in the center of my inner core.

I pull my sweatshirt hood back over my head and, with my useless fingers, I retie it as best I can. Then I zip up my jacket so that the collar covers my mouth and reaches the bottom of my nose. Slowly, I return to my rhythm of breathing and reps. All that goes through my mind is, Relax! Think logically! Stay calm! Discipline. Focus.

There is a small section of my face that I am unable to protect—my nose and the area that is usually covered by ski goggles. I simply do not have enough clothes to cover my entire face. My lower forehead, nose, and cheeks begin to tingle slightly. Lying down in the cave with my blinded left eye facing the opening to the cave, I begin squinting, making funny faces, and stretching my face muscles trying to stop the tingling.

The sensation finally overwhelms me. I reach up with my left hand and rub my face. As I slide the glove across the scrapes and gashes there, the glove feels wet and slippery. I think, No way.

Suddenly my attention is drawn to this new development. I roll over on my left side so I can see toward the cave entrance with my right eye. Snowflakes are gently blowing into the cave entrance. Greeting the white beast with the highest respect, I begin talking to the flakes as they enter the cave. I try to focus on individual flakes as they gracefully float down to the ground and begin to assemble and interlock, forming a white solid base. Thoughts about the natural purity of each snowflake lead to a darker realization. Though beautiful, they cannot be underestimated. As the snowflakes make contact with unprotected skin, they melt and change into water. While the body melts the frozen flakes, it has to work harder to maintain its core temperature. The ice water can be absorbed into clothes, leading to a frozen carcass in just a few short hours.

The snow flurry lasts for a while, then passes. I continue to maintain my breathing and reps. Several times throughout the night I catch myself rolling onto my left side so that I can see whether it has started to snow again. Several hours pass, and I know soon I will be on the move. The light of day has not yet revealed itself, but the darkness seems less dense. As I observe the change, all of my senses are heightened and my adrenaline starts to pump with excitement. I know I have survived a very long and brutal night.

Although my body is weary and the pain ever present, I am eager to abandon what turned into a refrigerated hell. I crawl to the opening of the cave, look out to the west, but see only darkness covering the mountains.

Once out of the cave, I use my walking stick to help me rise to my feet. Immediately I pick up where my trek left off yesterday. I move cautiously because the pre-dawn darkness makes it difficult for my good eye to focus on the steep, treacherous terrain.

As I begin to traverse the mountain, I immediately realize that the texture of the snow is considerably different than it was yesterday. Now, unless I drive my heels down hard, my boots do not penetrate the snow. The snow is so frozen from the subzero night temperatures that I can break through the frozen surface only about an inch. Each time I drive my left foot down, a sharp, piercing pain shoots up from my swollen, shattered ankle. To mitigate the pain and conserve the destroyed ankle, I just skate my left foot along the surface and I drive my right foot down to get enough traction to keep me from sliding down the mountain.

I am cheered by another sign of progress as well. I have spotted small traces of blood each time I cough, but nowhere near as much as I noticed yesterday. During the ten to twelve hours I was lying in the cave, my system may have had some time to heal. Unfortunately, this proves to be wishful thinking. As I trudge through the snow, I gasp for air and start to cough with greater frequency. After a series of coughing jags, I see that my phlegm is tinged with streaks of red.

Since I now have been coughing up blood for two days, I must check my urine. I procrastinate, because in the back of my mind I don't want to know the result. But finally, reluctantly, I urinate. Much to my surprise, I experience no physical pain. But I grind my teeth while squinting my right eye, and once again the flow of urine transforms the white snow to a golden yellow and then to a darker yellow that is laced with a red bloody tint. All I can think is, This is not good! Still, I have no option but to push on until I drop.

Finally day breaks. In several hours I will be exposed to the direct dehydrating rays of the sun, once it rises above Olancha Peak, some forty-five miles to the east. I need to plot a course that will protect me as I hike.

Having hiked west for about a quarter of a mile, I need to climb high enough to get a bird's-eye view of the surrounding terrain. I especially need to determine what the area to the south is like, where the Kern River snakes its way through the mountains.

Before attempting the vertical climb, I take a short break. The frozen snow has caused my shattered left ankle much more pain because it requires me to dig my heels in for traction. But it's also given me one major advantage: since I don't have to expend the sheer brute strength necessary to wade through waist-deep snow as I did yesterday, I consume less energy.

I soon reach a technical section, requiring mountaineering hardware, at an elevation of about 7000 feet. Before me a wall of rock protrudes from the mountain's southerly face. Almost vertical, it is about 60 feet high and 15 feet wide. Because the sheet faces south and is unobstructed by the trees, it has high sun exposure and the center is clear of snow and ice. Small trees grow out at angles through the cracks and imperfections in the rock's smoky gray surface.

I scan for an alternate route, but all I see are snow-covered jagged cliffs with giant icicles about six feet long hanging from underneath their ledges. Several frozen waterfalls are visible in the distance. In a few areas the snow- and ice-covered terrain is open, but it is extremely steep. Although these open areas look more appealing than the sheet of rock, there are two very important factors that I must consider.

One, these open areas also face south, allowing them to heat up and cool down daily. Second, in winter the Sierra Nevada gets snow on a regular basis. The combination of new snowfall and the heating and cooling of the existing snow and ice base creates unstable layers, making the area a perfect breeding ground for avalanches.

I stand with my stomach flush against the wall. Wearing my tattered gloves, using only my left hand, I feel above me for cracks and imperfections to use to pull myself up. At the same time I shift my feet about, searching with my toes for a place to grip the rock and push upward with my legs.

Progress is slow and tedious. With each repositioning I manage to advance six to eight inches. I try to use only the heel on my left foot because of my shattered ankle. After I cover about twenty feet, I look down. I'm awkwardly clinging to the rock like a spider by only a small portion of my left heel, right toes, and left fingertips.

By pressing with my right toes against a small knob, I'm able to maintain traction and add stability while resting. The circumference of the knob is about the same as the neck on a beer bottle. I stretch my left arm over my head with my fingertips pointed down, pushing against a small crack, which helps to reduce the pressure on my feet. Although my glove serves as a cushion between the deep cuts on my fingers and the fine saw-bladed surface on the tiny crack, it does not allow me to probe the rock and get a feel that instills confidence. My right arm remains at my side, in reserve, waiting patiently for that critical moment to come to my rescue. I know my right shoulder was destroyed, so I will use it sparingly.

I reach a spot just below a small bush growing out of the rock. It is about eighteen inches above my chin and slightly to my right. My left hand is strategically positioned so that I am anchored against the rock. I cannot let go, or I will free-fall over thirty feet onto the rocks below.

I'm in a tough spot, and I need to use that bush. Instead of using my left or right hand to grab it, I stretch my neck and upper torso as far as I can, trying to slide my chin over the root of the bush so I can help pull myself up. But the effort is useless. Even after I am fully extended, I am still about a foot shy of the root.

While holding on securely with my left hand, I search with my left heel and the toes on my right foot for alternate holds. I find new positions slightly higher up on the rock, but they are less secure. Ready for another attempt at the root, I cautiously extend both legs. My traction is minimal. I can feel my toes on my right foot sliding off the rock nipple they're perched on.

Desperately, I press against the rock wall with my chest, hoping that my jacket will create enough friction and allow me to reduce some pressure off my toes. Temporarily stabilized, I can see the base of the bush is still several inches away from my chin, but there are several limbs hanging down near my face.

I close my right eye so I will not puncture it as I move my head toward the wiry mesh of limbs. I then pin one of the limbs against the rock with my left cheek. Systematically, inch by inch, I slide my cheek up the limb toward the base of the bush. With my cheek now firmly gripping the coarse prickly limb, I can slowly push with both legs and capture another four inches. As I fully extend both legs, I can feel my toes on my right foot slipping loose.

With the base of the bush only a tongue's length away, I hook my chin around it and drive my chin down toward my upper chest, securing myself to the base. Although now secure, the prickly base is pressing into my Adam's apple, causing me to choke. I quickly place my left hand on another hold and pull myself up enough to stop from choking. The tricky section has been conquered.

Once I feel secured to the rock and properly balanced, I look south. In the clear sky at a 10:30 position, I see a star. How extra-ordinary! Stars aren't supposed to be visible after the sun has risen. But this star is burning brightly.

It is almond-shaped and positioned with the tapered end pointed downward. An exceedingly bright white light radiates from the outer edges and a diagonal line from the top right to the bottom left burns just as brightly. The two interior halves emit a dimmer light, one having a grayish quality. The inner area appears to be illuminated by the intense light from the outer edges and the diagonal line.

I do not know what to make of this weird star. Terrified, I look down, hoping that it will go away. Moments later it is still there. I feel torn. I want to get closer to it, but at the same time I want to escape its existence. Here I am, atop a mountain, bewildered by what I see, yet trying to remain rational. I can only wonder, What's going on here? Am I the only one who sees this? Is this even possible? Even though I have suffered severe physical trauma, I should not experience delusional attacks. It is still premature for me to experience hallucinations from starvation. Considering that I just scaled a wall and made a number of crucial technical climbing decisions, I believe my mental faculties are intact.

The light remains fixed. I still do not know what it is, but I am convinced it is not a star or a plane or a helicopter. My right eye becomes hazy as tears roll down my right cheek. Holding myself secure with my left hand, I rub my right eye and cheek on my right shoulder to blot my tears. I want to see this bright light with perfectly sharp focus. Still holding on, I lean away from the wall, stretching as far as I can to get closer to the light so that I can talk to it. But as I open my mouth to ask the bright light a question, I stammer.

My right eye is forced to blink repeatedly as I try to open it wider and wider in order to understand this phenomenon. As I gasp for air, my right eye starts to tear again and then I begin weeping. I stretch my neck up and finally gain the courage to talk to this powerful bright white light and ask, "Mom, is that you?"

It takes all the strength I have to utter those four simple words. When I do, I am relieved, but I do not know what to think of all this. I think perhaps my time is up. I have seen the light and they are coming to get me. Then I have another thought: Is it possible that it is some type of guiding light that will be with me throughout this journey? With that, I begin to experience an inner peace.

Heartened, I turn my head back to face the rock and continue to climb. I advance about seven feet upward, still at the same slow pace. After a couple of minutes pass, I want to look up at the light again, but I'm reluctant. Finally, after I reposition myself, I look up and there it is, bright as ever. There is nothing else in the sky. I am not alone.

Filled with a well of inner strength, I now believe I can do anything. I experience what feels like a spiritual orgasm as this feeling flows out and along my veins and arteries. It's a sensation unlike anything I've experienced before. I am convinced that I can climb up the rest of this rock face assured that "they" are not going to let me fall. I'm going to live. I cannot die.

When I reach the most difficult section on the rock face, I work it with authority. I move past the section until I reach a ledge—a great place to rest. I look to the south but the burning light is gone. I cry out for it, I am frightened without it, but it does not reappear. I look to the east and then the west. Nothing. I am alone again.

When I climbed this last section, I came up with several questions to ask the white light. But in trying to work up the courage to face it, I waited far too long. Now it is gone. Many people devote their whole lives to studying and waiting for a spiritual experience like this. In my case, it came, but I did not recognize it. Not only was I frightened, but I failed to greet it with the praise and respect that it deserved. How pathetic. I still feel strong physically, but now I am deeply saddened. I close my good eye and lower my head in disgust.

Five
Crossroad

November 28

The Kern River is clearly visible from my present elevation of about 6500 feet, but I need an even greater view of the vicinity to weigh all my options. I continue to climb, pacing myself by walking a couple of feet, then pausing before going on.

While resting I eat snow in moderation. I want to achieve a maximum liquid intake, but I'm careful not to overindulge and induce hypothermia. My understanding of hypothermia is that drinking cold liquids while the body is exposed to severe cold can lower the body temperature.

Eating the snow in moderation never quenches my thirst, but I know I must be disciplined to survive. My bones are still chilled from spending the night in the cave, and the toes on both feet are burning with the early stages of frostbite. I know what the signs are. When the blood circulation slows enough, the exposed tissue area turns dark blue.

The sun is beating down intensely. While stopping for a break, I notice to my right, ten feet away, a rock about the size of a backpack with no snow on it—a clear indication that it is absorbing the heat from the sun.

In the soil, at the base of this warm rock, the snow has melted. I remove my left glove, and with the fingers of my bare hand, I mix the wet ground in a circular motion to make mud. Once it becomes creamy, I spread it on my face, neck, and ears. This thin coat of mud will act like a sunscreen and will also help prevent dehydration.

Around 11:30 I reach 8500 feet, which provides me with the broadest view yet of the entire Kern River region. From this vantage point, I can devise a feasible plan. But first I must attend to some housekeeping chores. At this high elevation, with the ground already warm and dry, conditions are perfect for drying my clothes.

Only my socks, boots, and T-shirt are wet—my T-shirt from perspiration. After removing the liners from my boots, I place the wet items on top of a large, dark rock to dry. In addition to exposure from the sun the rock gives off radiant heat, which also helps my clothes to dry.

While I wait, I take cover under a gigantic sequoia. At its base is an immense mound of pine needles, which is warm, soft, and dry because of the southern exposure. This natural plush bed made of needles offers my exhausted, battered body a comfortable place to rest. I position myself with my back against another sequoia tree, which has fallen on its side. Right now all I want to do is rest.

As I chew on snow, I scoop up a handful and press it to my left eye to help reduce the swelling. As I feel its cold burn, Lloyd and Wave suddenly come to mind. I recall the plan Wave and I devised—hike south and find the Kern River, then follow it to Johnsondale.

Below me lies the beauty of the Kern River, snaking its way through the deep, treacherous canyon walls of the mountains. The river is flowing with such speed that chunks of snow and ice at its banks are violently captured and whirled into the freezing water. One choice is to follow the course of this raging river. Not only is it warmer at the lower elevation but it will require no navigation. All I have to do is hike down the mountain, then follow the river to civilization. I attribute its rapid flow to the abundant snow that fell during the night, plus the natural runoff from the snow and ice as they melt during the day.

The gorge through which the river flows has no sunlight, only shadows. Obviously, the only time the gorge gets sunlight is high noon.

Within the troposphere, the layer that starts at the earth's surface and extends about an average of seven miles into the sky, there is a term known as *the standard lapse rate,* which means that the temperature drops as altitude rises. The average decrease of temperature is 3.6 degrees Fahrenheit per thousand feet. Since the river is at an elevation three to four thousand feet below my present position, my current elevation is 10–14° F. colder than the river.

I look out to the south, the east, and the west. From my perch, all I can see are snow-covered mountaintops, which seem to go on forever. I feel like a shipwreck survivor who is forced to tread water while looking out across an endless sea of whitecaps.

To the east two mountains converge to form a very small V-shaped valley. A frozen stream within the valley is fed by several runoff streams, including one not far from where the Maule crashed. The valley terminates at the foot of another 9000-foot mountain. My guess is that it would take several days of hiking to reach that mountain from here.

Holding my undivided concentration are several dark spots in this miniature valley. The spots are evenly spaced and appear as a straight dotted line. Because my immediate surroundings are mountainous wilderness, the dotted line is an unnatural pattern and becomes imprinted in my mind.

I turn my attention back to the Kern and ponder some of the problems the river presents. It receives sunlight for only about an hour a day. If I follow it, how would I dry my wet clothes? The noontime sunlight would not be adequate. Also, what if the clouds block the sun during that critical hour?

I consider another factor. Although it is warmer at lower elevations, the snow is wetter and heavier there. In all likelihood I would become soaked while trying to move through slushy snow up to my chest. It would take so much more energy to sludge through the dense wet snow that I would be exhausted and frozen by sundown. In addition, if the mountains received precipitation, the temperature at the lower elevations might rise above 32 degrees Fahrenheit, and I would get drenched from rain.

An alternative would be to hike west and try to reach one of the small towns east of Fresno in the San Joaquin Valley. I could move along south peaks and take advantage of the sun's warmth during the day.

But how would I cross the Kern, the fastest-flowing and largest river in the area? The likelihood of finding a fallen tree spanning the river is highly remote because the force of the river is much too powerful for anything, even a fallen sequoia, to become lodged across its path. Moreover, since people shoot the rapids every spring and summer, the river would probably be free of any obstacles.

A northerly path would take me to Yosemite National Park, but I would be dead, frozen solid, before I even arrived there.

To the east I would have to hike forty to forty-five miles to Highway 395, which connects Los Angeles to Reno and Lake Tahoe. Following an easterly route, I could still move along the south-facing peaks. By staying away from lower, warmer elevations I would not encounter rain or wet snow. At higher elevations, the snow would be dryer and colder and perhaps frozen, as it was this morning. This would allow me to glide across its surface and use less energy, particularly if I started hiking at the crack of dawn and continued until about 11:30 a.m., when the snow usually turns wet and the crust weakens. At that point I could stop, dry my clothes on a peak facing south, and build a shelter for the night.

I revisit the plan I made with Wave to follow the river. If I alter it now, what would I use as a method of navigation? I know from childhood and from my adult reading that when one is lost in the mountains, the most common problem is that the hiker is apt to wander in endless circles. I need an accurate navigation method and a way to double-check myself. I would have to use the stars and the way the snow melts on the peaks to maintain my directional orientation.

That leads me to wonder whether Wave has already been rescued. If so, the search-and-rescue team is going to look for me along the river while I might actually be several peaks over—perhaps fifteen or twenty miles away.

Again, I gaze to the south, overlooking the Kern River. As I study the winding river, suddenly an image appears in my mind of an old wooden coffin, the ones that you see in western movies. The thin wooden top is not fully nailed down yet, and as I look inside the coffin, I see myself lying flat on my back, motionless. A man is starting to drive the last few rusty old nails into the weathered wood, securing the cover. When I look at the man's face, it is me. I am driving the last of the nails into my own coffin.

Deciding which direction to follow—south, east, or west—is critical and will ultimately seal my fate. Recognizing that I have come to a crossroad in this expedition, I decide to stay put, consider the problem overnight, and make my decision in the morning. In the event that I decide to move east or west and if the sky is clear tonight, I will select a star pattern that will remain unforgettable, regardless of the direction it points. The key is that I never forget which way the arrangement of the stars points. By determining one direction, I will be able to figure out the other three.

Again I look east at the V-shaped valley. As I eye the dark spots in the snow, I keep asking myself, What the hell is that? Maybe it's an orchard, with trees planted evenly apart. Or the spots could be the tops of fence posts. If either hunch is right and they are man-made, there could be a phone, shelter, food, clothes, perhaps a way to start a fire. I might possibly find materials that will allow me to build a shelter or construct snowshoes.

With my right eye closed, I take a few deep breaths to clear my mind. I remember the bright white light. Faced with overwhelming obstacles and natural elements that are beyond my control, it is now time for me to make my peace, while I am still strong. I'm afraid if I get really weak or sick, I will become desperate and begin begging, which I don't want. I could fall through the ice of a frozen river and get sucked under, or get buried in an avalanche. Should any of these events occur, I believe that I will not have had the opportunity to properly give thanks and to say my good-byes.

Heck, I can't complain. I'm still strong and I have my wits and I'm not ready to give up. But if it all comes to an end, that's OK. If I'm going to die, can there be a better place than this? I'm surrounded by nature and peace and beauty. I'm not lying in a hospital bed tethered to monitors, being force-fed intravenously while my family and friends stand over my still, discolored, withering body. They don't have to suffer as they stare teary-eyed at my emotionless face, with its bluish gray lips and eyes sunk deep into my skull, while I'm incapable of recognizing them.

In the biting cold my reflections lead me to revive a memory of a time I almost froze to death as a child. My best friend was my dog, Sanjaya. I named him after a friend in school whose family emigrated from India. We'd rescued him from the pound, where he was about to be put to sleep.

Sanjaya had a shiny golden coat, and his personality and charm ruled our house. If I slept over at a friend's house, Sanjaya would go from one friend's house to another looking for me. At each house, he would bark and scratch at the door to see if I was inside. When he found the right house, my friend's parents would awaken my friend and me, tell us that Sanjaya was here, and usually let him in to stay the night.

During the harsh Connecticut winters, when the temperature fell well below zero, everybody preferred to stay indoors. Everybody, that is, except Sanjaya and me. We would head out for adventures, hiking across the backyard in snow that was above my knees. With each step, Sanjaya leaped out of the snow like a kangaroo. We would head down to the snow-covered sand pits, cut through the woods, and go into the apple orchards. We were always alone, although on occasion we encountered my brother, Rocco, returning from hunting.

Rocco took me hunting every season of the year. The winters were especially brutal, because I was always in snow up past my knees. I always seemed to be running just to keep up with him while he walked at a normal pace.

Rocco did the big brother thing. He would catch a fish, hook it securely, and tell me there was nothing at the end of the line. Then he would hand the pole to me and walk away. Suddenly the pole would bend. I heard the reel go *zzzzzz* and I started fighting a fish, believing that I had actually caught it. Soon I was hooking my own fish and learning to shoot a BB gun. Rocco also taught me how to make bows and arrows and slingshots using materials from the forest. Before long, I was teaching my friends how to make them.

My favorite hike with Sanjaya took us to a spot I called the Den, an area filled with large pine trees. The large full branches hung down, almost snapping from the weight of the frozen snow and ice that clung to them. Inside this tree cave I was protected from the wind. I loved that soft, dry, peaceful place. I frequently spotted owls here, and on the way to and from the Den, I often saw deer.

On one of my adventures with Sanjaya, I was crossing a frozen pond when I heard the ice start to crack. The sound echoed as I watched the ice crack the length of the pond. Sanjaya knew what the cracking ice was saying. He started barking as he dug his nails into the ice and headed for the shore. As soon as Sanjaya reached safety, he turned around and stared at me while jumping and barking out of control. Caught in the center of the pond with cracking ice all around me, I spread myself out on all fours, distributing my weight. I wasn't sure which was the safest way to go. But although I moved very slowly, just a couple of inches at a time, the ice continued to sound off. I couldn't isolate the specific area where the noise was coming from or determine how far away from me it was. But the cracking noises grew louder. Finally, at the last second I realized that the cracking noises were directly below me. Suddenly I fell through the ice.

As my head plunged through the icy water, I tried to keep my arms up so I would not lose my fix on the ice hole. If I lost that hole, I would be trapped under the ice. I repositioned myself—my feet now beneath me and my head above the water—and reached out to climb back onto the ice. But it continued to break off, first in large sheets, then in smaller chunks. I heard Sanjaya barking, but I could not see him. I tried to pull myself onto the ice again, but the ice kept breaking. Finally, I got my upper torso up on the ice and slithered along until my legs were out of the water.

There was no time to rest. I had to make it home quickly, about a mile away, or else I would freeze. As I started to walk across the pond, about fifteen feet from the shore, I fell through a second time and went straight down. Again I threw my hands up, a natural reflex, so I would not lose the hole. I tried to climb back on top of the ice, but it continued to break all the way until I reached the shore, where I was finally able to stand up.

I started to jog through the thigh-high snow, repeatedly saying to myself, "Just make it . . . You can do it." As my wet clothes began to freeze, making them inflexible, it was harder for me to run. My hair was completely frozen. Sanjaya ran slightly ahead of me, occasionally turning around to see if I was going to stop. The weight of my freezing, soaking wet clothes tired me out so that, at one point, I wanted to stop and rest. But, again, I told myself, "No! Keep on going."

When I finally reached my house, I banged my head on the front door. As soon as my mother saw my condition, she asked, "Can you make it to the basement door?"

I nodded, walked through the snow, and waited at the basement door. By that time she had grabbed a butcher knife and some other tools and started filling pots with warm water. As soon as she opened the basement door, I stretched out on the concrete floor and she started chopping away at the ice that covered my body. Then she said, "I'll be right back."

She returned with the pots of hot water, which she poured on my boots. The water melted most of the ice. She then cut the laces with the butcher knife and pulled my boots off. Then she poured hot water on the ice that covered the zipper on my jacket. During all of this she kept saying, "Peter Joseph . . . Peter Joseph, what am I going to do with you? You are not going outside anymore . . . no more . . . never." Sanjaya stood by and watched the whole time as my mother raced to get my clothes off.

When I was stripped naked, she covered me with a blanket, helped me up two flights of stairs, and put me in the bathtub. She had already started to fill it with lukewarm water. I was so cold I wanted hot water, but she said no. She explained that my skin was frozen and the hot water would burn it. As my body acclimated to the water temperature, she added more hot water. All the while, she continually adjusted the water and covered my head with towels so I would stay warm. Sanjaya lay on the floor, just four feet away, staring at me and occasionally whimpering.

It was a close call, but now that I look back on it, maybe it was an omen of what was to come. I have to keep my spirits up just as I did as a boy. I pulled through then and with enough determination I can pull through now.

Denise calls my house in Long Beach again, but she receives no return call. She wonders whether I have had to take my father to the hospital. By this time Kevin has also left several voice-mail messages throughout the day wanting to discuss some business matters. My HyperSoft customers are calling—business as usual. Wave's roommate, Jim Hallorine, feels something is amiss; he contacts Wave's ex-wife and tells her Wave went flying on Sunday and never returned. They decide to play it safe by filing a missing-persons report with the Civil Air Patrol.

Expecting the sun to drop below the peaks to the west in a little while, I check my boot liners and socks. They are dry. My boots are still damp, although much drier than they were last night. The time has come to prepare my shelter for the night.

The best place is out in the open so that I can see the stars. I find a relatively dry spot but it's on a steep incline. After gathering thin branches into a pile, I break off some fresh branches from the surrounding pine trees. Needing bark, I strip several large sheets off a nearby fallen sequoia. I position myself so that my feet are locked into the base of a fallen tree so I cannot tumble down the mountain even if I doze off in the middle of the night.

Using only my left hand, I start to cover my feet with the branches, pressing them down while folding and tucking the limbs to insulate my clothes from the freezing air. I continue to interlock the branches up my legs. I place the bark over the top in case it begins to snow or ice up. Then I cover my chest as best I can. Finally, I place a bunch of branches against my face and shoulders. I position my head so I can look straight into the sky. I am not going to blow my chance for celestial navigation.

After the sun has been down for a few hours, while I wait patiently for the stars to start twinkling, I slowly put myself into a deep rhythmic meditation by inhaling through my nose and exhaling through my mouth into my jacket. The clouds are broken at about fifteen hundred feet above the mountain peaks. As they pass overhead, I start to see the stars between the gaps in the clouds. Just when I think I am going to be able to select a pattern, my view is blocked by more clouds. If the cloud cover stays all night, it will be warmer, but I need to get a fix on the stars. The principle behind this is simple. The sun heats the ground during the day and the air masses just above the ground are then heated. Warm air rises because it is lighter and less dense while cold air sinks. The clouds act as a natural barrier, keeping the warm air masses from dissipating, thus keeping the cold air from sinking to ground level.

Finally a big break appears in the cloud cover and I spot a shooting star. I am about to make a wish, but then stop. In all my years I have never used a shooting star to make a wish for myself but always for someone else. If I am doomed, so be it, but I am not going to make a wish for myself. Laughing, I remind myself that I will see plenty of shooting stars in the next few days and have an opportunity to make a wish for myself. So I make a wish for my dad. Then I go on to my more serious task. I spot three stars that point to the east, and right next to them are three others that point to the south. Yahoo! Mission accomplished. If I decide to go east tomorrow, I have a way to guide myself.

In the serenity of the mountain wilderness, my thoughts race furiously as I consider the various routes I could follow. Within hours, the decision I make will determine my fate, and perhaps Wave's and Lloyd's as well. My thoughts shift to the crashed plane and I wonder, Is Wave executing the plan? Is Lloyd still alive? Then my thoughts leap back to how cold it is. I am holding my own, but I remind myself that I dare not fall asleep; if I do, I will die. I keep repeating what has now become my mantra: Discipline, discipline.

I return to the problem at hand. What's it going to be, DeLeo, south, west, or east? The black patches in the snow to the east or a Kern River crossing to the west or following the river to the south, based on the plan I made with Wave. Over and over I run every detail through my mind. Perhaps I am leaving something out, another option. No, I don't think so.

In the silent darkness I hear a noise—a very light noise. Probably a deer. I listen patiently to hear it again. Within moments comes the cracking sound of a huge branch. It can't be a deer—they move too gracefully. And a mountain lion is too swift to snap anything that large. I concentrate on the noise and where it is coming from. Again comes the sound of a branch cracking. Whatever is making those sounds is massive.

I hear snapping branches and trampling sounds as it comes my way. I can't tell if I am downwind and the creature can smell me. I must warn him that I am here, that I am buried under the brush, and prevent him from walking on top of me. Otherwise, I'd be forced to move because of the creature's immense weight stepping on me. This would only scare or harass it, causing it to attack.

It stops in the area where I spread out my clothes to dry. I can hear it breathing and snorting as it picks up my lingering scent on the rocks and trees. It is a bear.

It pauses, then fearlessly it heads right for me. Because of its enormous size, I can feel the earth beneath me tremble each time the bear plants one of its powerful paws on the ground. From under the brush I begin to sing lyrics from an old song:

> In the jungle, the mighty jungle,
> The lion sleeps tonight.

I repeat the lines a few times, then I hum the tune. The bear pauses, but does not retreat, so I start singing the only other song for which I can remember the words:

> What the world needs now is love, sweet love,
> That's the only thing that there's just too little of.

I begin to hum the tune a few times. Then I repeat the words, singing as loud as I can.

The sound of the cracking branches stops. As I stop singing to catch my breath, on each adrenaline-charged heart thump I hear my blood pumping in my ears, surging though my head. Intently listening for the bear's next move, I feel like I'm playing cat and mouse. The bear pauses. I believe it senses my presence but does not know what I am.

The food supply is scarce this time of year because of the snow blanketing the mountains, making that bear more curious and aggressive in its search for nourishment. My experience with wildlife has taught me that an animal that is hungry or is protecting its young can be very dangerous and unpredictable. Animals are like many people that I know: hunger makes them agitated and short-tempered.

In the Sierra Nevada black bears do not hibernate during the winter, although they do remain dormant. Their movements are slower and less frequent. During the past winter I flew over the California Sierras many times. On some of these flights I spotted black bears in the open snow-covered terrain. Many times from the air I've seen large quantities of dark stool lying on top of the clean white snow. Along with the stool I could see a bear's tracks leading away. I would make a couple of passes to see if

I could spot its large dark furry body against the bright snow.

Doing some research on them, I learned that while their hair varies in color from white through blond, cinnamon brown, and chocolate brown to black, most black bears are indeed black or a dark shade of brown. They are approximately five to six feet tall, with small eyes and poor eyesight, rounded ears and good hearing, and a keen sense of smell. The black bear, though the smallest bear in North America, still weighs 300–400 pounds. The largest known black bear weighed 802.5 pounds and the oldest recorded was thirty years old.

The silence is broken as the massive creature slowly advances, placing its paws on the ground just a short distance away. I make an imaginary line between me and the bear. If it crosses that line, I must uncover myself from the brush, rise to my feet, and shake my walking stick to show it that I'm in control.

I start to sing again, praying the bear will retreat. After I sing and hum a few bars, the bear approaches even closer. I know black bear attacks are rare, but this animal is hungry and agitated. All I can think of is its forty-two razor-sharp teeth ripping through me.

Black bears have been reported running at speeds up to thirty mph, so I can't outrun it. I would never be able to climb a tree fast enough either, because the black bear's claws allow it to climb trees easily and quickly.

Singing as loud as I can, I try to make the beast redirect its path. The bear smells and hears me, but it's curious about what is making the noise. Black bears in state parks have been known to rip open car doors and pry out windshields to get access to food. Some bears have been seen swimming to island campsites in order to raid the food and supplies.

I have read that playing dead with a black bear is a no-win solution. It will tear through something just to see what it is. If the bear attacks me, I may have to let it bite me a few times, to see if it will stop and move away. If the bear rolls my body over on my back, exposing my stomach, I must protect my vital organs by continuing to roll back over so I'm facing the ground again. If the bear continues to shred me, I must try to fight it with all the strength that I have left.

The bear is still walking toward me very slowly. As it crosses my imaginary line, it pauses. As the creature exhales into the cold wilderness air, I can smell its hot foul breath as the small clouds of dense gamy odor drift toward me. I believe the bear is testing me, seeing how close it can come to me before I try to defend myself.

I'm on the verge of rising to my feet when the bear changes its direction, slowly positioning itself behind me. I can hear it stepping on some snow-covered bushes just a couple of feet from my head. I keep singing, but I'm wondering, What the hell is this thing doing? So far the bear has not attacked; maybe the singing is working.

It stays within a couple of feet the whole time as it completes its circle. Now, with the creature directly behind me, I sing as loud as I can, hoping it will stay away. As I pause to catch my breath, I can hear it stretching its mouth, then chopping its jaws together while swishing its tongue around the outside of its snout.

It starts to move around again, but I'm not sure which direction it's headed. As I sing, I pause and, between breaths, try to identify the bear's direction. Suddenly, a noise that sounds like thunder causes me to nearly jump out of my skin. The bear has just stepped on another large branch, snapping it clean off the tree. I can hear it walking, but I can't taste or smell its breath anymore. Maybe I'm not downwind anymore, or it's retreating.

I stop singing and hear the sound of its paws sinking into the snow as it walks away. With each step the bear takes the sound fades. It's headed north, up the mountain. With the brush still covering me, I cock my head to listen. The last few sounds the bear makes are like those of a deer walking gracefully in the distance.

Six
Needle in a Haystack

November 29

Straining to hear, I heed only the sound of the trees capturing the wind. I'm alone again and I like it. During the encounter with the bear, I failed to do the reps and breathe into my coat to heat my chest. A quick inventory of my feet and hands reveals that my hands are numb, my fingertips are stinging, and my feet are numb from the tiptoes to my ankle bones.

Now that my life is in no immediate danger, I start to breathe rhythmically, exhaling into my jacket, heating my chest. I start to wiggle my toes inside my boots to increase their circulation in hopes of keeping them alive. Soon the numbness in both feet is replaced by a dull, piercing pain. It is so severe that it causes me to arch my back, twist my neck, and grind my teeth all at once.

Just as I stop wiggling them I think, Discipline . . . As long as they hurt, they're alive . . . Yes, keep on moving and squeezing them. I love pain, I can't get enough pain . . .

Late into the bitter cold night I continue to focus on breathing and doing my reps. I continue to flex my abdominal muscles while I try to squeeze my fingers in both hands. As my fingers just touch my palms, I'm relieved. The deep lacerations I got on both my hands when they smashed against the instrument panel in the crash are slowly healing. Now that I can squeeze my fingers to my palms, I know I have a better chance of survival. I will be able to lace up my boots, which will help prevent the snow from seeping down inside them—hence keeping my feet drier. I don't want my feet to be amputated because of frostbite.

After a few hours the moment I have eagerly been waiting for arrives. It is the time before the birds sing and the rooster crows. Darkness shows its first signs of retreat and daybreak starts to conquer the quiet, peaceful, frozen night.

I uncover myself from the brush, lace up my boots, then rise to my feet ready to continue my journey. The surface of the snow is frozen, at its peak strength, allowing me to glide on top of it. Standing on the frozen white crust with my walking stick in my left hand, I look to the east, then south, then west. For the last time I ask myself, Which way is it going to be, DeLeo?

I decide to move along the south peaks and head east to the dark patches in the snow. As I start to hike, I'm haunted by the thought that I'm abandoning the plan I made with Wave. Each step I take I'll be headed farther away from the Kern River, the area where a search team could be looking for me if Wave is rescued. I try to focus on my goal, the dark patches in the snow to the east, so that the nervousness in my stomach will pass.

Although many of the mountains are still covered in shadows, daylight is upon me. I look south at the facing mountain's north side. Sticking out of its snow-covered ridge is a giant rock structure. The formation looks like a knob or knot in a piece of wood. The structure is unique so I am able to take advantage of it in two ways.

First, it allows me to hike in a straight line, but it does not determine my direction. The stars and the way the snow melts on the south peaks will identify north, south, east, and west. As I head east, I will be forced to hike up and down ravines, around cliffs and maneuver through other tricky sections. While I hike, I will slowly lose my imaginary line to the east.

In a dense forest, the trees, cliffs, and rocks all start to look the same. It is extremely difficult to maintain a straight line while hiking without a compass. The only way I know is to choose a point and hike to it. Since I left the compass with Wave in case he decided to move himself, I'm forced to use natural landmarks to maintain a straight line.

My experience has taught me to pick at least two natural landmarks and correlate them. In the best-case scenario the landmarks are in a straight line like dominos and aligned in the direction that you're headed.

In my case, I can see only one good landmark, the natural rock knot on the crest of the mountain. Although this rock is not in my path, I can still use it as a reference point. It will prevent me from wandering too far off my line to the east.

The second advantage that the knot offers me is a way to gauge time. As I continue to hike east, the knot will no longer be to my south but to my southwest, and in a day or so, it will be directly west, behind me, where the sun sets.

As I hike I can estimate the time that it takes for me to change my position relative to the rock structure. If it changes noticeably within a few hours, I know I can take time to rest. If my perspective to the knot remains constant as I hike, I know I'm moving slowly or not at all.

This morning completes the second night and starts the third day of the ordeal. Unknown to Lloyd, Wave, and me, a search-and-rescue mission is under way.

Wave's roommate and ex-wife are aware that he went flying on early Sunday morning and has not yet returned. This raised a high level of concern about his whereabouts. Wave's employer, Cherry Aviation, was contacted yesterday by Wave's roommate and asked if they had seen Wave or Peter's plane, the Maule. The two owners of Cherry Aviation reported that Wave never showed up for work on Monday and never called in sick. They also said that the plane was not tied down out next to the hangar and Peter and Wave never said anything about going on an extended flight.

They increased the concern about our whereabouts when they said they thought Wave and I had planned to do some mountain flying over the Sierra Nevadas to take photos of the fresh snowfall.

Yesterday afternoon, the Civil Air Patrol (CAP), a heroic organization that answers the prayers of downed and distressed flyers, was informed that Maule N5629J had departed Long Beach on Sunday for a one-day photo flight to the mountains but never returned.

The CAP consists of more than sixty thousand members and is active in all fifty states. CAP volunteer pilots fly 85 percent of all inland search-and-rescue (SAR) missions directed by the Air Force Rescue Coordination Center at Langley Air Force Base in Virginia. The organization has eight geographical regions divided into fifty-two wings, one for each state, Puerto Rico, and the District of Columbia. Wings are divided into groups, squadrons, and flights. The ages of CAP pilots range from teenagers, who are the cadets of the CAP, to seasoned vets, who are professional retired adults.

The CAP's services are not solely for fellow flyers. SAR missions are often initiated for campers, hikers, or hunters believed to be lost in the woods, mountains, deserts, swamps, etc.

CAP assists federal and local authorities on many missing-persons missions. Because of CAP's extensive training in large coordinated missions, it usually controls the search and the flow of all information to and from the CAP members doing the search.

The CAP searchers report back to a central location, known as the mission headquarters. If possible, it is established close to the center of the search square, usually at an airport or other facility that has easy access, power, and phones.

Shortly after I received my pilot's license, a few members of the CAP Squadron 150 asked me if I would like to become a member of their wing. My Maule, being a bush plane, was a perfect search and spotter plane. I started going to the local CAP meetings once a week and I learned that CAP does much more than just perform SAR missions. Its services also include disaster relief, humanitarian relief, and counterdrug operations.

When an area is devastated from floods, earthquakes, tornadoes, or hurricanes, CAP is asked to perform disaster relief. CAP volunteers provide support in the form of manpower and leadership, including air and ground transportation, as well as an extensive communications network to local, state, and national disaster relief agencies.

I found the humanitarian relief program especially interesting. I could see that the CAP members took pride and deep satisfaction in their missions to transport time-sensitive medical materials for organizations such as the Red Cross. The CAP's live-organ transport program is credited with saving an average of ten lives every year.

I learned that if I joined, I would have the opportunity to work with the Air Force, the Customs Service, the Forestry Service, and the Drug Enforcement Administration. The CAP's counterdrug operations program provides aerial reconnaissance, airborne communications support, and airlift support of law enforcement personnel in the war on drugs.

When CAP launches a mission, intelligence is gathered, and a stringent paper trail accompanies every step of the mission. The controller's log is kept at the mission headquarters of that particular operation. It tracks date, time, initials of the person who made the entry, and notes on that entry. On a particular day there can be several entries into the log, and they can be grouped together at the same time.

Last night, November 28, 1994, at 11:24 p.m., just thirty-seven hours after the Maule went down, CAP made its first entry into the controller's log for Maule N5629J.

CONTROLLER'S LOG			
DAY	TIME	INIT	
28	2324	JTS	To RANCHO MURIETA FSS (JJ) 916-354-0161. Received ALNOT. OBJECTIVE WAS EST. INTO S. TAHOE, CA. ON THE 27 NOV. DID NOT ARR. WIFE CALLED RANCHO MURIETA. SOMEONE WAS WAITING FOR THE OBJECTIVES @ S. TAHOE. NOT A LOT OF INFO. PILOT DEP. LONG BEACH ENROUTE TO S. TAHOE. NO FLIGHT PLAN THAT HE KNOWS OFF. HAWTHORNE IS THE FSS WE NEED TO TALK TO ABOUT WX CHECKS & FLIGHT PLAN INFO.

CAP knows from past experience that SAR missions in the Sierra Nevadas and the surrounding desert areas usually change to recovery operations, where CAP is looking only for wreckage, no survivors. As the mission status is changed to a recovery operation, CAP scales back its resources and sets an exit date for that mission.

CAP established a mission base at the Bishop airport. This location, just north of California's Inyo National Forest, was selected because the intelligence gathered by the CAP put the Maule somewhere in the Sierra Nevada near Mammoth Mountain, Lake Tahoe, and Yosemite National Park.

Bishop airport is within striking distance of all three of these locations and sits at an elevation of 4120 feet with a runway length of 7498 feet, which can accommodate all CAP aircraft. The airport is approximately eighty-five miles away from both Wave and Lloyd's and my own present position, as the crow flies over snow-covered mountains ranging from 9000 to 14,000 feet in elevation.

As a SAR mission for a missing aircraft gets under way, CAP calculates the maximum distance that plane can fly on a full load of fuel by multiplying the hours of fuel aboard the aircraft by miles per hour it can fly. Then CAP draws a circle around the last known position of the aircraft. The radius of the circle is equal to or greater than the distance the aircraft can fly on full tanks. This is the search containment circle.

When CAP believes it has a search containment circle, it breaks that area into smaller grids. CAP members are assigned grids in teams consisting of at least two members per plane, preferably three, a pilot and two spotters. Each time a search plane takes off for a specified grid, it is counted as a sortie. Only when the aircraft enters the grid does the clock start ticking for that grid. The clock stops ticking as the aircraft exits the assigned grid. A single aircraft can fly several sorties per day.

The CAP now rallies its dedicated members, and the SAR flights begin.

■ ■ ■

I push onward until the sun has risen above the peaks to the east at roughly a 10:30 position in the sky. The snow glare is blinding, so I reach into my jacket pocket and remove the remaining half of my sunglasses. Wearing the mangled right lens, I continue heading east.

Exhausted, too tired to keep my right eye open, I lean against a giant sequoia tree gasping for air. Focusing solely on breathing, I try to inhale deeply through my nose, filling my left lung with oxygen, then pausing just slightly before exhaling through my mouth. After several minutes of this controlled breathing, I have the strength to open my eye again.

About fifteen feet away I spy animal tracks in the snow. I move until I am standing directly over coyote tracks. I can see that two sets of prints are heading east, the same way I'm going. I decide that the coyote knows the easiest, fastest, and flattest trail. The tracks lead to a rocky cliff, however, where I'm forced to climb up and around a stony patch. Midway on the climb I lose my footing. Catching myself before it's too late, I lose my half sunglasses as they slide off my right ear, then off the ledge. As the glasses make contact with some jagged rocks about fifteen feet below, I think, *Shit!* I need that lens. I watch and listen to it go *ting, ting, tong,* shattering into little pieces, twirling through the air like paper confetti hundreds of feet below the cliff.

Discouraged, I follow the coyote's tracks until I reach the top of the cliff. Then I sit down on a fallen tree trunk. Trying to catch my breath, I'm paralyzed by the image of the sunglasses falling, then shattering onto the rocks below me. Without rope and climbing aids, I could just as easily lose a foothold or handhold while scaling a rock face or cliff.

I need the use of my left eye. I remove both gloves to get ready to spread my eyelid apart to see if I can sense any degree of light. I rest my right palm on my left cheek so that my fingertips are holding my bottom eyelid down. With my left thumb I search around the swollen, bloody mass for the remains of my top eyelid. It's difficult to identify because of the scabs, massive swelling, and lack of a mirror. Slowly I begin to push up on what feels like shredded skin and the swollen mass over my left eye. As the crusty dried-out scabs begin to crack, the pain from the tearing of the tissue is too intense for me to continue.

Using my left hand I grab a handful of snow to place against my eye to moisten the scabs, allowing the eyelid to split easier. After holding the snow against my eye and forehead for about fifteen minutes, I decide to try spreading the eyelids again.

As I start spreading my eyelids apart, I press against the swollen mass that overhangs my eye, pushing it partially up out of the way so that light can enter my eye. Even with the gash thoroughly moistened, making it more flexible, I can still feel my eyelids tearing as the wound opens, so I stop again.

My desire to know if my left eye has been destroyed outweighs the pain. I start again. Though bleeding and in wrenching pain, I split the lids and am rewarded with blinding sunlight in my left eye. I can still see. But the process has worn me out.

I peel some large sheets of bark off some fallen trees, and spread them out on top of the snow under a tree. After breaking and cracking the sheets so that they form a crude mattress, I lie down gingerly on it, checking to see if it's insulated from the snow.

Convinced that I'm insulated from the cold, wet snow, I shut my eyes to take a catnap. Fatigued, starving, my entire body numbed by the pain from all the broken bones, I immediately fall into a light sleep where color images of past life experiences filled with sound flicker through my mind.

The sensation of my cheeks sizzling, like they're almost on fire, awakens me from my dream state. Groggy, craving sleep, I open my good eye to find that I'm now in the sun. I have been napping so long the sun is penetrating the overhanging branches.

Realizing that I can use the sun as a natural alarm clock, I rearrange the bark bed so that it's in the shade but in about forty-five minutes will be directly in the sun. Exhausted, I fall back asleep, waiting for my sun alarm to go off.

Thirty minutes or so pass and the sun alarm strikes, beating me with its scorching rays, forcing me to move or be dried up like a raisin. With the help of my walking stick I rise to my feet, then eat a handful of snow.

Rested, I get up and continue tracking the coyotes to the east. Up ahead the two sets of tracks are joined by another. I feel as though I'm not alone. Excited, I eagerly anticipate the moment when I will see these three wild animals.

My stomach and the right side of my rib cage have been taking a pounding for three straight days, and I continue to explode into uncontrollable coughing attacks every couple of steps. The deep, scraping hacks force me to close my right eye while I position my body to lessen the pain during the hammering.

Nonetheless, I am showing improvement. The phlegm I spit up has no signs of blood. Encouraged, I prepare to check my urine and rectum. The urine is a deep yellowish color with an orange tint, revealing the lack of minerals and nutrients.

Because I have been eating snow steadily during the daylight hours and have not experienced diarrhea, I don't believe the color of my urine indicates dehydration. The color and the putrid odor that lingers are signs of starvation. A quick visual check of my underwear shows no new signs of blood from the rectum.

Greatly relieved, I brush off some snow on a fallen tree so that I can sit while I eat snow. I find myself gazing back to the area where the Maule went down. As always I wonder how Wave and Lloyd are doing. Is Lloyd still alive? How is Wave holding up? Did he set the ELT on the ridge? I have not seen any smoke from a campfire or any black signaling smoke made from pouring oil on a fire. This fills me with foreboding, but I must push on.

Seven
Animal Instincts

November 29–30

After following the three sets of coyotes tracks to the east for several hours, I stop to take a break and glance back to the southwest at the rock knob so that I can gauge how far I've traveled. In an attempt to keep my wits and sanity, I chuckle as I stare at the knob, which reveals my dismal progress.

Within moments the reality of my inability to conquer distance takes over my nervous, almost panicking mind. Fear prevents me from resting and catching my breath. As I rush to go a few steps farther, I can see that the coyotes have split up. One set of coyote tracks heads north while the other two sets of tracks continue to head east.

In an effort to regain mental focus, I say, "Come on, you can make it. Relax, think logically. If you panic, you can't think. The dark patches in the snow are only one to two days away. Let's make it to the dark patches, and then see what they have to offer."

Since early this morning my voice-mail has been logging calls from HyperSoft clients, Susan, Kevin, and my sister, Denise. Denise has been calling repeatedly, hoping someone will answer the phone. When the voice-mail clicks on, Denise hangs up.

At 10:34 a.m., Denise makes her final attempt of the day to contact my dad and me. Frustrated and scared, she leaves a message pleading for my dad or me to return her call. She tries to find Susan's and Kevin's numbers, but Susan's is unlisted and Kevin's only phone is the X-ALLOY number.

At 2:30, Kevin sends his brother, Rick, to my house to pick up an order of X-ALLOY material in my garage and to find out why I have not been in contact with them since Saturday. Rick finds my dad alone, nervous and concerned. Dad explains that I went flying early Sunday morning with some friends and have not yet returned. Rick, immediately thinking the worst, that the plane went down, decides to stay with my dad. He makes sure that he has food, picks up the order from my garage for X-ALLOY, then calls Kevin.

At 7500 feet, exhausted from hiking all day, cold, out of breath, and starving, I stop to rest against a tree to keep from tumbling down the steep incline. As I lean forward, my head droops down because my aching neck muscles are too tired to support the weight. As I labor in pain to draw the cold mountain air into my left lung, I glance to the west and spot the little sunlight remaining. I estimate the time at 3:45.

Although my plan for each day was to stop hiking at 11:30 a.m., then dry my clothes and construct a shelter, today I was able to extend the hike because the conditions allowed me to stay dry. But as the seconds tick by, it gets darker and colder. Any snow and ice that were melting during the daylight are now freezing. I'm soon engulfed in darkness; the start of another long brutal night has begun.

While searching for shelter, I continue to follow the coyote tracks to the east. I'm hoping to find a sequoia tree with full branches from top to bottom and a thick bed of needles at the base. A cluster of sequoias including a few fallen trees would be ideal.

I stop abruptly and stare at the two sets of tracks as they change direction from east to north, straight up the face of the mountain. Although I never saw the coyotes, I found myself talking to them throughout the day. The anticipation of spotting them provided me with some company and helped temporarily relieve the burden of my struggle.

Shivering from the dropping temperatures, I pause. Standing on the steep, dark terrain in snow above my knees, supported by my makeshift walking stick, I'm mesmerized by the clouds of breath that I exhale into the frozen air. With each exhale a slightly diseased scent lingers momentarily before the vapor is swept away by the increasing winds. As I break from the spell, I scan the immediate area and spot what looks like a cave fifty feet away.

The cave has a dry, level dirt floor and is much larger than the one I stayed in two nights ago. Protecting the entrance from the weather are a few small sequoia trees with low-hanging branches. The two exterior sides of the cave have a full winter's buildup of snow and ice with an occasional tree or bush spiking through the frozen crust.

After flirting with death from hypothermia Sunday night in that icebox of a cave, I told myself I could not take the chance of exposing myself to frozen rock unless I could start a fire or devise a method to insulate myself. Tonight, I reluctantly make the decision to hold out in this cave. This time will be different. I will insulate myself by constructing a mattress made out of branches and needles from the sequoia trees.

First, I snap off live healthy branches that are full of needles. After I have enough branches to make the mattress five to six inches thick, I interlock the branches, forming a branch bed.

Next, I fill in the gaps of the interwoven branches with needles until the bed is level, soft, and smooth. Then I tramp on the newly formed bed to compress the needles farther into the branches.

Last, I spread a thin layer of needles to top off the compressed mattress. With the mattress now completed I collect another round of fresh branches and pine needles to use as a blanket to cover my entire body.

Before covering myself, I lean out the cave entrance to peek up at the clear night sky, hoping to catch some stars twinkling. It's about seven o'clock and already the temperature feels below zero.

I crawl over to the mattress and start covering my feet, legs, and lower torso with pine needles. After I have a thick blanket of needles over the lower half of my body, I cover the needles with some branches. Lying down on my back, with a branch under my head acting as a pillow, I begin to cover my upper torso, right shoulder, arm, and hand with pine needles. It's a tedious process, but with persistent effort I'm able to cover almost my entire left side.

Within twenty minutes my body starts shivering moderately. I combat the shivers with the reps and by exhaling my warm breath into my jacket. After continuing the battle against hypothermia for about thirty minutes with no progress, I'm tempted to carry the branches and needles to another location. But I decide to stay in the cave and increase the reps and alter my breathing. Instead of drawing cold air through my nose and blowing warm air out through my mouth into my jacket, I will inhale and exhale through my mouth.

Although this makes a difference, I continue to shiver. After about twenty minutes, it feels like I'm trying to breathe with a plastic bag over my head. I fight to inhale a couple of warm breaths of air before I'm forced to expose my nose and mouth to the cold so that I can fill my lungs with fresh air. But inhaling this extremely cold air reduces my internal temperature and makes my body burn calories in order to maintain normal core temperature.

Since there is nothing else I can do, I decide to alternate between breathing warm air inside my jacket and the cold mountain air. When I start to suffocate from inhaling the air inside my jacket, I switch for a couple of breaths to the frozen mountain air until I feel I have enough oxygen in my system.

After an hour, the mild controlled shiver turns into me violently hopping and shaking off the mattress. With each jolt, the blanket of branches and needles falls off my body, leaving me exposed to the subzero air. I try to tighten all the muscles in my body to stop the overwhelming convulsions, but I'm helpless against the onslaught.

In the back of my mind a very faint voice tells me, "Get up and leave the cave now. In just a few minutes it will be too late. You must get up now! Get up! Get up!" Each time the voice speaks I mentally reply, In a minute, I'm comfortable. Just a couple of more minutes, I'll be OK. It's gonna be OK.

My body is now trying to protect itself by halting the blood flow to my extremities in order to conserve heat in my chest, groin, and brain. Vasoconstriction, the frostbite in my feet and hands, is rapidly advancing.

With my branch and needle blanket scattered alongside me, I'm fully exposed. My body has gone from extreme violent convulsions to an almost peaceful calm. In my quest to hike across the frozen Sierra wilderness to bring back a rescue team for Wave and Lloyd, I have committed an unforgivable blunder. It's clear that my body has now entered the third stage of hypothermia.

Hypothermia occurs when the body's core temperature falls below 35° Celsius (95° F.), the clinical state of subnormal temperature when the body is unable to generate sufficient heat to efficiently maintain functions. Once hypothermia develops, the heat deficit is shared by two body compartments, the shell and the core. The shell is the skin and the core is the interior of the body.

Wave, Lloyd, and I entered the first stage of hypothermia (impending hypothermia) when the Maule crashed. In this stage the core body temperature drops from the normal 98.6° to 96.8° F. I felt a few signs of mild hypothermia on Sunday afternoon when I stopped to rest. My muscles would tighten up and my body automatically responded to the drop in body temperature by shivering.

Shivering is the body's attempt to generate heat. It is an involuntary contraction and expansion of muscle tissue occurring on a large scale. The muscle action creates heat through friction. Even at this first stage, mental and physical fatigue set in and signs of weakness begin to show.

Stage two hypothermia (mild hypothermia) came Sunday night in the cave. In this stage the core body temperature drops to between 95° and 93.2° F. Some of the symptoms of this stage are uncontrollable intense shivers and a lack of coordination. Another indication of this stage that I have been experiencing for three days is the extreme pain and discomfort from the cold. At this stage, one remains mentally alert.

For mild hypothermia there are several simple external body-rewarming methods that I could use if I had some additional camping gear or if I could start a fire. Not only would the fire keep my body warm, but I could melt snow into hot water then drink the hot liquid, which would help heat my chest cavity.

It's my guess that because Wave has the tarps, the plane cover, fuel, and a lighter, he might have been able to treat his second-stage hypothermia and prevent his body temperature from further declining.

I know if I fall deep into stage three hypothermia (moderate hypothermia), I may not return. At this stage the body's temperature drops to between 91.4° and 87.8° F. The shivering slows or stops completely. Muscles stiffen and mental confusion and apathy set in. Speech becomes incoherent. Breathing becomes slow and shallow, and drowsiness and irrational behavior may occur.

At the final stage of hypothermia (severe hypothermia), death is imminent. The core body temperature drops below 87.8° F. The skin is cold and bluish gray. The eyes may become dilated. The person is very weak and delirious. He denies any problems and resists help. Gradually he loses consciousness. Breathing may slow to the point that he appears dead. The body becomes rigid.

Alone in the frozen wilderness and with no equipment, I have no way to treat moderate or severe hypothermia. At that point help from other people is vital.

The young and old are more susceptible to hypothermia. This puts Wave and Lloyd at greater risk than me. An infant's core body temperature will cool more quickly than an adult's, since infants have a larger body surface relative to total mass than adults, allowing greater heat loss. Infants also cannot produce as much heat as adults. Older individuals have a lower metabolic rate than the young, which make it more difficult for them to maintain normal body temperature when ambient temperature drops below 66.2° F.

Again a faint voice in my mind sounds off, "Get up now! If you

stay here any longer you will die." My right eye opens and I wait
for it to adjust to the pitch-black darkness in the cave.

Rising to all fours, I push the mass of branches and needles to
the edge of the cave entrance so that I do not have to enter the
cave again to transport the material to another location. Above
the cave to the right is a sloping area, but it offers me some small
rocks, bushes, and tiny trees that I can lock my body securely to
while I rest.

With the new bed made there and the blanket of branches
covering my body, I return to the focused breathing and the
reps. As my body returns to a slow controlled shiver, I break the
silent darkness of the frozen wilderness with "Huhhh, huhhh,
I'm so cold . . ." Alone, with my spirits declining, I think of the
star.

About ninety minutes before dawn, I decide to start hiking so that
my body will generate more heat. As I advance, each step is slow
and difficult because of the lack of light, the steep incline, and the
uneven icy surface.

When I pause, my mind fixates on the ten brutal, nightmarish
hours that I have just gone through. Weakened from the second
attempt to use a cave as shelter, I think about Wave and hope he
has made a fort and a fire. My thoughts darken as I wonder
whether Lloyd is still alive.

As daylight arrives the forest remains silent. I hear only my
boot heels digging into the white crust, my walking stick spearing
the frozen dense base, and my ragged breaths.

While I stand facing east in the dense sequoia timberline, I position myself so that my view of the snow-capped mountain peaks
and sky is unobstructed by trees and branches. With the sky clear,
no wind, and the temperatures already increasing, my spirits rise.
I believe I will see smoke from Wave's fire. Overall it's going to be
a good day.

Stopping at the edge of a ravine twenty feet wide, I spot on the
other side what looks like snowshoe tracks heading down the

mountain. From my angle and distance it looks like a semishort snowshoe, one that would be used in dense woods because of its ease of mobility.

Quickly I lean up against a very small tree and scream, "Help . . . help . . ." Because I have the power of only one lung, my decrepit scratchy voice is absorbed in the surrounding sequoia, dense bushes, and rocks. Still leaning against the tree, I straighten my body so that I can take a deep breath and let out a scream that will echo through the mountains. Yet when I try to scream, my voice is nothing more than a whimper.

Racked with disappointment, I start talking to myself. "How much worse can it get? A search team is here, and I can't even call for them. I wonder how they got here. I did not hear any snow-mobiles or helicopters. Maybe they set up a base camp in the area. I'll follow the tracks that will lead to them."

Time is a vital concern. I'm afraid the rescuer has too big a lead and I will not be able to catch up with him in my physical condition. I decide not to follow the S-shaped tracks down the mountain, but to intercept his path at an angle.

Still at altitude, with my senses fully alert and my adrenaline pumping, I march aggressively like a wounded soldier through knee-deep snow until I reach his tracks. As I lean over to inspect the large tracks for their freshness, I think, "These tracks aren't from a snowshoe."

Since the imprint in the snow is clean, showing no signs of freezing or melting, I believe the tracks are less than an hour old, headed east, and are probably from the same bear that I encountered Monday night.

Because breathing is becoming much harder due to the thin air, I decide to hike down to a lower altitude. Once I'm nearly at the bottom of the mountain, I stand in waist-deep snow looking all about.

I hear a faint but consistent *shhhhhh*, the sound of wind blowing through the trees, but I don't feel any breeze. As I tilt my head to zero in on the sound, I suddenly realize it's the sound of running water. Only fifty yards away, separating the mountain that

I'm on and the adjacent mountain to the south is a snow- and ice-covered stream about ten feet wide.

At the stream's edge all other sounds in the forest are dampened by the sound of rushing water. After finding a hole in the ice, I kneel down, remove my glove, and submerge my left hand in the icy water. Instantly it burns my frostbitten fingers and I yank my hand out of the water and put it inside my jacket underneath my right armpit to warm it.

Putting my left glove back on, I get on all fours and start lapping the water with my tongue like a dog. After swallowing only a few tonguefuls of water, I develop an acute headache that causes me to stop. I have to pace myself. I spend the next thirty minutes drinking the cold water very slowly.

Breathing is easier at this lower elevation, but as I expected, the snow is too deep to hike through. Descending into this sunless gorge was a mistake.

Heading east, I decide to regain some altitude by hiking at an angle up the mountain. With the stream now at a distance, its sound soothes my tense mind. When I get tired, I lean up against a tree. A large sheet of bark is separated from the trunk. Just then an idea comes to me. I strip off a three-foot section of bark and spot what looks like several frozen moths clinging to the trunk.

I pick off the insects and mix them with a tiny bit of snow in my palm. Then I reluctantly pack my mouth with the snow-covered moths. Surprisingly, as I chew I find the moths are soft and bland. Needing nourishment, I now plan to position my breaks near trees so I can look for insects under the bark.

By noon I finally reach the altitude that I started the day at. Glancing to the west, I see the rock knob is now behind me. I see how far I traveled. Excited with my progress, I shake my walking stick above my head and scream, "Yeah, I can do it!"

As I continue to hike, I now observe the forest through a different set of eyes. I no longer view trees, logs, and bushes as obstacles, but as materials for construction and potential food sources. I now hear the subtle sounds in the forest that have been muffled by the wind or absorbed into the dense plant cover. With my animal instincts now surfacing, I'm alert but calm. While I hike, I can smell, taste, and feel the minute differences from one area in the forest to the next.

I wade through the knee-high snow until I reach an area where there is no snow at all. Standing on the bare ground, I spot what looks like a tag from a T-shirt or a label from a bottle. Excited to have spotted a man-made object, I immediately look for other signs of human activity and notice several trees that have been cut down with a chain saw in order to clear a trail.

Changing course, I follow the trail north through waist-deep snow. After losing it in the snow and veering off my easterly heading for about a hundred yards, I retrace my tracks back to the clearing.

I look to the east and estimate that the dark patches in the snow arc still about a day's hike away. As I glance to the northwest, toward the Maule, I still see no smoke.

My heavy water intake has worked its way through my system, and I can now check my urine for blood. Although the urine has no sign of blood, it's still a yellow-orange color with a putrid smell.

That morning Denise, still in Colorado and unaware of the plane crash, awoke from a disturbing nightmare. In it she ordered a size six black dress and shoes to match for a funeral. Shocked by the dream, she lies under the warm covers thinking about it. Although neither my father nor I has returned her phone calls, she has the strong feeling that we're both still alive. But she is still convinced she will be attending a funeral within a week.

With the CAP search under way, the Long Beach police doing an investigation on a missing-person report, and hangar gossip at Long Beach Airport, the *Long Beach Press-Telegram* prints a story that morning. The headline reads: AIR PATROL SEARCHES FOR TRIO.

At 1:00 p.m., Kevin makes a difficult phone call to Denise. He explains that I departed the Long Beach Airport in my Maule with two friends, Wave and Lloyd, on the twenty-seventh and have not yet called in or returned. Although Denise has sensed something is wrong for the last few days, she goes into a state of shock.

Shortly after Denise hangs up, Susan phones her and asks her to sit or lie on the floor while she explains the situation in detail. Since Denise is unaware of CAP's existence, Susan explains the role CAP plays in the general aviation community and the methodical steps it follows while trying to locate aircraft that are late to their destination or missing.

As Susan informs Denise that the CAP search started yesterday, Denise squeezes the phone tighter, and knots begin to form in her stomach. Susan explains that yesterday's CAP search included forty-two personnel launching fourteen aircraft that flew twenty-five sorties totaling 64.5 flight hours. Denise holds the phone close to her ear with a death grip. At last she keels over on the floor from an anxiety attack and curls into a fetal position.

Since Denise is suffering in silence, Susan is unaware of Denise's condition. She goes on to explain that CAP has almost doubled its deployment today and gives her the current mission statistics, which include sixty-nine personnel launching twenty-six aircraft with fifty-four sorties totaling 132.4 flight hours with 60.7 hours in assigned grids.

Denise, now physically ill, excuses herself from the phone and remains on the floor in the fetal position. With her breathing short and choppy, her eyes bloodshot, tears streaming down both cheeks and dripping down her neck, she begins to wail.

After venting her anger and frustration, Denise goes into her bedroom, lies on her bed with her head on one pillow, wraps both arms tightly around another pillow, then continues to cry. As she starts to calm down, she begins to pray to God for our safe return. Then she says to herself, "I must get a grip."

As she considers the horrifying news she just received, she begins to make a series of painful phone calls to friends. She tells them that she's headed to California to be with her father and to assist in the search any way she can and asks them to set up prayer chains for Wave, Lloyd, and me.

With my boot liners, gloves, pants, and jacket soaking wet from today's hike, I stop for the day in an area with several large dark-colored rocks fully exposed to the sun. Fifty yards away is a mixed grouping of large sequoia trees, logs, and bushes that I can use for tonight's shelter. Once I've set my clothes and boots drying on the rocks, I hold a handful of snow to my left eye and look for smoke in the northwest, but still I see no signs of a fire.

The gash on my left eyebrow, eyelid, and the bridge of my nose gets wet from the snow I've been pressing against those areas, and as I spread my upper and lower eyelid apart, I can feel the soggy scab starting to split. Able to control the pain by how fast I work the wound open, I let my pain threshold adjust to each incremental movement until I can sense sunlight through my left eye.

After glimpsing daylight and blurry objects for the second time, I'm convinced that the eye is intact and that within days I will be able to see through it.

During the few remaining hours of sunlight, I move my clothes on the rocks several times to take advantage of the sun's changing angles. They are still damp, but I believe I can survive the night with enough insulation. Under the cover of several sequoia, with a branch and needle mattress now constructed and sufficient material gathered for a thick, dense blanket, I cover myself and mentally prepare for the night.

At my house in Long Beach my father is unaware of the media frenzy building and the CAP and police involvement in the search for the three of us. Kevin, Kevin's girlfriend Judy, and Rick are sitting with my father when a local television station breaks the story and flashes pictures of Lloyd, Wave, me, and the Maule across the TV sets of the L.A. area. While the report paints a very gloomy scenario, Kevin, Judy, and Rick tell my father that there is a good chance we're all still alive.

Denise's vigorous spirit has now kicked in. She has made airline reservations, packed her bags, and called several friends who are pilots so that she will know what to expect from CAP. Since this will be the last night she will have the opportunity to get any rest until she finds out what has happened to us, she decides to go to bed early.

While she lies on her bed sobbing, in one arm she embraces a framed photo of me on my race bike. The picture was taken during a 750cc Super Sport road race in Georgia. In the other hand she gently holds a bandanna against her cheek. The bandanna was a Christmas gift from me last year, and imprinted on both sides is a map of Yosemite National Park and the surrounding Sierra Nevadas. The southern border of the map is less than seventy-five miles from my present location.

Eight
Second Wind

December 1

Because the cloud layer did not form until about 10:00 p.m., most of the heat from the day dissipated into the upper atmosphere. In the early hours of Thursday morning, with an inch of snow covering my branch, needle, and bark blanket, I continue to fight the borderline convulsive shivers with weakened bursts of reps and by steadily exhaling into my jacket.

Knowing the facts—forced to fight extreme cold and hypothermia, severe lack of sleep and rest, nutrition intake consisting solely of dead bugs found behind bark, and the high energy output required to hike through the remote snow-covered backcountry—I don't think I can last more than another seven to ten days.

From the sound of the sequoia branches swaying back and forth, I estimate the wind speed at 30 mph plus. The mattress and blanket insulation is proving to be quite effective, as I feel no direct temperature drop from the windchill factor. After several windy hours, the clouds have disappeared; the sky is clear and I can see the stars again.

Remaining stationary for ten hours has allowed me to forget temporarily about my broken bones. I remove my blanket; then, using my walking stick, I prop myself up on both feet while I get reacquainted with the throbbing pain that surrounds each of my fractures.

After hiking for several hours, daylight finally greets me. Still high up on the mountain in knee- to waist-deep snow, I can see that the dark patches in the snow, at the base of the mountain I'm on, are less than a two-hour hike away. Glancing to the west, in the distance I spot the rock knob. While I used the knob to gauge the distance that I had hiked for the last three days, a sense of confidence slowly begins to infuse my whole body. Humbly, while closing my right eye, I bow and say softly, "I can do this . . . I'm alive and I've got a chance . . ."

While making the mountain descent, through the deepening snow, I come across a fresh set of tracks left by my furry friend. It appears the bear has changed its direction from east to north and is headed toward the ridgeline. Its trail leads me to believe it had been watering earlier this morning at the stream at the base of the mountain. Knowing the bear could be close by, I make as much noise as I can while I hike, occasionally humming verses from a song.

At nearly the same time, Denise boards a plane in Colorado Springs that will take her first to Phoenix, then to Long Beach. As she sits in her seat she is overcome by the terrifying thought that the plane I had been flying crashed and I might be dead. Crying, her body shaking, unable to maintain her composure, she leans forward and puts her face in her hands. The woman sitting next to her asks, "Are you afraid to fly?"

During the second leg of her flight, she begins to make a list of people to call and things to do as soon as she steps into my home office. While prioritizing the list, she notices that the man sitting next to her is reading medical literature. The two of them begin to chat and he tells her that he is a lung specialist. Denise asks him if he had any training or knowledge in trauma related to the outdoors, cold weather, or accidents in the wilderness. She tells him that two of my friends and I might have been in an airplane crash and she is gathering information on what they might be facing and how long they could survive. The doctor is full of compassion and hope. He asks about my personality, temperament, age, and physical condition. He believes it's possible a man could survive for two weeks in the wilderness in winter. He further explains that he has found that patients who come from loving, supportive families do far better than patients who do not. They discuss the power of faith and prayer.

Meanwhile CAP expands the search into remote backcountry of the Sierra Nevadas. The Squadron Forty commander phones Captain C. E. Judd at ten o'clock this morning and asks him if he can participate tomorrow morning in the search for the three missing men. The commander tells the captain that the search will be taking place over high-elevation terrain and that they need him and his aircraft.

Since all search aircraft owned by CAP, which are corporate aircraft, and most of the aircraft owned by CAP members themselves are lightweight single-engine aircraft, Judd is called in because he is one of the few members who operate a semiheavy twin-engine airplane.

In high-altitude searches a twin has some advantages over a single-engine aircraft. Although most twin-engine aircraft cannot climb or maintain altitude with only one engine operational, the pilot does have the option to shut down one engine if it experiences trouble or catches fire. With one prop still rotating under power the glide distance for the plane can be extended, allowing the pilot or crew to find an airport in its glide path or suitable terrain that can be used for an emergency landing.

Captain Judd knows that with himself and two crew members aboard the twin and with a full load of fuel, he can stay airborne for five hours while searching at altitudes of 10,000 feet to 14,000 feet.

After Captain Judd agrees to participate in the mission, the commander asks the captain to fly his plane to John Wayne Airport in Santa Ana tomorrow at 8:00 a.m. to pick up his two crew members. Captain Judd agrees to the rendezvous time and location.

The commander further informs the captain that the search

base has been moved from Bishop to General William J. Fox Airfield in Lancaster, California. Captain Judd tells the commander that he should be able to touch down at General Fox by nine.

With the logistics of the mission now settled, Captain Judd asks the commander who his crew members will be. When the commander names Howard Selleck and John Soley, the captain is pleased because he knows both men. Howard, like the captain, is fairly new to CAP, while John, the youngest of the three men, is ironically an old-timer in CAP.

Both men served in the military. Howard piloted B-24s over the skies of Europe during World War II. The captain, a World War II vet himself, was a Navy enlisted man in the Pacific and didn't start his flying career until leaving the service. Howard's experience made him an excellent choice for the front right seat in tomorrow's search. John's background and his highly tuned observation skills made him a perfect fit for the third seat.

Also at ten o'clock Denise's plane arrives at Long Beach Airport, the same airport that I took off from in the Maule four days earlier. Rick picks her up and drives her to my house. As Denise enters the house, she is greeted by our dad, Susan, Kevin, and Judy.

My father tries to be strong, but Denise strongly senses his fear that he might never see me again. She sits down close to Dad, talks with him for several minutes, and assures him that I am alive and will return. She excuses herself, then walks into the office with Susan, Kevin, and Judy, where she is briefed on the search in private.

In the meantime I forge onward. Although the large rocks and the dense growth obstruct my view of the dark patches in the snow, I catch a glimpse of a large meadow that has no snow and borders the area where the dark patches are. Amazed at what I see, I increase the pace of my descent. Meanwhile I think, Why is there no snow there? Is it warmer there? It makes no sense. Even with the sun beating down on the meadow, there should still be a blanket of snow. There are lots of meadows with snow; why not this one?

Presently my view of the mountain's base is totally blocked, but I sense I'm near the bottom because the sound of wind is faintly present, the same sound I heard yesterday when I was close to another runoff stream at the base of the mountain.

Soon I'm standing in six inches of snow at a stream's edge. I see no ice covering the stream in the immediate area. Looking twenty feet, then thirty feet beyond the stream into the open meadow, I see only small scattered patches of snow in the high grass and on the ground.

Tired and thirsty, I cross the stream, remove both gloves and lie down on the soft sand and dead grass at the stream's edge. While lapping up water, I think, I can't taste or smell anything irregular in the water or in the air that would explain why there is no snow here. Why is there no snow?

With my thirst quenched and gloves back on, I rise to my feet to further investigate the barren meadow. As I walk across the clearing I feel energized, but I'm not sure why—perhaps because it's not the same old thing, snow and more snow.

While standing in the center of the meadow I scan the area with a full 360 degree turn, but see or hear nothing that would explain this snowless wonder. I inhale very slowly through my nose, hoping to detect a scent that is out of the ordinary from the fresh mountain air. Then I inhale through my mouth, trying to catch something on my taste buds that will explain this phenomenon.

Still playing nature detective, I start walking south, where the ground turns from frozen to semimushy. As I spot a palm-size puddle of water that is about three inches deep I ask myself, Why is this not frozen? Any small puddle or standing water should freeze.

I stare at the puddle, thinking I know why it's not frozen, but unable to confirm my suspicion because there is no sulfur odor. Suddenly a bubble rises from the bottom.

Knowing it's possible that the bubble was caused by an air pocket trapped in the soil located underneath or immediately surrounding the puddle and was squeezed into the water as I compressed the mushy ground by stepping on it, I hold off before getting too excited.

I put the fingertips of my left glove in my mouth and bite down, holding the glove in my teeth while I pull my left hand free. With my hand exposed and the glove hanging from my teeth, I slowly kneel down on both knees and position myself to touch the puddle.

Extending my hand toward the puddle, I say, "Come on, baby! Please!" Instead of using my frostbitten fingers, which have lost their sense of feeling, to check the water temperature, I make a fist and dip my knuckles in the small pool. As I feel the warm water, I slowly close my eyes and say softly with thanks, "Yes, thank you, God, for these hot springs. Thank you."

A hot spring is any spring whose water is at least fifteen degrees warmer than the annual air temperature and is formed from water that is heated underground and returned to the surface. In certain areas, magma or lava has worked its way up through the earth's crust to relatively shallow depths below the surface. Groundwater percolates downward, comes in contact with the hot rock, and is heated. As the water returns to the surface, it collects into pools known as hot springs.

In the nineteenth century it was legal and often quite profitable to claim that mineral water could cure an impressive list of ailments. Numerous hotels and boardinghouses sprang up near hot springs, catering to visitors looking for relaxation and cures. Many hot spring sites can be found on the national forest land along the lower Kern River canyon.

Native American tribes have long accorded many hot springs special status. They used hot springs for healing and, believing the waters had other powers, they would declare a hot spring a neutral zone, devoted to peace and healing.

Although I started learning about hot springs in high school, my first encounter with one came when I moved to California for college and started taking motorcycle road trips with a friend. Brian had a bike and was eager to throw a leg over the seat to head out to explore the West Coast. Every holiday we packed our bikes with rain gear, tarps, sleeping bags, spare clothes, and whatever money we could cough up. We were road warriors combing the national parks of California, Nevada, Utah, Wyoming, Montana, and Arizona. Yosemite, Lake Tahoe, and the roads to Las Vegas became our backyard.

One day I received a call from my friend Stewart, who was still living in Connecticut. Stewart told me he wanted to come take a motorcycle trip through the California Sierra Nevadas.

His timing was perfect because at the time I had a spare street bike set up for road trips. I immediately phoned my road trip partner, Brian, and we began planning the trip. We decided to head to our routine stomping grounds, Yosemite and Lake Tahoe.

After a couple of cold nights in the mountains, the three of us pulled into Bridgeport, California, and headed to the hot springs off Highway 395. As I started unpacking my bike, we were greeted by several girls who had been enjoying the springs. Soon Brian, Stewart, and I submerged our tired bodies into the steamy waters.

After about thirty minutes I climbed out and crashed in my sleeping bag. Morning came too quickly when Stewart started shaking and kicking me, trying to wake me up. Trying to remain calm, he told me that a bunch of beautiful girls had just pulled up in a jeep, stripped down naked, and were now in the hot springs.

I can stay up all night, but I love to sleep in the mornings, and I was not going to fall for that line. I fell back asleep, only to wake about an hour later to see Stewart smiling and listen to Brian's comments about the bathing beauties who had driven off fifteen minutes earlier.

Brian and Stewart kept on telling me how gorgeous the girls were and tried to convince me that I missed the opportunity of a lifetime. While packing my bike, I was thinking about the egg omelet, potatoes, English muffin, and large glass of orange juice I was going to have when I heard the sound of a four-wheeler coming up the trail.

Immediately I thought it was the ranger coming to give us tickets for sleeping at the hot springs. As the vehicle turned the corner, we could see it was a jeep. Just a split second before Stewart or Brian could say anything, I thought about the girls in the jeep they were talking about earlier.

Stewart, unable to keep his excitement in, said, "That's them, check this out." Right before my eyes four angels jumped out, stripped down while laughing and giggling, and walked right past us to the springs. With our bikes packed, ready to go, and our helmets in hand, it was obvious that we were headed out, but Brian said, "I forgot to pack my flashlight, and it goes in the center of my pack. I'm going to have to completely unpack and then repack. It's going to take a while." Of course the flashlight was a miniature Maglite that easily fits in any pocket.

Smiling at the memory, I continue to walk southward across the meadow until I come upon a pool of water that is covered with scum. After checking the temperature of the spring and finding it quite inviting, I skim the scum off with my walking stick.

With the pool clear, I start the painstaking chore of removing my clothes. I have lost a lot of weight in four days. I can slide my pants over my hips and buttocks without unbuttoning them. With my clothes spread out on the ground to dry, I slide my carcass into the pool, buttocks first. As I submerge my body in the warm water except for my head, feet, and hands, I let out a sigh. "Ahhhh, ohhh boyyy. Thank you, Lord! Thank you."

In less than thirty minutes the magic of the natural hot tub raises my body temperature enough to partially arrest the hypothermic shivers. Estimating the time at 10:30, I momentarily consider returning to the Maule to bring Wave and Lloyd back to this haven. Yet a round trip will take me at least five days. Plus, if I return and Wave has built adequate shelter and a fire, the trip will have been wasted. The only thing for me to do is continue hiking, as Wave and I had planned.

My buttocks begin to burn from resting on the silt on the bottom of the spring. Shifting my body, I lower my feet and hands into the pool's edge, the area where the water is coolest.

Within moments my frostbitten extremities begin to sting from the hot water, forcing me to quickly lift them out of the tub. I allow them to cool before redunking them. After dipping and redipping my feet and hands for thirty minutes, I dunk them for a final time, keeping them submerged in the hot water while I grit my teeth.

Believing that a force greater than I can explain guided me to these hot springs, I relax in the miracle water with only my neck and head exposed to the brisk mountain air. With each breath I take, I can feel the power of this sacred area reviving me, breathing life back into my mind and body, helping me capture a second wind.

Completely relaxed with my head pointed toward the clear blue sky, I start dozing off, almost dreaming. Immediately my survival instincts kick in and prevent me from falling into a deep sleep. With my right eyelid fluttering, trying to open, I remain in a semiconscious state.

Suddenly, for no apparent reason I calmly open my right eye and spot a military tanker headed south at about 30,000 feet. While the tanker refuels a conventional fighter plane, a C-117 stealth fighter flies in formation to the left of the tanker.

I know the three jets are flying too high for Wave's smoke signals to be seen. At that altitude those planes are silent, leaving Wave no time to create a signal. Even if Wave did make smoke, by the time the first black oily cloud rose above the peaks, the planes would be long gone because of the speed at which they travel.

Our only good chance of being rescued would be if one of the three jets is monitoring the ELT's radio frequency. I sigh, then silently say, "Wave, buddy, I hope you have the ELT going."

During Denise's hourlong meeting with Kevin, Judy, and Susan, she learns that a media storm is building. Today's *Long Beach Press-Telegram* story is headlined: STILL NO SIGN OF MISSING AIRPLANE, THREE L.B. MEN.

As Denise leaves the office, she sees our father starting to cry. Trying to be strong herself, she sits at his side and gently hugs him. Although it is tough for Dad to admit he is scared, he confides in her. Trying to comfort him, she tells him that she had a dream that I was hurt but still alive.

Thinking my father might know where I've gone, Denise gives him one extra-large shoe box of mine that is filled with photos of motorcycle trips, family, friends, holidays, birthdays, and some adventures with the Maule. She's hoping that if he reviews all the photos with the plane, it may give him a clue as to an area where I flew often. These photos could then be handed off to CAP, which could determine where the trees, rocks, rivers, and mountains in the picture are located. CAP could then concentrate their search efforts on the areas depicted in the photos.

Denise, seeking support and advice, also phones an old friend in the Long Beach area. After she describes the impact that the tragedy is having on her father, her friend suggests that Dad be taken to the hospital, where he can be seen by a doctor and sedated if necessary.

Her friend, a public relations man, advises Denise that the media storm may be just starting. He thinks it wise that the family not speak to the press, but let CAP handle all media inquiries.

In fact, making contact with CAP is one of the first items on Denise's list, and she phones Lieutenant Colonel Sydney J. Wolfe of CAP to introduce herself. Wolfe, the liaison between CAP and the family members of victims, has many sad memories of confirming tragic news to surviving kin. Experienced with worry and grief, the lieutenant colonel starts briefing Denise on the mission. Wolfe's briefing includes the CAP efforts for today: fifty-three CAP personnel launching twenty aircraft, which perform forty-eight sorties. They log 129.2 hours of flight time with 50.2 flight hours allotted in the search grids.

He also has the painful job of telling Denise that the chance of survival for the three of us is minimal. Even if we were trained to live in harsh conditions, he says, it is the fifth day since our flight, and the military window of survival is only thirty-six hours. The mission is now recovery of a wreckage, looking for three corpses.

Wolfe tells Denise that he is surprised someone from the DeLeo camp did not come forward sooner. Denise explains that she had just received the news yesterday and then flew out immediately from Colorado.

She asks for the phone numbers of Wave's and Lloyd's families, but Wolfe says that CAP policy forbids his giving her that information. He can pass the request on to the families and give them her phone number.

Immediately after hanging up the phone with Wolfe, and against the advice from her PR friend, Denise decides to go public with the story. Since the plane has been missing for five days and no new clues have surfaced, she believes that she must help fan the fires of the story.

By blitzing radio and TV stations, she may reach somebody who saw the Maule or has some information that could lead to our rescue. Most important, her gut instincts tell her that CAP is getting ready to halt its mission. By feeding the growing media storm, she may be able to pressure CAP to keep searching. By two o'clock she is in full swing. She has written several press releases and obtained contact information for radio and TV stations.

One of Lloyd's closest friends and fellow pool players, Jim Mashburn, also comes forward. Jim knows time is critical in rescuing the lives of hurt, stranded people in the mountains, so he heads 230 miles north to Lone Pine Airport. Jim speaks with Bill Woodward, the airport operator, who is also a Maule M-5 owner. Bill tells him that he knows my plane and Wave, because several times we had landed there for gas and then Bill had driven us into town so that we could have dinner.

Jim hires Bill to fly him over the Sierras to search for the missing plane, and they log two hours of search-and-rescue flight time.

In the silence of the hot spring, the burning sensation in my feet and hands has worsened. My limbs are so discolored that I know the tissue is close to death, but the pain is a good sign, evidence that the tissue is still alive and that the hot water is increasing the blood circulation, giving the numb limbs feeling again.

I'm so relaxed in the pool, I feel as if I'm waiting for a waitress to take my order. As the sun touches the top of the peaks to the west, I estimate the time at three o'clock. The steady drop in temperature makes it tougher for me to get out of the warm security of the spring.

With less than an hour of daylight left, I exit the celestial water feeling revived. Steam rises from my body as I get dressed. I can feel the cold breeze on my warm skin. Ready to slide my long johns on, I notice that the ground where I laid them to dry earlier has been oozing water and now they are completely drenched.

Since I have no towel, I use my soaked long johns to dry off. Once I'm done, I wring the water out. The garment will take at least two days to dry so I nervously scout for shelter. I'm drawn to a long, thick fallen tree that I spotted when I first entered the bare meadow. Although I know I cannot build adequate shelter from the downed tree and from its immediate surroundings, I still gather bark and branches and form small useless piles of pine needles.

For reasons I cannot explain, I do not want to wander into the shadows of the woods surrounding the meadow to find a better location to construct shelter. The unspoken bond that I share with the springs of life restrains me.

Knowing that if the night proves to be too much for me, I can wait out the cold darkness submerged in the pools, I try a different method for constructing shelter. Using my walking stick, I dig a trench underneath a downed tree, trying to create a cavity that is just large enough for my body to fit into.

After snapping my walking stick several times from trying to use it like a shovel, I realize that it's hopeless and that I'm expending my energy uselessly. Sitting down with my back leaning against the downed tree, I stare at the dark patches in the snow only 150 yards away.

Draping my long johns and sweatshirt over the tree to dry, I walk back across the meadow and reach a second stream that is joined by the one I drank from this morning. This stream (Nine Mile Creek as I later learn) snakes its way between the mountains and merges with the Kern River about five miles to the west. From here I can see steam arising from several hot springs that I did not see earlier today. I cross over the gushing stream on an old wooden plank that spans the stream's width. Walking on the slippery, wobbly plank, I stick the end of a new walking stick that I've found into the stream to keep my balance.

As I approach within fifty yards of the dark patches in the snow, the mystery ends. The patches are the tops of weather-beaten fence posts that are evenly spaced apart, forming a horse corral. Entranced by the dark, round post ends protruding from the white glittery snow, I reflect on my travail of the last three days. Never did I imagine that I would suffer so much, physically and mentally, to unravel such a simple, insignificant riddle.

As I let out a loud sigh of laughter, the dull raspy sound echoes lightly across the meadow. All alone, I shout a single word, then wait for its echoing response. I continue calling out single words, pausing between each word burst, waiting for the comforting echo to talk back to me before I release another word into the wilderness, finding hope and companionship in the mirrored sound.

Trying to stay upbeat and focused, I scan the area beyond the corral. I notice several large sequoias with their massive branches weighed down from snow and ice, forming what looks like a tree cave. Remembering the image of the tree cave I visited as a child with Sanjaya, I approach the overhanging branches with a sense of déjà vu.

The snow rises to my waist as I advance toward the overhang. Suddenly, my shattered left ankle breaks through what I thought was solid ground and becomes trapped in a wooden catwalk.

With my ankle twisted below the snow's surface, I start screaming in distress. The pain is so great that just a whisper magnifies the spiking throbs. After hearing my anguish echoed across the meadow, I scream at the mocking sound, pleading for it to leave me be while I wait for the pain in my ankle to reduce to a tolerable level.

I begin slowly moving my ankle, feeling with my foot and toes, trying to work my boot free from between the wooden planks. Once my ankle is free, I have reservations about moving forward again. Still unable to see the snow-covered ground beneath me, I'm afraid I will crash through the walk altogether or become snared in some other man-made device that lingers in the area, bringing my journey to an end.

A thought occurs to me: Why would somebody build a horse corral and catwalk here without building a cabin? The hot springs are a perfect location for a cabin. Some type of shelter has to be here somewhere. There must be a cabin close by.

Sure enough, a few steps later I spot a group of buildings. There are three cabins and what looks like an old country store near the main cabin.

I can see that the main cabin is in great shape, but the windows are boarded up and bolted from the inside. The massive front door is locked shut. A thick chain has been threaded through the hole where a doorknob would be installed, wrapped around the doorjamb, and padlocked.

With a pistol the meaty lock would be no challenge. I think back to Sunday morning, when I was getting ready to leave my house. I purposely left my Smith & Wesson .44 Magnum revolver in my drawer, thinking I would not need it, though I'd taken it on almost every other flight.

Because the cabin is locked, it's obvious that this is the one cabin with supplies stored inside it that I so desperately need. I walk around to the left side, but it doesn't have a window. The back too has been boarded up and sealed from the inside and the windowless right wall matches the left.

I notice that whoever uses these cabins has bear problems. They have built a hoisting device made from a pulley hung high in the trees and a basket to hold food, garbage, and other material that a bear may forage for. Hoping to find food, I lower the basket. Sifting through several paper and plastic bags, I find only useless garbage.

I walk over to the old country-store building and enter it

through the back door. The interior is filled with junk. I keep my eyes open for something that will either help me break into the main cabin, start a fire, or construct snowshoes. I spot a generator and think that there might be gas somewhere. If I could find gas and a small container to store it in, and matches or a lighter, I could make small campfires as I continue on my journey.

I spot a large clear jug on the floor with a tiny bit of fluid in it. Assuming it's gas, I twist the top off the container and take a whiff. The gas is old and stale, the odor is weak. I rock the container back and forth. The fluid flows like mixed egg whites in a bowl, and the heavy collection of sediment reveals the breakdown of the compounds and additives in the fuel.

My eyes roam about, bouncing off one piece of junk after the next, looking for other survival options. I find a chain saw resting on the floor only three feet away, but it's broken, left behind by the owner to decay. There are several large plastic colored buckets that were probably used to carry horse feed. Scattered on the floor are some flowerpots. They look like they're made from clay. I stop and think, If I were to hide a key, where would I put it? On a shelf? Above the door on a support beam?

After sifting through the junk, I come up with only a piece of steel and a discarded, rusty fire extinguisher. Carrying both relics back to the front of the main cabin, I stop to take a short rest and prepare to break off the lock.

First, I rig the steel rod in the loop of the lock. Then I raise the fire extinguisher over my head. Finally, I let the weight of the extinguisher crash down on the end of the steel rod, trying to force the lock open. The lock, though shaken violently, remains intact.

Thinking about the canned food, extra clothes, snowshoes, and other riches that may await me on the other side of the royal door, I become obsessed by the ten-dollar piece of metal that separates me from living like a king. I try again and again, but the brute lock defies me. Soon I become too weak to hold or swing the extinguisher.

A massive sequoia has fallen on the roof of the center cabin, demolishing it. Upon closer inspection it looks like this tree destroyed the cabin several years ago and nobody ever cleaned up the mess.

The third cabin appears to be intact. Advancing to it, I can see the door is open about four inches. There is a hole for a door-knob, but there is no chain preventing entry. As I get ready to enter the cabin, I wonder if a bear or mountain lion has taken refuge in this abandoned shelter. Cautiously I peek through the hole. Seeing nothing, I stand to the side while I slowly swing the door open. I burst out laughing when I find only three homemade bed frames, made from trees and baling wire, and an old dirty carpet covering the wooden floor.

Entering the small cabin, I am protected from the cold. The shelter consists of one room and a closet. I kneel in one corner to examine the condition of the carpet. Grabbing one end, I begin to slowly peel it off the floor, trying not to rip it.

After separating about two feet of carpet I stop, elated. I think, My home is here for the night, in this humble shelter, rolled up in this dirty carpet. This is going to be a great night.

Excited that I don't have to construct a shelter and that I will be warm and protected, I decide to fetch my long johns and sweatshirt from the tree.

Captain Carl Kennedy, the CAP mission intelligence officer, calls Denise at my house. He needs a clear description of my plane since many planes are painted with unique paint schemes.

Captain Kennedy rattles off the separate surface areas—top of fuselage, belly, elevators, vertical stabilizer, underside of wing, struts, top of wing, cowling—but Denise is confused by the termi-nology. She tells him that the plane is red and white and she can send him several large color photos of it if that will help.

Denise is suddenly overcome with worry. She asks Kennedy to hold and tries to compose herself. When they start talking again, he tells her that two forest rangers spotted a plane fitting the description of the Maule on Sunday morning along the Kern

River. Charged with hope, Denise quickly relays that information to my father.

Conserving energy and trying to stay dry, I retrace my footprints to the fallen tree. I arrive back at the front steps of my palace after dark, wearing my sweatshirt underneath my jacket and carrying my soaked long johns. I leave the door open so that any reflected light from the white blanketed forest will shine inside the cabin.

While waiting for my eye to adjust to the pitch black, I think about how to move the three heavy bed frames out of the way while I roll the carpet up, creating a sleeping bag. Soon I can faintly see. The bed frames, still just hazy silhouettes, remind me of being a child in a dark unfamiliar room.

Shutting the door, with my long johns stuffed in the hole of the door, prevents the cold air from seeping inside the cabin, completely insulating me from the wind. I drag and push the bulky bed frames out of the way and then roll up inside the carpet.

After I'm settled inside the carpet, relaxed and warm, I suddenly have a strong urge to urinate. I don't want to unroll myself from inside the carpet, sit up, and go out into the cold to take a leak. I cross my legs and squirm, trying to fight the pressure in my bladder. After thirty uncomfortable minutes the pressure is too strong. I must now urinate so that I will be relaxed and able to sleep for the first time in five nights.

Hating the idea of facing the cold air, I eye the small closet in the back of the cabin. Standing at the closet entrance, against my moral upbringing, I expel a foul stream of urine against the closet wall. Midway through the process, I start laughing. I'm worried about pissing in this old dilapidated cabin when I might be dead in a couple of days! What the hell am I thinking?

I walk over to the window by the door and stare in Lloyd and Wave's direction. I can picture their warm kind faces in the cabin's glass. I see Lloyd's smile from a time when we were shooting pool. He dropped one ball after another, then shot and sank the nine ball, winning again. I can see Wave laughing, free-spirited as always, as he walks across the hangar carrying an aviation chart, asking me, "Where we going this time?"

Once I'm lying on my back, rolled up in the carpet, I quickly realize that I do not need to do the reps and controlled breathing tonight. Since the carpet has never made friends with a vacuum cleaner, some of the sand, dirt, and hair that clings to its surface starts to trickle in my nose, mouth, ears, and right eye. I stretch my sweatshirt hood over my face and softly suck air from the corner of my mouth, using the hood as a filter as I fall asleep.

Nine
Adrift in an Ocean

December 2

Late Thursday evening, Susan, Rick, Judy, Kevin, and some other friends leave my house to get some rest at home for the night. Because Denise lives in Colorado and my dad splits his time between Connecticut and California, this is the first time in several years that my father and sister are alone. Clinging to each other for emotional support, they cry and describe how powerless they feel. All they can do is let time run its course. Even though the statistics on missing aircraft lead to only one logical outcome, they agree not to give up hope. They vow to continue thinking positive thoughts, trying to send me their love and strength, praying for a miracle.

Tired and emotionally drained, they lie down to sleep. Thanks to the medication my dad takes for his condition, he immediately nods off, but Denise twists and turns, wondering where I am and what I'm doing. She prays, hoping somehow I will contact her, my father, or my brother, so that they can come to my rescue.

Unable to sleep, Denise gets up at 1:00 a.m. and heads into the office to start faxing radio stations a letter that pleads for help locating the missing trio. Soon there is a knock at the front door. Worried about Wave, Lloyd, and me, Judy is unable to sleep and returns to my house. She and Denise stay up all night, faxing over a hundred radio stations and several TV stations—they call this "dialing for hope"—and digging through the office for missing clues that may help locate the aircraft.

Around 4:00 one of the TV stations calls the house, asking for a live interview. They make a date for 6:30 to 7:00 a.m., featuring Judy, Denise, and Jim, Wave's roommate, at Judy's house.

Although I'm cozy rolled up inside the carpet, my survival instincts prevent me from sleeping. Each time I drift asleep, my right eye suddenly springs wide open while my torso lunges off the dirty old wooden floor. Instinctively I think I'm in danger, that my limbs have frozen solid while I've been asleep. Out of fear, I start doing the reps to increase my blood circulation and say aloud, "You sleep, you die." I try to calm myself by taking slow deep breaths while trying to yawn, putting myself back to sleep.

I've been sleeping for about four hours when my right eye spikes open. I can sense a slight change in the darkness. I try to will myself to get up so that I can continue my journey, but my body refuses to budge. While I rest, warm and secure, I glance up at the window—and I remember the images of Wave and Lloyd that I saw in its reflection last night. They are depending on me to bring back help.

Finally standing, I tuck my T-shirt into my pants and reposition my ski bibs so they'll be more comfortable for today's hike. I limp over and sit down on the edge of one of the homemade wooden beds. Slowly I pull my smelly socks up over my shrunken calf muscles. My right boot slides on with ease, but while trying to slide the left boot on, I find that my left ankle is now too swollen to fit into the boot.

Immediately I recall when my left ankle crashed through the catwalk. The already shattered bones were jammed again, causing increased swelling. For the next several minutes the serenity of the cabin is filled with screams and moans as I force the boot over my throbbing fractured ankle.

Trying to quell the pain, I start taking deep breaths. Long minutes pass. As I stand, tears of pain roll down my cheeks into my filthy six-day beard. Standing completely still with my face down, I can feel the tears dripping off my jaw onto the cabin's old wooden floor. At last I zip up my jacket over my chin and pull the hood of my sweatshirt over my head. Next, I have to tie my boots. I sit back down on the corner of the bed frame. For the first time in six days I'm able to open and close my hands with effort, moving my fingers with little restriction. I think, I can make it. No matter what, I can do this.

I grab my walking stick and look out the window at the snow-covered forest. My thoughts return to the food and supplies likely waiting in the main cabin. I still want to break into it in hopes of finding matches or a lighter so that I can make fires.

As I continue to gaze out the window, my spirits begin to climb. I'm in better physical condition than I was yesterday morning. The hypothermia treatment in the hot springs has arrested the nasty constant shivers that accompanied me for the last five days.

My fingertips and toes are dark blue, indicating frostbite, but I still have complete feeling in them, a sign that they're alive. The muscles surrounding my fractures feel a little less tight. I don't exactly feel well rested, but I did sleep off and on.

I focus my attention on my long johns, which are still packed inside the hole of the door. I try to remove them but they have frozen solid inside the hole. After aggressively twisting, turning, and tugging, I work the garment free. The long johns do not flex. I lay them on the floor and begin to trample them with my boots, trying to flatten them out. That done, I drape them over my back and tie the frozen legs around my neck.

Reluctant to leave the safety of the hot springs and cabin behind, I swing open the cabin door and stare into the frozen darkness. My stomach begins to knot just as it did on Sunday when I parted with Wave to start the trek. Fear creeps up my spine and pulsates at the base of my neck. Purposely I shiver, trying to shake the dark feeling of death that now surrounds me. The bitter cold lashes out at me, whipping the skin on my exposed face, reminding me that the hot springs, cabin, and carpet were a gift, and that I must still soldier on.

Hiking back toward the hot springs, I follow the footsteps in the snow that I made on my way to the cabin, trying to conserve energy and stay dry. Looking back over my shoulder, I see that the cabins are hidden from the overhang of the trees. I recross Nine Mile Creek on the old wooden plank. Heading east alongside the creek, I can see the silhouette of the 9000-foot mountain that I must climb today.

While staring at today's objective, I straddle the border between the snowless meadow and two feet of snow. Out of nowhere an unknown force restrains me from putting both feet into the snow, from leaving the warmth and security of what I later learned was Jordan Hot Springs behind.

I remain split between the warm ground of life and the frozen shadows of death. Fear takes over and my frail body shivers, trembling in terror. Yet I know it's now or never. I must move.

Mechanically I lift my right leg from the dead grass to place it with my left foot in the snow. Facing east, staring at today's climb, I put the springs of life behind me. They are now only a part of my past memories.

After trekking through waist-deep snow, I reach the base of the mountain, admiring its majesty in the dark. The sharp penetrating fear that plagued me before is now buried in my trail of deep snow-prints. The tremble of terror has become just an occasional quiver that travels up the length of my spine. I pretend it is a chilly burst of mountain air.

I come to another plank spanning the gushing creek's width. Even though it has two feet of snow on its surface, I can see that half was rough-hewn from a tree, with the flat surface on top for walking. From the end I also see that the snow camouflages several inches of ice underneath. If I were to walk across the plank, I would slip into the icy drink.

My experience tells me the only way I can cross is to use the snow as traction. Kneeling on the log with both knees at the stream's edge, I gently pat down the snow. That way my knees and palms can sink down and rest on the ice, getting traction, but not slipping. In the center of the bridge all sounds in the forest are drowned out by the freezing, gushing water just two feet below my nose.

Reaching the other side of the stream safely, I spot a cabin at the edge of a snow-covered meadow. The high pitch of the cabin's roof tells me that whoever constructed it anticipated heavy snowfall. Thinking there might be another catwalk below the snow's surface or a barbed-wire fence, I proceed with caution. After advancing only ten feet, I'm forced to stop because the snow has risen to just below my chin.

With the shadows of the night dissolving into the early dawn's light, I remain planted in the snow, staring at the weather-beaten cabin. Although I expect no signs of life to appear, I still wait several minutes, fixated on the lifeless structure, wishing for help. It's probably locked up tight, too. It's not worth getting soaked for.

I recross the log bridge, debating whether I gave up too early in my investigation of the cabin. Although I know I must head east and climb the mountain before me, mentally I'm frozen. I cannot commit to any direction. I'm looking for an easy way out. I want to avoid the pain and the struggle. I simply lack what it takes to reach the top, desire.

I scan the area hoping something will catch my eye and help lift my spirits. I spot a sign fastened to a thick tree about thirty feet away. Brushing off snow, I see two arrows engraved on the weathered homemade wooden sign. One arrow points to the west and engraved next to it is "Kern River." The other points to the north and reads "Red Rock."

As I stare at the sign, I review my options. To the west, in the distance, I believe I can see the mountains that border the Kern River. Staring back at the engraved arrow, I start laughing aloud as I say, "No way. I'm not going back there. I just spent three days getting here."

I have no idea where Red Rock is, except it's to the north and I'm going east, but it's a trail sign and the trail could snake around the mountain and head east or lead to other cabins. One thing is for sure, the snow is too deep at the base of the mountains for me to hike through. It makes logical sense that the trail that heads to Red Rock is probably cut along the base of the mountains, twisting and turning, trying to avoid steep ascents and descents. It is probably closed during the winter months because the entire mountain range is inaccessible.

I have another option. I could follow Nine Mile Creek to see where that leads me. But I have a plan, and I'm still alive because my survival instincts have guided me. Both my mind and my heart tell me to dig deep and find the strength to conquer the mountain before me.

As with many new things that I must overcome, it seems the hardest part is simply taking the first step. I find myself caught in a trance while I stand and stare at the mountain's steep snowy base. I'm looking for stairs covered in red carpet to lead me to the top. I want to prevail, but I do not want to commit the energy or suffer the pain that it requires to ascend the peak.

I picture myself standing on top of this mountain, shaking my walking stick in victory, looking back down at the springs of life and saying, "Yes, I crested another peak, that's one less mountain I must climb." Sighing, I place my left foot forward to begin the ascent.

At mission headquarters the candles burned all night in preparation for the CAP sorties planned for today. The sun is up, the sky is clear, and it's a cool morning, a perfect day for flying.

As planned, Captain Judd lands at John Wayne Airport just before 8:00 a.m. and Howard and John load their gear into the aircraft. Within fifteen minutes Howard and John are strapped in, and the twin-engine plane is airborne again. After Judd establishes the twin into a climb, he says to Howard and John, "Our estimated time for General Fox Field is a little after nine, but with a little luck we should be on the search sortie by ten a.m."

The twin sets down at Fox Field as scheduled. The weather in the California high desert is even better than in the Los Angeles basin. The smog in L.A. is dark, ugly, and thick. As soon as you fly over the mountains that box in L.A., the air is clean and the visibility seems endless.

Since the twin still has enough fuel for four more hours of flight time, Captain Judd decides not to add any more fuel, which would decrease the plane's performance during the high-altitude sortie. CAP intelligence briefs the three men for thirty minutes. Their search assignment covers a grid southwest of Mount Whitney near the Kern River, close to the very area where Lloyd, Wave, and I are fighting to survive.

During the briefing the trio decides to fly up Owens Valley to a point where they can follow one of the lower highway passes across the mountain ridges and head west at a lower altitude. This would allow them to pick up the Kern considerably south, then head north searching along the river on their way to their search site.

Shortly after ten o'clock the twin Beechcraft Baron rolls down the runway and heads into the sky. The air is still cool and smooth, the winds light. The weather is forecast to remain this way all day, perfect conditions for this type of search.

In mountain searches, winds aloft are just as important a factor in determining whether a search continues as weather obscuring a grid site. High winds above mountain ridges can make searches very uncomfortable, even hazardous. They create updrafts and downdrafts. If the plane gets caught in a downdraft, it can be pushed right into the mountain. An updraft can cause the plane to gain altitude even without the pilot applying throttle.

As the twin climbs above 4500 feet, Judd notices that the aircraft is not climbing as it should. He quickly scans the instrument panel: flaps up, both engines functioning normal, trim tabs positioned normally, and no landing-gear warning light on. The aircraft's climbing ability continues to deteriorate and the crew discovers that one or all of the landing gear did not fully retract, creating drag. Judd checks the circuit breakers on the gear to see if a circuit popped out, but they are functioning.

Judd says to Howard and John, "I'm going to try and lower the gear." But nothing happens. The three men discuss their options and decide to return to General Fox Field before attempting to lower the gear manually. Judd radios CAP operations at the field to inform them of their situation.

While on the twenty-minute flight back to Fox Field, Judd makes radio contact with the Fox tower, which is already aware of their problem. As he communicates with the tower, Judd makes a mental note that he has been in the air forty-five minutes and now has only enough fuel for about three hours and fifteen minutes of flight. The tower asks, "What are your intentions?" Judd requests a low, slow fly-by so that the tower can make a visual check of the landing gear.

As the twin glides past, the men in the tower think all three wheels are partially retracted, but they're unable to make a conclusive statement. On the second pass from the opposite direction the control tower confirms that the landing gear is not fully retracted. Since it is critical that Judd know how far each wheel is extended, he asks the tower, "Can you tell whether they were extended evenly or to different degrees?"

The tower replies, "Not sure."

Judd radios, "We're proceeding to an area north of the field, clear of your traffic area to try lowering the gear manually."

Tower responds, "Affirmative. There is another aircraft in the area, a T-34 from Edwards Air Force Base Aero Club. They asked if they can be of any assistance to you."

Judd asks, "Can I get a common radio frequency? I will radio them."

The crew decides to climb to 4500 feet, giving them 2000 feet above the surface to work in. Judd turns the aircraft over to Howard and suggests that he keep her in a shallow bank and maintain a speed of 120 to 130 mph.

While Judd prepares to operate the landing gear using the manual crank, John starts reading off the checklist for the manual gear extension to Judd, double-checking each of Judd's steps. After repeated attempts it becomes obvious that the crank handle is engaging as it is supposed to, but the captain feels no back pressure on the crank, an indication that the gear isn't catching.

The captain and John try to manually engage the landing gear four times with no success when the T-34 arrives, and Judd asks, "Can you fly wing on me, but slightly lower to ascertain the condition of the landing gear?" After several minutes the pilot of the T-34 radios back, saying, "It does not look good. All three wheels are partly extended at different degrees with the left wheel down about thirty percent, the right one ten and the nose wheel fifteen." The first rule that Judd learned as an airline pilot was if one makes a wheels-up landing, be sure it's not by accident—that is, don't forget to put the gear down during landing. The second rule was try to get the main wheels fully retracted.

The T-34 pilot radios, "My observer is a trained Beechcraft mechanic. Would you mind some suggestions?"

Judd responds, "By all means."

The mechanic asks, "Did you try the manual method more than once?"

Judd radios, "Many times."

Next the three men buckle up their belts and put the twin into a dive. Once the plane is descending, Judd pulls back on the yoke hard, trying to force the gear down using gravity. They make several dives with no luck.

The mechanic aboard the T-34 tells Judd to leave the manual crank engaged while resetting the circuit breakers, giving the electric motor one more try. Before doing so Judd warns John to keep his hands clear of the crank because if it works, the handle will start spinning like crazy. As Judd puts the gear handle in the down position he can hear the electric motor running, but the handle does not spin, indicating that the worm gear between the crank handle and the electric motor is not engaging the sector gear, which lowers the landing wheels.

The captain confirms with the mechanic aboard the T-34 what he already knows: the gear is hopelessly jammed in its present position. As the T-34 banks to head for Edwards AFB, the Baron crew thanks them for their help. The two men aboard the T-34 wish the crew luck as they disappear into the blue skies, leaving the crew aboard the broken twin alone.

Frustrated and out of options, Judd radios CAP operations at Fox Field to update them on their progress. Since CAP operations was out of the communication link while the crew was in contact with the T-34, after radioing operations the crew must now wait several minutes for the operations officer to return the radio call.

The officer radios, "Do you wish to land at General Fox Field?"

Judd asks, "Do you still have search planes in the air?"

The operations officer responds, "Affirmative."

The crew and the operations officer decide not to tie up the only runway they have in operation. The operations officer asks, "Do you have enough fuel to reach Van Nuys Airport?"

Judd responds, "Yes, we have enough fuel, but I do not want to interrupt operations at a commercial field."

While the twin Beechcraft sails through the blue skies burning precious fuel, the three men discuss their options. They agree that since they still have about two hours of fuel on board, they can reach several airports that are better equipped to handle a potential disaster than Fox.

There is silence in the cabin while all three men mull over the options: long runways, not much traffic, and lots of emergency equipment. Suddenly John Soley says, "Why not El Toro? It is our squadron base and familiar territory."

Judd agrees, then radios the operations officer at Fox asking him to call El Toro to see if they will accept the twin.

A few long minutes later CAP informs them that El Toro is awaiting their arrival. The crew thanks operations for their help and gives an estimated time of arrival at El Toro. Since the weather forecast at El Toro is clear, with winds light and variable—perfect conditions for a forced landing—the captain is upbeat.

Silence fills the cockpit as each man thinks about the old bird making her last landing. Judd continues to fly the plane, Howard keeps to himself, and John stays busy writing as he has throughout most of the flight, except when helping Judd with the emergency procedures.

They have been in the air about three hours; Judd is feeling fatigued and assumes Howard must be feeling the same and that must be why Howard is so quiet. When Judd glances back and sees John writing, he thinks, He is probably recording all this for the CAP newspaper; a very thorough man he is.

When the twin is ten miles northeast of El Toro, Judd radios the tower with their position.

Judd asks, "Are you aware of our situation?"

Tower replies, "Affirmative. Do you have enough fuel to stand a short delay?"

Judd responds, "Affirmative. The more gas we burn off the less chance for a fire."

The emergency equipment is ready, but the ground crew needs a little more time to remove the arresting gear, a restraining cable used for practice carrier landings. It crosses the runway about a thousand feet from the approach end and extends about fifty feet beyond each side of the runway.

Judd holds a pre-landing briefing. John already has both emergency exit windows in the back unlatched.

Judd says to John, "Once the aircraft comes to a full stop, do not hesitate. Leave by either window exit that is free of fire."

Howard's job is to open the cabin door and exit as soon as the aircraft stops. When time permits during a crash landing, one of the checklist items is to unlatch windows and doors beforehand because the airframe may bend and twist after slamming into the ground, jamming the exits and making an escape from a smoke-filled burning aircraft impossible.

Judd tells the tower that he and his crew are ready whenever they are. As the twin makes its final circle over the field, Judd thinks through the approach and landing one more time. If we could land with both engines shut off and the props feathered, the chance of fire and/or major damage would be reduced greatly, he decides.

He tells Howard, "When we are established on left base leg for landing, I am going to shut down and feather the right engine. At that time you unlatch and crack open the cabin door."

He then says to Howard and John, "When we turn final, if everything looks good as planned, then I am going to shut down and feather the left engine."

Both agree with the plan. Howard's only response is, "Are we landing on the runway or in the grass?"

"On the runway as close to the fire trucks as possible."

Howard smiles slightly but says nothing. As Judd continues to fly the bird, he thinks how Howard's question was so unusual, but he seems to be in agreement with the plan. Judd vows to talk to Howard later about it.

As the plane turns onto the downwind leg for landing, it's quickly abeam of the touch-down spot on the runway. Judd lowers the flaps fifteen degrees for landing. Normally he uses full flaps, but he believes he will have more control of the powerless bird down the runway if the flaps are not hanging all the way down out the bottom.

At this point he closes the right engine throttle and moves the mixture control to idle cutoff position, killing the engine. Next he puts the right prop control to feather position. Howard and John complete their pre-landing duties.

As Judd turns the twin onto base leg, he purposely swings it wide in order to give himself enough time on final landing so he can establish a glide path that will get the twin to the touch-down spot before shutting down the left engine.

After turning on final, he checks airspeed and distance to the touch-down spot. Satisfied that all looks good, he shuts down the left engine and feathers the left prop. The Beechcraft Baron, with the engines so close to the fuselage, is a very noisy airplane, but now with the plane gliding on no power, the silence is disconcerting. It takes Judd a few seconds to get back to the job at hand.

He knows that the initial contact with the runway has to be on the left side because the left landing gear is hanging down the farthest, but, more important, he must fly the plane just inches off the deck and keep the full weight of the aircraft off the left gear for as long as possible, flying the plane in what's called *ground effect*. This happens when a plane is a wingspan's length above the ground, but the effect is much stronger when at one-half the wingspan's length. Ground effect can make the airplane float on landings.

As the twin glides down to the tarmac with the flaps down only fifteen degrees, Judd tries to set the bird's nose slightly lower than for normal landing. This technique will give him elevator control for a longer period and allow him to keep the full weight of the airplane off the landing gear until the bird has slowed, allowing her to rest gently on her belly.

Just six hundred feet from the fire trucks, the twin begins to nick the pavement. As Judd continues to ease back on the yoke, trying to keep the old bird flying for as long as she can, the emergency ground crew can hear it scraping its belly, giving off long bright sparks that they watch intently for signs of fire or explosion.

The old girl's airspeed bleeds and she slowly starts to settle her weight on the black landing strip. With the tires and metal grinding, filling the cabin with smoke, the three men start to inhale burned rubber. Although the fire trucks are still in sight, Judd feels like everything is happening in slow motion, that he is scraping, grinding, and skidding down the runway for over a thousand feet.

Airspeed now falls below the limit at which the old girl can fly in ground effect. Still grinding her belly and shooting sparks off the tarmac, she settles her full weight on the runway. Judd continues to give the controls input, trying to keep the right wing tip off the ground until the last second. He is afraid that if they have too much speed when the right tip finally touches, they may cartwheel, causing the remaining fuel aboard to explode, burning all three men to death.

Suddenly the nose swings to the right about twenty degrees. The plane grinds down the runway for another hundred feet, giving off sparks and smoke until she comes to rest almost directly in front of the emergency crew.

With raw tire smoke filling the cockpit Judd yells, "Everybody out!" Wasting no time turning off the fuel switches, he exits the dead plane. He quickly sees that his crew is safe and runs over to join them, well clear of the emergency crew, who are securing the bird.

Everyone is all right.

Then Judd remembers the question that Howard asked earlier. "What did you mean when you asked me, was I landing on the grass or the runway?"

Smiling, Howard says, "Several years ago I was in almost identical circumstances as today. The pilot decided to land in the grass. The aircraft was destroyed. How we got out without serious injuries I will never know."

Judd turns to John. "What was all the writing about?"

John replies, "I have all the confidence in the world in you, Ed, but I was writing my will just in case."

Despite the forced crash landing, that day fifty-seven CAP members launch eighteen aircraft totaling fifty sorties with over 100 hours of total flight time, and 35.2 hours of that in the grid.

Adding to the search sortie count, Lloyd's friend Jim Mashburn hires Bill Woodward for the second day. They fly over Tunnel Meadows, which is seven air statute miles north of the wreck. Included in their two hours of flight time is a search of the Mount Whitney area.

The media momentum builds as the *Long Beach Press-Telegram* releases another story. The headline reads: AERIAL SEARCH FOR MISSING SMALL PLANE TO CONTINUE TODAY.

As I struggle to reach the mountain's peak, I have a view to the west, where I can see the general area where the Maule went down. Gazing out toward the wreckage site, again I wonder, What is Wave doing? Why no smoke? Is Lloyd still alive? Is it possible they were rescued and I never saw or heard the rescue team? Does the rescue team think I'm dead?

Still able to use only one lung, I gasp for air as I continue my ascent. My inner clothes are drenched from sweat. My mouth is dry. I'm thirsty and just short of vomiting from exhaustion. The deadly combination of steep rugged terrain mixed with deep unstable snow and ice has forced me to scale down my climbing goals to just five- to ten-foot sections.

While resting I scan the terrain, looking for downed trees sloping downhill, which can form a logged path to the peak. A downed tree is a valuable aid. I can grab its branches and pull myself up the mountain. I also can use the branches for footholds. The giant ones also come in handy when I need to rest. I just wedge my body into the branches until I'm secure.

I resume the vertical assault, zigging and zagging from tree to downed tree. I think I see the mountain's summit some fifty feet ahead. After climbing steadily with only a few breaks, I'm just steps from an area where the terrain opens up, what I believe to be the top. Although fatigued, I push extra hard to claim today's victory. Just as I get ready to cheer and shake my walking stick above my head, I realize that the mountain has tricked me again.

As my gaze slowly follows the choppy contour of the mountain upward, I feel my energy evaporate. The summit is higher yet. I stand and stare at my overwhelming opponent, who has fooled me time and time again. While gasping for air I scream, "Why are you testing me? Why do you let me think I'm close to the top, then slap me in the face with this?" The only answer I hear is the sound of my labored breathing and my heart pounding in my chest.

I think, Maybe I should just head back to the hot springs and wait for a search team. In desperation I scan the immediate area, seeing only cold lifeless snow in all directions.

My breathing calms. I say nothing, not even a whisper.

First I think, It's OK to die. You're in God's country. Then I ask myself, Is it OK to give up? Is it? This is so tough. I don't want to do this anymore.

Moments pass. Even as I get ready to tell myself, Keep moving, you have to do it, you told Wave you could make it, I realize that somehow I'm already moving. I'm not going to give up.

With my clothes and boots soaking wet and my long johns still tied around my neck, I reach the 9097-foot summit. I stare at the spectacular 360 degree view while the merciless wind burns my unprotected earlobes and chapped face. Desperately I listen for unnatural sounds of possible search-and-rescue helicopters, snowmobiles, or a Snow-Cat, but I hear only the solitude of the wilderness.

With clear skies and the sun just past its zenith I may have enough time to dry my clothes on the large rocks that surround the area. The rocks are a light gray and do not absorb as much heat as dark rocks, so I have to leave my clothes out until the last minute of sunlight.

Sitting around naked out in the open can quickly lead to dehydration. Against my discipline, I sit in the sun on a natural bed of sequoia needles and chew on some snow.

Both my feet are dark blue and burning from frostbite, so I slide them into my jacket, then fold the jacket halves over them so that the heat will not escape. Then I zip it up, wearing the garment upside down.

As the minutes click by, I visualize the sun's rays tapping my remaining pool of minerals and nutrients, depleting me of energy, leaving me to die. I decide to limit my sunbathing spell to the time it takes for my ski bibs to dry, a thirty-minute warming delight.

Clothed with my ski bibs, the exterior jacket layer on my torso, and the outer rubber shells to my boots, I hike eastward below the summit to a copse of sequoias with several large needle beds. Because the trees and rocks form a natural protective perimeter from the heavy winds, I decide to gather needles and bark to rest here tonight.

Soon enough the sun is almost touching the distant mountain peaks to the west. I hike back up to my drying clothes. The boot liners are damp and the long johns are still too wet to wear.

Fully dressed, I scan the rugged mountain range one more time before the sun goes down. As I gape at the snow-covered mountaintops rippling endlessly in all directions, I feel as if I'm adrift in an ocean with no land in sight. Six days have passed and I'm in the same situation I was in from day one. I start doubting my navigational skills. Could I be wrong about my direction? Am I completely lost?

I'm overwhelmed with fear and panic. A negative landslide of emotions attacks my ability to reason. I envision myself wandering aimlessly, starving and freezing, then keeling over in the snow to become a frozen carcass.

I respond to the mental assault by grabbing cold handfuls of snow. Using both hands, I rub wet freezing snow against my cheeks and temples, trying to snap out of the panic attack. My eye falls on the rock knob in the distance, and I tell myself, The knob is to the west, I'm headed east. I've hiked in a straight line so far. I can make it. I'm in the center of the mountain range. It's going to take some luck and a couple more days to hike out of here.

The sun falls below the peaks to the west and darkness blankets the mountain range. Before I hike down to my shelter, I stare in the direction of the wreckage site in hopes of spotting light coming from a campfire. Although I don't see any signs of light, I continue to watch because this is the last chance I will have to see the area where the Maule went down. Once I'm over this mountain I'll be unable to look back to the crash site.

I'm soon buried under the needles, branches, and bark as has become my ritual. I listen to the increasing howls of the freezing wind as I stare up at the dark sky, waiting for my star formation to appear so that I can reassure myself of my eastward heading.

As the nightly shivers begin, I think, If I have to, I can return to the hot springs. After all, it's a downhill hike.

With the clear frigid sky picture-perfect and full of bright shooting stars, I make several wishes for my mom, my dad, Lloyd, and Wave. While doing the survival reps throughout the night, I think about the bright light in the sky on Monday late morning.

Ten
Whiteout

December 3–4

I'm unable to get a wink of sleep throughout the endless, torturous glacial night, and I welcome the long awaited change in the darkness. After uncovering my body from the needles and bark, I push myself to my feet. While my entire body quivers in the frigid wind, I lean on my faithful tree-branch crutch. As I remain planted in the knee-deep snow, my body sways about from the wind's hammering ferocity. I raise both hands to protect my face from the swirling snow crystals pelting my body.

From yesterday's summit perch, I set today's goal: the sister peak to the east. This lofty aim is based on a simple principle I have learned. If on today's trek I get trapped at the bottom where the two mountains meet, I will freeze for sure because the snow is deep and wet, and the shaded rocks do not offer enough radiating heat to dry my clothes. In order for me to have a chance, I must attain the top of the next peak before 11:30 a.m., so that I will have a few hours of strong sun. Such are the simple rules of survival.

As I descend the steep rugged mountain, the wind of the exposed peak settles to a calm because I walk in the cover of the giant sequoias.

Although my trek to the bottom is downhill, wading through the knee- and waist-deep snow exhausts me. The early morning daylight is blocked by low, thick dark clouds, forcing me to keep my sweatshirt hood over my head and my clothes tightly bundled around my body.

After three or four hours I reach the base of the mountain and rest for thirty minutes. Kneeling at the fast, wide ice-covered stream that separates the two sister mountains, I slowly lap its freezing, numbing water.

I search up and down the stream for a safe dry crossing. I'm able to find only a thin tree that has fallen across the banks. When I mount the snow-covered frail tree, it begins to shake, twist, and sag, immediately almost throwing me off its saddle into the water. I wrap both legs around its thin branches. I grab the limbs with my left arm and hook its sharp pointed branches with my chin, face, and neck, holding my body secure against the trunk while it whips about.

The pressure of curling three of my limbs and chest tightly around the wiry tree causes my broken bones to explode with piercing pain. I scream in agony as I slither inch by inch. Reaching the center point, I stop. With my head just inches above the frozen stream, I listen to the rushing water beneath the thin layer of ice. Before continuing my slither I think, What the hell am I doing out here? This is nuts! If I fall into the water I have no way to dry my clothes. I will freeze in just a few short hours.

When I'm almost across the stream, the tree suddenly sways out of control from my weight, nearly bucking me off onto the jagged rocks at the stream's edge. Using all my strength, I wrestle the last section of the thin icy trunk and the toothpick-size branches. My reward for reaching the end is a slide off into waist-deep snow.

Before attacking the next mountain's heights, I bust a hole in the thin ice for more of my animal lapping. After twenty minutes of drinking and resting I rise to my feet with the help of my walking stick. Then gripping it tightly in my left hand, I stare at the mountain's first twenty feet of vertical climb, thinking, If the entire climb is this steep, it's going to take me several days to reach the top.

As I climb, I check the dark cloudy skies. I'm not going to gain any respite from the sun. With my wet clothes I pray for the sun's strength to burn through the overcast, but deep within me I know a storm is brewing.

As I continue to ascend the mountain, visual navigation is difficult because of the lack of sun and reference points. Unlike the past six days, where I had the rock knob and some opposing mountains to use for navigation, I now have nothing to help me hike in a straight line. At times I feel like I'm headed north, then I feel like I'm headed south. I'm unable to hold my course heading. Stopping, I turn around and scan the mountain that I descended earlier today, searching for reference points, but I see nothing; the rocks, trees, and cliffs all look the same. Finally I use the mountain peak where I survived last night to realign my easterly heading by mentally drawing a line from it to the tip of today's climb. That gives me little confidence. I'm so nervous that I may be veering off my hiking line that I catch myself realigning my heading when I'm forced to stop every two minutes because of my gagging outbreaks caused from lack of oxygen.

I'm also fighting through a thick, wet, heavy snow base much tougher than anything I've had to wade through in the last six days. It's bitter cold and strong winds are blowing from the southeast. The wind velocity has increased to the point that I use the waist-deep snow to anchor myself so that I'm not blown down the mountain. Snow eddies swirl everywhere, limiting my visibility. I have to accept the inevitable. A storm is coming. How am I going to shelter myself from its unforgiving assault?

At last I spot a large fallen tree, offering grip holds and a dry place to rest. Using the dead branches that protrude from the massive trunk, I pull myself closer. Once I'm seated on the giant downed pillar, I lock myself onto its branches, resting and hiding from the wind's pelting snow. No longer is the wilderness a place of serene silence. As the howling wind increases, low, dark clouds race overhead.

I use the branches from the tree to secure me on the steep terrain as I urinate. Although I don't see any signs of blood in the yellow orangish urine, the smell reminds me of one night in L.A. when I ventured down a dark alley among a group of vagrants. The smell in that alley nearly caused me to vomit.

I have been living on only small helpings of bugs for seven days. I have not passed any stool, and my body's deterioration shows in the color and smell of my urine and in my extreme weight loss. As I break into a fresh series of gags and scraping coughs, I spit onto the tree and inspect the phlegm for blood. Luckily I see no red tint. Finishing my physical examination, I check my rectum and underwear for fresh signs of blood, but there too I am still OK.

Continuing the hike, I'm forced to exert all my energy on a vertical icy patch to the point that I can no longer breathe. During a violent cough attack, I fall into the snow. While in a fetal position I try to suck enough air to survive between the hacking attacks. I move on after resting in the cold snow for some twenty minutes.

At last I'm finally at the same elevation as yesterday's peak. As I near this mountaintop, I say with relief, "Man, what a climb that was!" Suddenly I realize that I'm still below the peak and that another mountain has fooled me.

From this mountain's vantage point, I see many new snow-capped mountaintops. The Sierras are so vast, it looks like a whole new range awaits me. My thought for the last couple of days was that if I hiked to the east the peaks would become lower in elevation, but now I'm confronting peaks equal in elevation or higher. As I stand in the knee-deep snow, leaning into the cold wailing wind, a chilling thought comes to me: What if I'm wandering in a big circle? Maybe I'm headed south and not east? Maybe I screwed up. Could I be going north toward Yosemite? Maybe it's going to take me longer than a couple of days to get out of here.

Although the wind velocity is still increasing by the minute and the storm appears to be headed my way, I decide that the storm will advance at an average pace, giving me a few more hours of hiking time.

Even though I'm struggling to wade through the snow, which

should warm my body, the lack of sun and the severe wind are making me shiver all over. Looking at the clouded skies, I estimate that I have seven hours of daylight left.

With the storm clouds racing overhead, the endless view of snow-capped peaks, the frostbite in my extremities, and the pain of my fractures, again I consider the good life in the hot springs. Maybe the hot springs spoiled me. Maybe they made me soft. Maybe they took the survival edge from me. Yes, I was spoiled and now I'm going to pay.

Despite the lack of sunlight I'm able to continue navigating to the east. Because it's still morning, the sun is at a low position directly ahead of me, showing as a yellowish stain bleeding through the clouds.

Cresting at what I believe to be the top of the mountain, I'm forced to alter my direction because right in front of me is a large collection of trailer-truck-size boulders. At least hiking around the side of this giant rock complex temporarily protects me from the raging winds.

As I try to push onward, I suddenly crash through a frozen layer of snow, leaving me standing in snow that is chin-deep. Struggling to get free, I search with both feet for the layer that I just crashed through, climbing back onto it so that I can return to a snow depth I can wade through.

I continue east along the boulders. After twenty minutes of hiking I leave the giant rocks behind me and become exposed to the pelting winds again. In the short time that I was behind the boulders the winds have increased further. Snow and ice are whipping through the air like sand in a violent desert sandstorm. I lower my head and raise both hands to my face, trying to protect myself from the crystallized chunks that are pelting me. Squinting between my gloved fingers I see that the mountain peak to the south is engulfed by the storm. I judge that leaves me less than a half hour before I'm in the middle of whiteout conditions.

Operating on animal instincts, I search for warm dry shelter where I can wait out the storm. My gut tells me that if I try to move during a blizzard, I will become disoriented and will wander aimlessly through the mountains. A mental image of my bleak future pops into my mind. I can see myself slightly hunched over with only my neck, head, and the top of my left gloved hand (resting on my walking stick) sticking out of the deep snow. The wind blows strong, and snow and ice collect on my already frozen head. I picture long icicles hanging from my beard, smaller ice fringes hanging from my eyebrows and eyelashes. I imagine that underneath the snow my body is encapsulated in a block of ice, where it will stay preserved until the spring when wildlife awakes, when the flowers blossom and the worms and insects begin to feed. Breaking from the horrible images, I take a few deep breaths, then say aloud into the stormy wilderness: "I'm not going to let that happen to me!"

CAP has had to call off mountain searches due to the storm. Sorties are now confined to the low desert. CAP pulls together seventy-four personnel who launch twenty-one aircraft that fly fifty-four sorties. They log total flight time for the day, Saturday, of 84.3 hours, but with only 12.7 hours of that in actual assigned grids.

Desperate, the families turn to psychic readings, hoping to turn up fresh clues on our whereabouts. With the TV media reporting the storm, some people lose hope. "Nobody can survive a bloody mountain plane crash, then live through a Sierra blizzard."

My brother, Rocco, flies in from Connecticut to be with Denise and Dad.

Knowing I need to find shelter before the storm swamps me, I look back at the giant boulders for a cave or some rock overhang, but my inner voice says, "No! Don't go near the rocks. They will steal the heat from your body. You will die for sure! You could be here for several days waiting for the storm to clear. If you can't find anything else to make a shelter, then try to find your way back to these boulders as a last resort."

I nervously increase my hiking pace through the deep snow, searching for shelter and aware that I have little time left. After a minute, I'm struck with an old memory. It's summertime and I'm in the fourth grade, spending a week with my grandfather and grandmother at their house in Connecticut. Each night before supper my grandfather would set up targets in the backyard for me to shoot with his pellet gun. After several nights of target practice, I told Grandpa that I wanted to head into the woods and hunt some animals. As Grandpa agreed, he said, "Remember, walk slowly and softly. Don't scare the animals. If you move too fast, you will walk right by what you're looking for. Everything you need is right there. Be patient and walk with your head up so you can see."

Replaying over and over in my mind what my grandfather told me, I pause and eye the storm that is headed my way. Stay calm. Scan the area for solutions. Remember, everything you need is right here.

My gaze bounces off every tree, bush, and rock in sight when suddenly, through the swirling storm, I spot a tree with a trunk the width of a small car. The base has been damaged by fire. About 30 percent of its diameter is burned away, exposing the center of the tree, creating a cavity just big enough for me to squat in. Just to the right of the tree trunk is a string of truck-size boulders that will help block the wind. Quickly I think, Maybe I can build a lean-to fort around the damaged area of the tree, then stay inside the trunk. It's warm and trees don't steal heat—they help insulate.

In the immediate area are several large sequoias and a few massive evergreens that form a small wilderness canopy over the ground below. At their base the snow is only a few inches deep and I am able to quickly gather large piles of needles.

The storm is now coming on hard as I feverishly prepare. Although full whiteout conditions have not yet arrived, I have only a few minutes to gather more branches and needles before visibility is zero. There are several smaller fern trees nearby. I hike over to them, then hastily snap off full live branches, piling them on the snow. I continue to work, trying to beat the storm, but my severe lack of nutrition and multiple body fractures impede my race against time.

The snow is coming down so hard, it creates a white blur. It's impossible to see which direction the trunk is located. I pick up a large pile of branches and mentally picture where I believe the trunk and the string of boulders are. While wading through the snow, I mark my trail by dropping branches along the way so that I can find my way back to the remaining piles. After several steps of blindly wading around, I question my heading. I proceed through the whiteout with caution, dropping a branch trail all the way, and make it to the tree.

While the blizzard continues to pound away, I spend the next thirty minutes transporting the remaining branches back to the trunk using the branch-marked trail. With all the branches now piled at the base of the tree's trunk, I need only one more component in order to build a windproof shelter that can withstand a violent Sierra snowstorm. I need a wall of twenty-five to thirty branches five to six feet long.

Luckily, before the blizzard started I spotted a branch-filled dead tree about forty paces away. I fill my arms, then lay a branchy trail behind me as I venture away from the trunk, searching for the downed tree. With the mixture of high winds and the storm dumping snow fiercely, my wooded trail disappears quickly. Just as I drop another branch to mark my trail, I trip over one of the downed tree's branches.

With the dead tree lying on its side, I'm able to get enough body leverage to snap the thinner branches off its trunk. Once I have about fifteen straight limbs loaded in both arms, using both feet I feel for my trail as I blindly hike through the snow. After several trips I clean my trail by picking up my dropped branches and carrying them back to the fort.

Now that I have piles of needles, branches filled with needles, and straight branches I can build a double-layer fort. First, I kneel down in front of the burned-out core. Using my left hand, I remove sticks, bark, and dirt until the entire center is completely

clean, leaving a giant hole in the ground. Using the gathered needles I fill the freshly dug hole, leveling the tree's center floor, creating a soft, cozy six-inch base. Testing out my perch, I cram
myself inside the trunk so that my knees are fully bent to my chest
and my chin rests on my kneecaps. I have six inches of clearance
between the top of my head and the tree trunk above, so I add
more needles to the trunk's floor to increase the insulation between the ground and my buttocks and feet. Sitting inside the
tree's cavity for a second trial, I find the top of my head now
touches the tree-trunk ceiling.

When I crawl out of the tree, visibility is still zero and I experience spatial disorientation. The snow is coming down so hard
that my tracks around the tree are covered in snow in just a few
minutes. With a sigh of relief I think, That was close. If I did not
find this tree, I would probably be dead by morning.

Before using the branches to construct the exterior layer of the
fort I transport all of the remaining needles to the trunk's entrance. Then I tightly stack and form the needles in front of the
hole, building a wall so that the hollowed-out core is sealed off
from blowing snow. Next, using the straight limbs, I drive the
thick end of each branch securely into the snow, then rest the thin
end up against the tree above the hole. After thirty minutes the
line of tree limbs extends three to four feet on each side of the
trunk's entrance.

Since the wind can penetrate the loose-wall construction, I start
weaving the live needle-filled branches into the straight limbs, creating a wind block. As I finish this stage, I press against the outside wall to test its strength and durability. To my surprise it's
sturdy and needs only minor patchwork insulation. To the right
of the tree I notice a small pile of needles I haven't used and I
cram handfuls of needles and strips of bark into the small cracks
in the fort's wall. The double-layer fort is now complete. Layer
one, the primary capsule, the center of the trunk, is sealed off by a
thick wall of needles. And layer two, the exterior wall, acts as a
wind and snow barrier.

Before I enter my tree-trunk home, I urinate off to the side in the snow. Relaxed, I get on both knees in front of the stick wall where the hole in the tree is located, then spread the limbs apart just enough so I can slither through my tiny opening. As I crawl behind the secondary layer of the fort, the shrieking of the attacking storm is completely muted. Before sliding the limbs back together, sealing off the fort from the weather, I reach outside to drag a snow block inside so that I will have access to water without having to leave the fort. As I slide the sticks back together, closing the fort opening, the lack of sound and light gives the fort a peaceful feeling of solitary contentment.

I reach up to the top of the wall of needles, then carefully drag enough needles off to the side so that I can crawl over the needle mound and into the center of the tree. Taking position in the center capsule, I sit with my knees bent into my chest and my kneecaps almost touching my chin. The pain from my broken ribs and right shoulder is magnified because the angle of the chamber's ceiling forces me to lean forward, but I'm just going to have to live with it. To seal the center compartment behind, I begin restacking the needles, forming the needle wall behind me. For fresh air I leave an inch gap between the needles and the top of the cavity.

Within twenty minutes, my body heat has filled the tiny insulated capsule enough that I unzip my jacket and remove the soaking wet outside shell to my boots. I cover my wet boot liners with pine needles, insulating them, trying to raise the temperature in my feet, hoping to keep the tissue alive. I know it's a long shot, but I'm hoping the warmth from the chamber will help dry out my boots and boot liners before the storm passes so that I don't have to slide the cold, wet, smelly old doggers back on my frostbitten feet when it's time to trek on.

I try to adjust to my fractures and the cramping of the dishwasher-size quarters by closing my eyes and slowly inhaling through my nose, then exhaling through my mouth, a form of pain-control meditation. Although I'm temporarily safe, the blizzard is pinning me inside this soundproof pitch-black chamber, making me feel totally disconnected from life. Occasionally I groan from the pain and hiss like a wild animal, a further testament to age-old instincts I barely knew existed.

After an hour of meditation, I'm able to doze off, taking intermittent catnaps. Whenever I wake I think, bizarrely, of exotic tropical foods. Starving, secluded inside a mountain tree trunk, I can smell and taste Caribbean juices and fruits. In my mind I can see the bowls of colored juices and the sliced fruits spread across a long table. While I continue my meditation breathing, my mouth begins to salivate as I sense fish, chicken, and meats being cooked with rich spices over a barbecue. As I slowly savor the aromas I think, When Wave, Lloyd, and I get out of here, I'm doing something I never have done before. I'm going on a cruise to the Caribbean, where it's warm and where they have giant displays of fruits, fish, and meats twenty-four hours a day. I can eat any time of the day that I want to. We'll sit at a table that overlooks the ocean while eating like kings!

With my food craving rising to a peak, I slide the wall of needles down so that I can grab a piece of snow from the snow block. I tell myself, All you need is water. Just keep on eating snow. This is 100 percent Sierra Nevada snow; it's simply the best!

After dozing in and out of sleep for about two hours, I can no longer take the pain in my snow-filled bladder. I push the wall of needles to the side, then climb out. The temperature drops drastically as I enter the secondary layer. Exiting the fort completely, I stand in the relentless blizzard with one gloved hand touching the boulders for security while I urinate in the snow.

After I finish I stretch my body before returning to the dwarf confines of the capsule. Returning to the pitch dark of the center chamber with the wall of needles in place, I slowly lull myself into a meditative state, then into a light sleep. As I wake I wonder, Is Lloyd still alive? What is Wave doing? How is he handling this storm? By now he must have a nice fort built with a warm campfire burning.

I ignore the pressing question: How long will I wait out this storm in the center of this tree? At what point do I push on? Although I have no input from any outside atmospheric data, like an animal that lives underground I sense the change in darkness. With the night coming I decide to check the rate of snowfall and urinate for the last time before the temperature drops. The storm is still pounding away. After peeing in the secondary layer, I return to the inner chamber, then restack the needle wall. With the center now chilly again, I wait for my body heat to warm the capsule.

For several hours I remain scrunched inside the capsule. With only inches of room inside the trunk to reposition my body, I periodically relieve pressure on my broken ribs and fractured shoulder. Yet no matter how I position my body, I'm uncomfortable and in severe pain. A dark thought leaps out at me: If I die in here, nobody will ever find my remains. Is this my tomb? I try to keep mentally focused while saying softly, "You can't leave. Where are you going to go? What will you do? Peter, stay put. It's warm and dry here. Discipline. Think with logic, not emotion."

I revisit a time when I was twenty years old. During that period of my life I studied computer programming at a technical college and trained several hours a day at a karate school. Master Lee made the students hold their karate stances for several long minutes while saying the English word "discipline" in a rough Korean accent. Some of the stances were unnatural and uncomfortable, making the body stretch, causing pain. Master Lee walked through the class with a bamboo stick, striking the calf or thigh muscle on a student who was cheating on his or her stance. If he found several students not trying their hardest, the whole class would suffer. He'd force us to hold our stances for twice as long. In the nine months that I studied under him, Lee never hit me with his bamboo. Weekly he worked with me privately, encouraging me to develop my techniques, helping me to find new levels of personal confidence.

I'll never forget Master Lee. He helped instill a sense of mental discipline that I have carried throughout my life. Remaining cramped inside the tiny dark capsule, I use that iron will he taught me to ignore the pain in my fractured rib cage and my shattered left ankle. Closing my eyes, I slowly begin breathing deep. Softly, calmly, and slowly, I say, "In three to four days the storm will pass. That's all the time I have to stay here curled up in this painful human ball. Come on, you can do it."

The peak of the frigid night is here. Cold air seeps inside the fort, lowering the small compartment's temperature, forcing me to do the survival reps and the survival breathing, channeling the warm exhaled air into my zipped-up jacket. As my bladder is pressured by my cramped position, I grit my teeth. I don't want to leave the capsule for fear the compartment will fill with subzero air. With my stomach in bloated pain, I count the seconds until the early morning change in darkness.

Yet such is the human body's need for rejuvenation that even with my fractured bones throbbing and my bladder feeling like it's going to explode, I drift off to sleep for twenty-minute intervals, awakening with a jolt in fear of my limbs freezing. I massage my feet with my left hand, trying to increase the circulation. With the manipulation, my feet begin to sting and burn, signs of feeling returning to the severely frostbitten areas. I am surviving the blizzard.

In the trunk's dark womb I now experience complete mental rest. My physical trauma seems to dissolve as I find peace cramped inside the tree trunk. I have never experienced such a feeling of removal from the human race—not even during the many times when I rode my dirt bike in the vast deserts of the west. This is preparing me for my unwritten destiny. This is cleansing my soul.

A sick man wants to be healthy. A lonely man wants love. A hungry man wants food. I'm a lucky man in this warm, dry shelter. Even with the blizzard still raging away, happiness fills me. I murmur the words, "I'm alive and I've got a chance." Lloyd's and Wave's faces appear in my mind and I say, "Hang in there, guys. I'll make it out of here, then I'm coming back for ya."

From within the dark tree trunk, I begin humming the trumpet sounds of this song while singing its lyrics,

> What the world needs now is love, sweet love,
> That's the only thing that there's just too little of.

After humming the song so many times that it runs unbidden like a tape loop, I stop singing, then whisper, "You must be disciplined. You're alone, there is no backup for you. Nobody knows where you are. You have no spare clothes. You must mentally hold it together. Move with caution, preserve life. Don't panic. If you don't make it, who will take care of Dad? You must make it out of here."

Whenever the wind velocity builds, the big old tree makes settling noises. I presume the exterior of the fort is holding up against the harsh elements because if the wall collapsed, the wind would whip through my insulated wall of needles like a tornado attacking a child's sand castle.

Although I'm isolated from the outside, I sense the early morning change in the darkness. Pressing slightly on the top of the wall of needles I peek through the air gap. Through a small crack I left on the north side of the stick wall I can see into the wilderness. Although it's still dark, I can feel and hear the blizzard pounding away.

Several hours pass and again I peek through both fort layers out into the white blur. The clouds are so dark and thick that they make the morning feel like night. Experiencing leg-twisting bladder pain and needing to stretch my cramped body, I exit the fort, stretching my fractured body in the company of the blizzard. I estimate the time at 10:30 a.m. After finishing my bowel movements I use the line of boulders as a lifeline, keeping my left hand against the rocks so that I don't get lost while wading through the snow, heading to the tip of the eastern end of the line of boulders. Before the blizzard struck, there was no snow on the top of the rocks; now there is over two feet of fresh white powder.

Returning to the fort, I enter the secondary layer, then slide the branches back across the opening. To prevent the center capsule from getting wet, I brush off the snow before going inside. With the pine needle wall in place, I slowly return to a meditative state.

With the daylight hours offering slightly warmer temperatures, I doze in and out for several hours, occasionally awakening to check the storm's status. But whirling snow still bleaches the air, preventing me from seeing even the nearby mountain gorge to the north. The storm appears to be easing, although it might be only a lull. In any case, it's too late in the day for me to make a move. Sure enough, after another half hour, the storm returns to ruthlessly dumping snow accompanied by what seem to be fierce 100 mph winds.

Although my rule is not to leave the capsule after sunset, the exploding pain in my bladder forces me to exit the warmth and security of the tree trunk. The sun has been down for about thirty minutes, and I estimate the time at 4:30 p.m. While urinating onto the clean white snow I smile for two reasons. I see no red, indicating no blood. And the fact that I'm urinating at all means my water intake is sufficient.

With my body shivering from the storm I cram my carcass back into the trunk. Waiting for my body to reheat the cavity I wonder, How is Wave handling this blizzard? I'm alive, and Wave had seven days to build shelter. He must be living like a king. Is Lloyd still alive?

Since the blizzard has already taken two days and two nights, when the weather breaks I'm going to have to push hard and fast to make up lost time. Yet I will face three problems. One, the snow depth will have increased four to five feet in areas. Two, new snowfall increases the chance of avalanches. Three, each day that I'm exposed to the extreme elements, I get weaker, so I have less strength to battle the snow.

Fighting the fear of dying alone inside the tree trunk, I try to use my low survival odds as a form of personal inspiration by whispering, "I know there are people looking for the three of us and that they probably counted us for dead when this storm rolled through the Sierras, but I'm going to prove them wrong."

Eleven
The Coffin

December 5

t's the crack of dawn. The storm is on its third day with no sign of letting up. Softly I whisper, "It's OK. You can stay here another day. Relax. Is it better to hike through a blizzard or stay put in warm shelter? Remain calm. Get some sleep."

An hour or so passes and full daylight arrives. I estimate the time at 7:30. Although the air is still filled with small dense flakes, visibility has increased. After trying to focus on trees and rocks for several minutes, I begin to see the dark silhouette of the canyon wall to the north.

Anticipating the end of the storm, I slide my boots over my bluish-colored feet. They burn with pain, but I thank God that they are actually healthier now than when I stumbled upon this fire-damaged tree two days ago. The tissue in my feet has had a chance to rejuvenate.

I push aside the wall of needles and climb out into the secondary layer. I recheck the canyon wall to the north, not sure whether the weather is playing a deadly trick on me.

Exiting the fort, I find myself standing in three feet of fresh snowfall. In places the snow rises clear up to my shoulders. If I stumble or hunch over, my face touches the snow and some seeps around my collar into my jacket, immediately making my clothes wet. When I'm standing still, the snow finds a way into my boots.

The peak to the south is now visible, and the sky is clear. I decide to continue my journey. Using the technique from the previous days, I hike from tree to tree, trying to find where the snow is shallowest.

During the storm the thick clouds held the warm air against the terrain, preventing the old layer of snow from freezing hard enough to support my weight. Now I break through on every step as I head east along the canyon ridge.

With less strength than ever, the only element in my favor is that the terrain now slopes downhill, allowing me to exert less energy. The wooded canyon opens out into a small meadow. Stopping at its edge in chest-deep snow, I scan the terrain, but realize that it all looks the same.

As I mutter, "Where the hell am I?" I'm filled with hollowness. As I try to think, my mind is blank. In an attempt to find something alive within me, I search for any old dream or memory, but nothing surfaces. Questioning my existence, I stare up into the clear blue sky asking, "Is this really happening? Could I be dreaming?"

While I'm in this mental zone I never dared to visit, a smile finds my face. A powerful glow so open and true turns to a cry of relief. With tears filling my eyes and rolling down my weather-beaten cheeks, I continue to stare across the meadow. I see nothing, I hear nothing, I smell nothing. Somehow I'm calm. I've entered into some sort of trance state.

I am snapped out of my fugue state when some snow falls inside my jacket collar. I cringe as it drips down my back.

The doubts that were plaguing me drop away as if with a flick of a switch. As the wind grazes my chapped face, forcing me to moisten the deep cracks on my lips, I taste the cold, dry mountain air. The scent from trees and bushes fills the air. The tall trees, jagged rocks, and snow-filled meadow have depth and color again.

Focused and alert, I start chanting, "Warmth water weather direction . . . warmth water weather direction."

I push through the snow until I'm several feet into the meadow.

Then I stop instinctively. Uneasy with the thought that water may be flowing under the snow-covered terrain, I probe with my walking stick while cautiously wading through the meadow.

Feeling the pressure of losing two valuable days of hiking because of the storm, I catch myself increasing my wading pace. So I say, "If you break through the ice and the current is strong, you will be swept away under the ice. Peter, even if you get lucky and climb out of the freezing water back up onto the snow, you will be frozen before sunset."

At a slow, methodical pace I continue to probe the blanket of snow first, then wade through it. Suddenly, I feel like I'm sinking very slowly into the depths of the snow. As I lift one foot a few inches out of the hole my other foot sinks even farther. The snow is almost completely over my head.

Since the powder is so dense, it may have muffled the sound of my breaking through a thin layer of ice that covers a fast-moving stream. With only seconds to spare and my body movements restricted by the tall, thick white base, all I can think to do is fall backward on my back into the powder.

Snow now packed in my clothes, I rise to my feet, then wipe the snow off my face and from around my neck. I'm already soaking wet and I haven't even crossed the meadow yet.

I stab the walking stick into the snow, searching for the edge of the stream. Again and again I stab the snow like a miner prospecting for gold. Finally the stick slides through the snow and makes contact with a hard slippery surface. Moving forward, I stab again. The stick disappears, making contact with nothing. Sliding the stick back out, I can see a water line measuring about two feet high.

Having located the stream, I begin to test the strength of the ice by driving my right heel down, trying to break it. Crossing the stream foot by foot, I continue to test the safety of the ice. On my next pounding the ice breaks, creating a hole the size of my boot print. The opening exposes the rushing water, and the burbling sound is magnified by the silence of the forest.

The snow that comes in contact with the icy water immediately changes to slush, then disappears under the white surface as it is carried downstream.

I have to cross this stream, but I'm not sure how wide it is. I can't jump because I don't know how far I need to jump. If I come up short in the jump I may punch through the thin layer of ice.

Gently I begin to slide one foot farther across the ice. I get about eighteen inches before the ice starts to break. The water is too deep and is moving too fast for it to freeze thick enough to support my weight.

The only way across is to jump. I kneel down, then slide the walking stick through the snow until the tip touches the surface of the ice. Slowly I push the stick across the ice until it stops abruptly. Where the stick stops is the other side of the stream. Making sure I can trust my newly devised technique, I run a parallel test a foot apart. The stick stops at the same point. On a third test the stick again stops at the same point.

The stream is about seven feet wide. I'm going to need some type of launching pad before the stream's edge in order to clear it in a broad jump. As I start to make a path in the snow just before the stream, I ask myself, "What the hell am I doing? What makes me think I have the strength to leap across this stream? What happens if I don't make it?" Yet my answer to this doubt is simple. What choice do I have?

After thirty minutes of hard work, using a big sheet of bark as a shovel, I manage to clear a path about twelve feet long and two feet wide. Before attempting the jump, I take a few practice limps to see if I'm able to get enough speed and to pinpoint my timing on the leap. During the warm-up runs I notice the path is a little narrow in some areas, so I carve out those areas, making them wider.

At the starting line of the snow trench I breathe deeply, filling one lung, focusing only on the narrow white path ahead. I break from the gate limping. I try to increase my speed knowing the takeoff is the most critical component of the jump. At the runway's end I jump over the stream into a wall of soft snow.

Standing on solid ground, brushing myself off, I am about to celebrate my victory when I realize there is another stream parallel to the one I just jumped across. I start spearing the snow, searching for the stream's edge. Eventually, I shovel out three trenches to leap over three streams.

Exhausted after all that effort, I stare at a clump of trees on the higher ground in the center of the meadow. The snow is shallow there, and I wearily forge toward it.

Taking cover from the sun, I sit down on a rock in the shady clump of trees. While chewing on some snow, I scan the landscape for anything that can be used for navigation. I see nothing. I'm unable to see any peaks or any landmarks. I'm totally disoriented. There is no way to navigate through the thick forest. Terrain like this causes people to hike in endless circles.

Trekking on, I spot a dark circular patch in the snow about fifty yards away. Curious, wading through the chest-deep drifts toward the unnatural dark spot in the snow, I can see that it is about eight to ten inches in diameter. It is the top of a wooden sign post. While leaning against it, I dig out the snow from around the wooden rectangular sign below. Soon I uncover an engraved arrow that points to the west with the word "Trail." Laughing aloud, I say, "No way am I going back that direction! I spent nine days getting here!"

The *Press-Telegram* runs another story today forecasting doom for Wave, Lloyd, and me. The headline reads, SEARCH FOR SMALL PLANE CALLED OFF BECAUSE OF BAD WEATHER.

Because of the two-day blizzard CAP scaled back its SAR operation, using thirty-six personnel to launch only six aircraft flying 6 sorties. They log 30.9 hours total flight time with 18.8 hours in grid.

Denise, Rocco, and Dad launch their first intelligence-gathering mission. Rocco rides my motorcycle 135 miles northeast into the Mojave Desert to the Daggett airport. Armed with a picture of me and the Maule, he asks everybody he sees whether they ever saw us.

■ ■ ■

This wooden trail sign promises hope, as does the change in the terrain. It's possible that I may soon hear snowmobiles or spot cross-country skiers, snowshoers, people on horses, or smoke coming from a cabin fireplace.

Figuring that in the opposite direction of the arrow the trail may lead to a cabin, I journey on. Exiting the meadow into heavy woods, I glance up through the trees. The sun is nearly directly overhead.

With only a few hours to dry my clothes, I journey east and search for shelter.

After advancing a hundred feet, I stop and look back at my tracks. They reveal the start of a slow arc to the left, a northerly direction. I'm starting to hike in circles, expending precious energy for nothing. Trying to navigate without any visual reference points is useless.

With refueled determination I reach the edge of another meadow. Here the sun rays have made the snow wet and difficult to negotiate. Plus, the snow glare is blinding. I stay in the cover of the trees at the meadow's edge. Soon I spot a potential shelter. It's a monster tree that has recently been completely uprooted. The base is still filled with dirt, and its roots extend in all directions twice as wide as I am tall. It's difficult to get close to the beast because its branches extrude from it like needles on a porcupine. On further inspection, I conclude that it would take too much time and energy to make shelter from this tree.

At the northeastern end of the meadow, the snow is only ankle-deep and in some areas just a few inches. I spot another massive tree resting on its side. The thick body is smooth with just a few branches near the top.

This ancient decaying torso will be my shelter for the night. With no rocks in sight on which to dry my clothes, I'm forced to hang them from the trees. This method means the garments dry only from sunlight and wind, not from the radiant heat of rocks.

Before constructing shelter from the downed tree, I peel off a large sheet of bark about three feet long and eighteen inches wide, fill it with snow, then place it in the sun. The bark will retain the heat from the sun and melt the snow, becoming a natural bowl.

Using a thick stick, I start digging out underneath the tree, making the existing hole large enough for my entire body. At last it's big enough to test. Sliding into the tomb, lying flat on my back with my legs extended, my nose just touches the bottom of the trunk.

Thirsty from the intense manual labor, I exit the hole to check the bark. The snow has melted, so I place some fresh snow on top of the water. Using the snow as a natural filter to keep the dirt and bark particles from going into my mouth, I begin sucking on the snow, drawing the water through the snow and into my mouth.

Since the chamber is a tight fit between the ground and the tree trunk, I dig out the floor another six inches so that I can lie on a six-inch needle mattress. I cram freshly broken pine branches against the inside snow walls, creating an insulation barrier. Except for a door hatch, the fort is now fully insulated.

Earlier while edging around the meadow, I spotted some animal dung. They were stiff and each pile was about 8 inches in diameter and 2¼ inches thick. Once when I was hunting with Rocco, he said, "Animal dung is a great insulator." I collect as many as I can carry, returning to the fort with twelve large dark donuts.

As the sun changes position, I move my clothes in the trees, trying to capture as much remaining sunlight as possible. Stripping a few large sections of bark off the downed dinosaur provides a hatch door and some bugs to eat.

With the clothes hanging in the trees to dry and the fort now complete, I have to address the problem of how to navigate tomorrow. Earlier, when fetching the dung, I spotted what looked like the two tallest trees in the area. I could climb one to get a great view of the meadow. Standing at the base of one of those trees, dressed in snow bibs and the shells to my boots, I slowly scan its thick abrasive trunk through its midsection to the top. I study every extruding branch, knob, and imperfection on its bark.

Fifteen feet up from the ground the branches are just close enough together to climb. Above its knees the branches begin to form a stretched staircase. From its waist up the branches are nested together. Six feet from the ground a single branch thick enough to support my weight extrudes from its ankle.

While returning to the fort, I think, Climbing that tree is going to take a lot of energy and a lot of time.

Studying the second tree, which is located right next to the fort, I see a starting branch about eight feet up. To climb this tree I'll need a log to stand on so that I can reach the first branch. The branches on this tree are staggered, making it a more challenging climb. I will save this problem for later. I have to prepare for the night first.

As the entire meadow falls into shadow, I crawl fully dressed down into the hole. Sliding the thick bark doors over the tiny entrance cuts off all remaining light into the tomb, making it pitch-black.

I lie flat on my back in the comfort of the needle mattress, using dung for a pillow, my nose a hair's gap away from the trunk. Using the remaining dung, I pack one on each side of my neck against my sweatshirt, two under each armpit, and three more between my legs. The remaining pieces I use to seal off the cold air that is seeping through the bark door.

Although the fort is helping to insulate me, within an hour my body is convulsing with cold. As I twist and turn within the tight confines of the grave, my nose, lips, and chin scrape against the barreled trunk ceiling. Restrained by the coffin's space, my repetitive motions are limited, but each warm breath I exhale is channeled into my jacket, heating my chest cavity. As I wiggle my frostbitten toes I mutter a scream from the painful burning.

After a 350-mile round trip Rocco returns to Long Beach and explains to Dad and Denise that he showed the photos to every pilot who landed at Daggett. He then went to two other airports in the

Mojave, Apple Valley, and Hesperia. He showed the photos to mechanics, pilot instructors, and other pilots. A few people remembered seeing a red and white tail dragger practicing in the pattern, doing touch-and-gos, but that was several weeks ago, possibly a month or two.

Back at home Rocco stares at the map of California on my office wall, then reviews my Maule flight history data for the second time. He tells Denise and Dad that the plane has crashed in the mountains and that searching the deserts is a waste of resources.

Rocco explains that if the plane went down in the city, we would have known about it. If we were forced to make a crash landing in the desert, there should be no problem. He says that I'm an experienced pilot who has flown all over the country, landed along lakes, on top of dried-up lake beds, grass fields, and short mountain runways. The Maule is a tough little bush plane. A desert crash would probably collapse the landing gear, bend the wings, and destroy the propeller, but for sure we would have walked away from the crash, reaching a road the same day. But a mountain crash in the remote backcountry would leave the plane destroyed, people incapacitated, and communications to the outside world severed.

Denise, Rocco, and Dad agree that the search should be concentrated in the mountains. Rocco makes plans to drive to the Sierras in the morning with a man he met the day before at Long Beach Airport, where I park my plane.

My family has not given up hope.

Twelve
First Search Plane

December 6

Straddling the peak of the night, I remove my left glove so that I can check the exterior of my clothes to see if they're warm. I rest my hand on my groin then slowly pad my body upward to my neck, finding my clothes are indeed warm to the touch.

My internal clock senses the change in the darkness. Pushing the bark doors to the side, I slide out from under the pillar. Feeling weaker and experiencing more pain, propped up by my walking stick, I stand outside the fort's entrance staring into the dark hole and whisper, "I've survived another night."

Although the left side of my face is still swollen, I'm now able to see out of my left eye. Still so early, the trees, bushes, and rocks are merely silhouettes. The only contrast I can detect is between the bright white snow and the dark objects that make up the forest.

I hike over to the tall tree that I studied yesterday. Yawning, completely tapped out of energy, I start rubbing my right eye with my left ungloved palm, trying to work the night's debris clear from my right eye.

Fifteen minutes pass and all I have done is limp around the monster, stalling, staring at it with disbelief. The longer I procrastinate the taller it gets. With a few fallen trees nearby offering a seat, I think, Let's rest and think about this when suddenly I shout at myself, "Get off your lazy ass and start climbing!"

Jumping straight up, I grab the lowest branch with my left gloved hand, then begin pulling my body up while trying to press my feet against the trunk to gain traction. Though I strain to hold on, in only a few seconds I fall into the snowy base.

Waiting for the pain in my rib cage and left ankle to subside, I slowly limp around the tree, studying it while I softly whimper, "How do I get started using only my left arm?" Again I jump up to grab the branch, then begin pulling with one arm. Both feet dangle against the trunk and instinctively they begin to scratch its outer surface trying to push, but they cannot gain a purchase. Fatigued, I release my left-handed lock, crashing into the snow.

Ten minutes later, still in the dark, I lock on to the branch, then begin to pull. But the muscles in my left arm are too spent, forcing me to drop to the ground.

I elect a different technique. At one section of the tree's base the snow is higher and frozen solid. With one foot on this section and the other against the trunk's base, I'm able to touch the bottom of the lowest branch with my fingertips on my left hand.

Determined to steal every inch that I can, I slowly push with my tiptoes, then hook the branch with my left forearm. Supported by only my left tiptoes and my left forearm I start scratching the tree with my right boot, trying to advance a few more inches. My boot finally finds traction against the trunk, allowing me to hook the branch securely with my left elbow.

Stretching full out, using my left shoulder, I begin pulling myself up while searching for footholds on the trunk. Laboring to breathe, now I use my chin to hook the branch, reducing the workload on my left shoulder. My right cheek grips the weathered abrasive surface while I temporarily rest.

Anchored by my chin and cheek, I quickly switch my elbow lock so that my left hand now grips on top of the branch. With all my strength I push with my hand and pull with my chin. I'm now draped over the branch like a wet towel hanging out on a clothesline.

Feeling the pain from my broken ribs and unable to breathe because of the pressure on my rib cage from my body weight, I move so that I'm sitting on the branch with my left side leaning against the trunk.

Standing on the branch, I'm able to grab another branch farther up the tree and find footholds to aid in the climb. The combination of the injuries from the crash and the irregular body positions that I find myself in while climbing a tree causes me to pant from the pain. With daylight arriving and only three branches climbed, I am on the verge of giving up this quest.

As I stare at the branches below, getting ready to climb down, I say, "Just climb one limb higher." Several hours of climbing pass and still I'm below the surrounding treetops, unable to see anything. Thinking this whole effort was a waste of time and energy I prepare to descend.

Sitting on a branch I start talking to myself. "Did you climb all this way to give up? You're almost level with the surrounding trees."

I keep climbing until I'm level with the treetops. Each limb higher offers a better view. A smile breaks on my face, then turns to a laughter of joy. Advancing one more limb allows me to see above all the treetops across the forest. As I say, "Just one or two more limbs higher," I'm hit with a surge of energy.

At long last I reach the top. With no more branches to climb, I cling to the six-inch diameter tip while it sways from side to side, almost snapping. Now that I'm higher than all the other surrounding trees, I have a bird's-eye view of the forest. To the east and slightly north in the distance, about three days' hike away, is a dominating mountain peak. Unknown to me at the time, it's Olancha Peak, elevation 12,123 feet. Of closer proximity is a smaller mountain, today's goal.

While the tree tip sways, I study the dense wooded terrain that leads to the first mountain. In order to maintain a constant course I will have to hike through this section until I reach the base of the mountain. Then the natural contour lines will lead me toward the top, where I should be able to spot the neighboring peak to the east, allowing me to plot a course.

Climbing down from the tree, I start hiking. The sun is already in the 11:00 position, telling me it's going to be a short-distance day. In this area the snow depth ranges between my knees and my lower waist. Little sunlight penetrates through the thick overhang of the treetops.

In short order I cross to the mountain's base. Slumped against a tree, sucking air from exhaustion, I thank God for helping me navigate through the dense woods. Headed in an easterly direction reaching the mountain's crest, I join forces with a man-made trail that heads to the east.

As I advance along the trail, the sound of rushing water drowns all other sounds. To my right, down a steep embankment, a stream flows east along the trail. Through the thicket of the trees, in the distance at a lower elevation, I can see a white meadow, almost the size of a small town. Unknown to me this is Monache Meadows, elevation 8000 feet.

Without warning the snow-covered trail makes a left turn to the north, leaving me five feet past the turn. Stopping to evaluate the trail's direction, thinking, Could that trail lead to a cabin? I conclude that it probably circles around in snakelike fashion, then leads out to the northern tip of the meadow.

Although the meadow is close by and would probably allow me to close distance fairly easily, in my present physical condition I do not want to expose myself to the open terrain during the height of the day. Also, if I keep to higher ground than the meadow, I will maintain an aerial view of the valley, and tonight I may spot light coming from inside a woodsman's cabin, allowing me to make a beeline to the beacon.

This unique location in the mountains is the border of two distinct types of terrain. From my location to the west it is heavily timbered with thick undergrowth. The east is high desert country with scattered groupings of trees and bushes.

Although I'm far away from the valley, I think I see signs of skag brush. Exploding with energy at the thought, I think, I'm getting close to Highway 395! Unless I get pinned down by another storm, I should be able to make it to civilization within two or three days!

With so many fallen trees lying on their sides, thick sheets of bark on their carcasses, I should be able to construct shelter and find dead bugs to make snow bug soup. This area is a mother lode of shelters. Scattered throughout the area are large patches of needle beds, further reducing the time and energy I will need to make a fort.

Without rocks in the vicinity, I hang my clothes from the trees in sun pockets in the forest, leaving me dressed in my underwear and the interior layer of my ski jacket. I go about my preparations. I am about to rotate my clothes in the sun pockets when I hear the roar of a piston-powered plane trumpeting over the forest.

Pumped with adrenaline, I make an awkward handicapped sprint as I head barefoot through the snow to where my exterior jacket hangs and rip it free from the trees. While quickly marching to a clearing about twenty yards away I scan the treetops for the low-flying aircraft.

In the clearing, desperately searching for the plane, I mount a downed trunk for greater height. As the roar of the plane rises I start waving my red jacket, trying to flag the crew. The low-wing aircraft flies rapidly overhead about a thousand feet off the ground. To my disappointment I see no tipping of the wings, the signal that they spotted me. But low-wing planes do not offer good ground visibility. Because the wing is below the fuselage, it obstructs the crew's view.

While shaking my fist at the plane's tail as it disappears, I have a second thought. I let out a cry of happiness, saying, "Good job, Wave! You and Lloyd have been rescued, and now you're searching for me."

Standing on the trunk in my underwear, with my bare frostbitten feet burning from running through the snow, I loathe the thought of hiking back to where my boots hang to dry. The low-flying aircraft might have been a CAP plane. I decide to wait on the trunk to see if it will make a second pass. If this is its grid, it will be making several passes shortly. Wondering how to flag this plane down, I decide that standing in the open valley would make spotting me easier, but that would take at least forty-five minutes plus the time I'd need to get dressed.

Waiting for the second pass, I sit down on the trunk with my feet wrapped up in my jacket. The chance of being spotted without smoke is slim. Heck, back in 1948 a Stinson 108-3, a high-wing general aviation plane, departed a private airstrip at Moose Creek, Idaho, then crashed only nineteen miles from takeoff. The remains of the plane and pilot weren't found until thirty-nine years later.

Earlier this morning Rocco and the man whom he met at Long Beach Airport headed to the Sierras in the man's four-wheel-drive truck. On the way they stopped in Bakersfield to purchase two pairs of snowshoes and a tent. Passing through Kernville, they reached a snow-covered road that led them to an area known as the Needles; Rocco's plan is to search this area on snowshoes until dark, then rest inside the tent during the night, resuming the search in the morning.

Rocco and his partner come within thirty miles as the eagle flies from the Maule site when they spot what looks like wreckage at the bottom of a steep ravine. Using climbing rope, Rocco rappels to the bottom of the ravine only to discover that it is an old car.

Rocco wants to bivouac in the frozen Sierras, but his partner tells him that it's far too cold for him. He wants to drive back to Long Beach. In the end Rocco agrees, but he is coming back. He won't give up until he finds me.

It's been four days since I could see the area where the Maule went down. A plane or helicopter may have spotted Wave or homed in on the ELT signal. If that happened, the searchers are probably concentrating their forces on the Kern River, according to the plan I made with Wave, but I'm several peaks over, some twenty miles to the east.

CAP increases their personnel to fifty-one, launching eleven aircraft. They fly thirty sorties, logging a total flight time of 56.1 hours with 26.1 hours in grid.

The search plane continues to fly, making a square pattern to the north. On his southerly leg of the grid I spot him through the treetops in the distance. The roar fades. I'm alone again. That was the first plane I have seen other than the jets flying at 30,000 feet I saw when I was soaking in the hot springs.

Softly, finding inner strength, I say, "It's OK they didn't find me. Wave made it and maybe Lloyd, too. And if I hold it together without making any mistakes, I'll make it, too. I'll live to see them again." Then again, I realize that seeing a search plane flying overhead does not mean that Wave and Lloyd were rescued. I still have to make it out of here for their sake, too.

Wearing my underwear, the shells to the boots, and the interior layer of my ski jacket, I gather bark and needles for tonight's shelter. After mixing a handful of snow with the collected dead bugs I find under the bark, I gulp down the cold trail mix.

Thirsty, I check the snow I left on a strip of bark to melt. It's only partially melted, not even enough to fill a coffee cup. With the burbling stream making me even thirstier, I yank my snow bibs from the trees, slide them on, then head down the steep, snow-covered embankment.

At the stream's edge in the snow, resting on both knees and my left hand, I slurp the icy water like a three-legged dog. Even though the water enters my system slowly, a tongueful at a time, my temples start to sting, then throb.

Quenched, I hike back to my clothes and rotate them in the sun for the last time. With darkness approaching and the needles and bark set for the night, I get dressed as I scan the valley with excitement, hoping to spot a light.

The valley is huge. I can't be alone. Soon someone will light a candle or take a midnight ride on a snowmobile. In a minute or two I'll see a light or hear a noise, and this nightmare will come to an end. Yet all my searching proves to be in vain.

Several hours into the lonely night, the cold penetrates the fort. Until this moment I thought I had eluded this creeping menace for the night. Responding with a sarcastic laugh, I say, "Only one way to combat." But before I can even finish saying the words the sarcasm turns to a scream of anger. Aloud I yell, "Fuck this shit! I can't take it anymore! I'm tired of this endless torture."

As the words roll off my tongue, the warm negative vapors dissipate into the freezing air. I begin to calm down. Without realizing it instinctively I am already doing the reps and channeling warm exhaled air into my jacket.

The valley is silent and offers no beacon of life. I'm soothed by the continuous splashing of the icy mountain stream. As a partially broken cloud layer passes overhead, I can see an occasional grouping of stars. Sensing a storm brewing, I remain focused on the sky, trying to spot my star formation through the open pockets. At last a large hole in the clouds opens at a 12:00 position, allowing me to spot the star formation, confirming the easterly heading.

I scan the valley and think I see a light. Forced to partially uncover my body so that I can look from another angle, I realize it was a false alarm.

While still making final touches to the re-covering of the pine needles on top of my body, I feel soft, cold wet flakes touching my right cheek. It's light snow, but it's collecting, forming a base on the top of my needles and bark blanket.

Deep into the night the flakes continue to fall. Remaining buried under the needles and bark, covered with two fresh inches of snowfall, I have no idea that my brother, Rocco, who taught me so much about the ways of the forest, has joined the search.

Thirteen
Almost Rescued

December 7

An early riser, Rocco awakes in pitch darkness and prepares to search the Sierra Nevadas alone. Knowing a gun can be helpful in the wild, he holsters my Smith & Wesson .44 Magnum pistol to his side and stuffs a fifty-round box of 240-grain hollow-point shells into his backpack. He dresses for an arctic expedition, then with a motorcycle helmet in one hand and a map of the southern Sierras in the other, he walks out to the garage. Leaving Denise the van for transportation, Rocco ties down his backpack filled with survival gear and a pair of snowshoes to the passenger seat of my motorcycle, and heads off.

With the headlight cutting the darkness, he leaves the warm beach city behind him. Averaging 90 mph, he heads two hundred miles north to Sherman Peak, a 9909-foot mountain located in the southern heart of the Sierras, twenty miles north of Kern Valley Airport, inaccessible in the winter. Today's search has started.

I begin uncovering my body from the snow-laden needles and bark. The freezing air sharply penetrates my exposed body, causing me to shiver. Attempting to rise to my feet, first I try to roll over on my left side, but my muscles and joints are frozen. I'm paralyzed.

The combination of the severe injuries, the intensity of the cold, and malnutrition has driven me into a state of shock, shutting down my system. With all my strength I try to force all four limbs to move. As they start to rotate and extend like a ragged puppet doll on a string, the pain is magnified and I do not have the energy to continue.

After several failed attempts at getting off the cold ground, I revert to one of the oldest tricks in my ammo box. As I try to move my limbs, I say, "It's only your arm and leg! So what if it hurts. It's not like it's your heart or liver."

Now, able to move my limbs like an arm on a rusty robot, I continue limbering them up, getting them ready for today's journey. Rising to my feet, then brushing myself off from the needles, I grab my walking stick and begin heading east, trying to absorb the pain.

After hiking a short distance, just enough steps to convince myself that I won't perish at this site, I stop and listen to the cold wind passing through the trees, swaying the branches. As I take a few breaths, I think, That plane I saw yesterday, was it looking for me or all three of us?

As I give more credence to the idea that Wave and Lloyd have been found, a smile of relief covers my face. Standing in the dark cold woods shivering, I begin to fade into the snow as my muscles feel weaker and my determination dwindles. With the thought that this endless, torturous journey centers only on my life, my mission assumes less importance.

With despair filling the air, I say, "What if Wave and Lloyd have not been found? What if that plane wasn't even a CAP plane? You have to keep moving no matter how much you hurt."

Having temporarily suppressed my thoughts of surrender, I head east, staying high on the ridge, trying to spot a light in the valley before daybreak. Stopping abruptly, I explode with a chuckle. I've run into a barbed-wire fence. I am near a ranch or a road.

With daylight peeking through the darkness and the splashing sound of the stream near at hand, I hike alongside and drink occasionally at its snow-covered banks.

Following the stream east, I pass along the base of Monache Mountain. It rises 9410 feet to my right and helps make up the western border of Monache Meadows. To the east, luring me onward, stands Olancha Peak.

Now that I'm a day's hike closer, I see that its face is steeper than I'd realized. It appears to be supporting the sky with its broad shoulders, extending as far as the eye can see to the north and south. Gaping up into the clear blue sky at its long ridgeline, I strongly suspect that Highway 395 runs parallel on the eastern side of this mountain-high blockade.

Entering the edge of the snow-covered valley, I become exposed to the sun. Concerned about being dehydrated, I try to stay in the shadows of the scarce trees. In order to avoid the sun totally I would have to hike completely around the valley, which could take days, so instead I aim for a small rise where a clump of trees offers shade.

Reaching the hill, I take cover in the shade while chewing on a snowball. I'm amazed I have not seen any cabins. Searching the valley, I ask myself, If I were to build a cabin in this valley, where would I build it? The key factors are cover from the wind and southern sun exposure. I concentrate on the east side of the valley, where the melted snow drains down from Olancha Peak. This area would supply cover from the trees and running water from the highland.

As I squint my eyes to scan the open land in the south, a structure begins to form. It's square and looks about the size of a cabin. But I think, Having a cabin in the middle of the valley, where the wind, rain, and snow can punish it day after day, makes no sense.

After starving and freezing for eleven days, I may be seeing things. More than anything I want to take shelter in a cabin. I could eat and build a fire, maybe call for help. Yet I can't start wandering around this valley, chasing chimeras in the distance that look like cabins. I have to be 100 percent sure before I commit to hiking toward it.

■ ■ ■

Rocco is just south of the forestry road leading to Sherman Peak that he is looking for when a sheriff parked in a four-wheeler waves him down. Sitting in the running vehicle with the heat blasting, the sheriff is stopping all vehicles, allowing only vehicles with four-wheel drive to head north over the mountain pass. Yelling loud enough to carry over both idling vehicles, the sheriff says, waving his hands, "Are you crazy? Turn your bike around! The roads are full of snow and ice! You'll get killed up here with that thing!"

With the Magnum concealed under his coat, Rocco does not want to draw extra attention from the sheriff. With a smile he says, "Snow on the road! Wow, that's dangerous. Thanks for the help, officer."

He releases the clutch and turns the high-performance machine around in front of the sheriff's four-wheeler. He proceeds down the narrow winding mountain road with the sheriff glued to his rear fender all the way.

Watching in the motorcycle's rearview mirrors, Rocco waits for the sheriff to turn off the main road. Finally, after passing a few turnoffs in the road, the sheriff elects one. Immediately Rocco spins the 1000cc bike around and returns to elevation.

Racing past the area where the sheriff stopped him, he wrestles the 472-pound sport bike over the snow-covered forestry road. With the rear tire spinning and the back end fishtailing, he tries to keep the machine moving forward, closer to Sherman Peak. Yet soon he is stuck in the snow. He pulls, drags, and pushes the bike until he has it upright on both tires leaning against a tree.

Abandoning it, he straps snowshoes to his feet, throws the backpack over his shoulders, then snowshoes over to a tree, snapping off a dead branch, making a walking stick. With the pistol now chambered, alone in the snow-covered wilderness he heads north to Sherman Peak.

Some two hours pass and still I'm searching for cabins and trying to plot a course. As I continue to stare at the shelter-size object in the center of the meadow, it looks more like a cabin. Hiking into the center of the valley through the three-foot snow base will burn a large portion of the day and expend a lot of energy. With no trees or clouds to provide shadows for cover, the intense snow glare will put me at risk of snow blindness.

And if it proves not to be a cabin—or if it *is* a cabin but I cannot gain entrance, or if it is an old dilapidated dwelling—I will have hiked and exposed myself for nothing. I would then have to spend several hours of strenuous hiking in the open terrain before I could take cover in the trees again.

Squinting at the cabinlike object again, I think, Why would anybody put a cabin there? Could that be a huge rock or boulder?

Although I am far from the eastern tree line of the valley, I'm convinced that if someone were to build a cabin, that location could be ideal. I head east across the valley to the western slope of Olancha Peak, where the tree line is the thickest.

Crossing the pristine valley quickly turns into a white-meadow gauntlet. The snow, two to three feet deep, covers jagged, wiry high desert skag brush. Half of my steps break through the snow crust, tangling my feet and ankles in the brush. Every time I have to twist my shattered left ankle out of the skag, bolts of pain ripple through my system, at times dropping me to my knees.

Panting from the pain, I stare at the tree line wishing that it could come to me. Searching for humor in my hopeless situation, I say, "This skag brush is a good thing. It means I'm headed in the right direction, east." Trying to force myself to continue, I say, "The end of the rainbow is right there. You can almost touch it. Crawl if you have to, just make it."

Moving forward on both knees and my left hand, I intersect some large prints in the snow. Just ahead of them is a large collection of bear stool. Although the stool is frozen, it's fresh. I believe it's from early this morning after the snow stopped. The prints show that the bear was headed west.

With the pain spikes in my ankle and knee somewhat subdued, I rise to my feet, continuing the hike until reaching a river's edge. Unknown to me, it's the South Fork of the Kern River. The river enters

Monache Meadows from the north, then snakes its way through the valley, splitting up into three separate water channels. Then all three streams reconnect, flowing south through the valley.

Standing in the snow at the river's edge, I stare at the tree line, which for a healthy person is only a five-minute walk away. An object about the size of a cabin begins to form. Charged with hope, I move along the riverbank looking for a place to cross. Here the river looks shallow, about two feet deep at its deepest point, but it's still too wide to cross. Another hundred yards to the north brings me to an area where the water is frozen, forming an ice bridge.

Fording the slippery bridge, aided by my walking stick, I listen to the freezing water passing underneath me. As the ice cracks, making sounds of thunder, I think, I have not eaten in ten days. I must be light as a feather.

Completing the crossing, I find another stream thirty feet ahead. Again the stream is iced over. The third stream is a combination of ice and water. But it's only ankle-deep, shallow enough for me to cross without water leaking into my boots.

Taking a quick breather, I gaze at the cabin and notice that it has a porch with new-looking propane tanks resting on it. Still breathing hard, I abandon my rest, limping and wobbling toward the castle, thinking, Heat, food, and communications.

Approaching the gray cement steps, I can see that the cabin is boarded up, the front door locked and wrapped with chains like the main cabin at Jordan Hot Springs. I grab the solid handle of the thick heavy wooden door and shake it, trying to free it from its chains, but I'm denied entry.

A big black six-burner iron stove is set on the gray cement porch next to the propane tanks. I slide the heavy iron mass into the sun so that the metal can absorb the thermal heat. I can dry my clothes and warm my body even if I cannot enter this cabin.

I twist the propane valve and listen for a hiss. The tanks have gas, so all I need is a way to create a spark, then I will have fire. Nearby a large thick black tarp covers a healthy pile of freshly cut wood.

Searching for something to create a spark, I spot a round color-ful dart board secured to a tree trunk. The dart thrower would have an endless view of Monache Meadows and the heights of Monache Mountain. In the shade, attached to another tree, like a clock hanging on a wall, is a large round thermometer, which reads 20° F.

To the east is a row of smaller cabins. The cabin with the tanks and stove is larger. I spot no electric wires or phone cables. All the cabins are boarded up and locked tight.

Limping around the cabins, I find a steel fence post used for stringing barbed wire. Armed with the post, I march over to one of the boarded-up windows on the main cabin and begin attack-ing it. After thirty minutes of jamming, prying, and slugging, I manage only to dent the surface.

I jam the fence post into the chained front door. After trying with all my might to pry it open, I release my one-handed grip and collapse to the cold cement porch from exhaustion. After catching my breath, I use my fingers to test the curves of the big black stove. It's hot all right. Quickly my arm snaps back, pulling my fingers from the burning surface.

With the hulk of black iron offering companionship and warmth, I strip off my wet clothes and drape them over my four-legged friend to dry. Since my boots and boot liners are the wettest, I place them on the hottest section of the stove to dry. Lying down on the cement porch dressed in my T-shirt and long johns, I hold my naked bluish-black feet against the sunny side of the stove.

At first I can't feel the heat, but after several minutes a small area on my feet feels as though it's being roasted, so I pull them away to allow them to cool before baking them again. Although my feet are discolored, the pain is a definite sign that they're still alive.

Frostbite has four degrees. First degree is a partial freezing of the outer layers of skin. The infected area is reddish; there is swelling and sometimes a peeling of the skin about a week later. Symptoms include a pins-and-needles sensation, periodic burning, stinging, aching, and throbbing of the skin.

Second-degree frostbite occurs when all layers of the skin have frozen. The skin is reddish with significant swelling. Blisters form. The symptoms are numbness and heaviness of the affected area.

Third-degree frostbite is life-threatening. The skin and subcutaneous tissues are completely frozen. The area has purplish blood-filled blisters. Symptoms include loss of sensation, and the area feels "woody." Later on, if one survives, the area has significant burning and throbbing.

Fourth-degree frostbite penetrates into muscle, nerve, and bone. The infected area has minimal swelling and is initially quite red, then becomes black. Gangrene can set in.

Both alcohol and smoking increase the risk of frostbite. Alcohol causes blood to lose heat quickly and smoking slows down blood circulation to the extremities.

Diabetes is another risk factor. Diabetics have poor circulation, leading to poor body temps.

Continuing to thaw out, I alternate between holding my feet against the hot surface and leaning my shoulders and upper torso against its tall fiery sides. Gradually my fingers have less discoloration and become sensitive to touching the hot black metal.

Relaxed and content, with plenty of remaining daylight to warm my body and dry my clothes, I think of the bright light I saw in the sky last week. Still with no explanation for it, I tell myself I am lucky to have chosen this direction instead of heading into the center of the meadow, where I thought I saw a cabin. That star was a sign of good providence.

Exhausted but comforted by the stove's heat, I fall into a catnap deep enough that my hands and fingers twitch. While in this resting zone, I hear the noise of a distant chopper. I'm unable to open my eyes and rise from my sleepy trance state. As the chop sound gets louder, my eyes slowly open, finding sunny southern skies. From the sound of the blades and the reflection of its fuselage, I'm able to spot the helicopter several miles to the south, a thousand feet above the ground.

Injected with an adrenaline rush, I jump to my feet, desperately waving my red jacket as the chopper flies northbound over the cabin at a height of fifty feet.

He hovers for less than thirty seconds behind the cabin, then slowly crawls fifty yards to the west, then south, hovering ten feet off the ground. My screams for help are drowned in the deafening roar of the blades. I continue waving my jacket at the pilot. I'm pelted by a wall of snow and ice from the rotor-wash as he hovers less than thirty yards from me. Blindly I keep waving my jacket while covering my face.

Confident that he sees me, I'm filled with joy. Waiting on the porch out of reach of the rotating blades, I think, How did Wave know to send a helicopter this way, east? Thanks, Wave.

The chopper slowly begins to rise, then lowers its nose forward, picking up speed, heading straight for me. He swoops to my right, continuing a 180 degree turn heading south. As the helicopter climbs into the blinding sun I lose visual contact with it. Using my hand to block the sun, I see the helicopter disappear for good, leaving me staring into the clear southern Sierra skies, straining to hear its fading chop in the distance.

Standing still, shoulders slumped, arms at my side with my jacket hanging from my left hand, I force a smile while tears roll down my cheeks. With the cold breeze chilling my chapped face and weather-cracked lips, I get into position to resume snuggling with my black iron friend while listening to the wind whisper in the trees.

I can only think of two explanations for the copter. One, the helicopter pilot was just out having fun. Or it was someone surveying the mountains for snowfall depth.

Throughout the mountains the California Water Department has visual meter sticks staked in the ground. These sticks resemble a ladder and each ladder has a unique number assigned to it to identify its location. Each rung on the ladder represents snow depth. Since these ladder meters are large enough to spot from the air, the water department used to fly a route taking pictures of the ladders (a practice since discontinued). Then back at the office they would study the photos, counting how many rungs were still exposed. Using this technique they would estimate the amount of water that would be available in the spring and summer.

Currently, where wildlife refuges exist in the mountains low-flying aircraft are not permitted. In these cases visual inspection of the ladders is made by cross-country skiers and snowshoers. Although some of the ladders are being replaced by electronic sensor technology, the ladders still remain because their size and weight makes it costly to remove them. That helicopter pilot may have been checking Monache Meadows for an early season inspection. I do not know how he could have missed me when I was standing on the front porch of the main cabin waving my red jacket while he was only fifty feet away, flying right at me. It's possible that he spotted me and then radioed for help. But he would have given me some sort of sign, letting me know he saw me, so that I would stay put while the troops were on their way.

If he was with CAP, he was one of today's forty-eight personnel who launched sixteen aircraft, which flew fifty sorties totaling 90.5 hours in the sky with 51.6 hours logged in search grids.

Between the low-wing airplane nearly clipping the treetops yesterday and the peppering rotor-wash today—the nightmarish experiences of coming within inches of being spotted only to see the rescuers dissolve into the thin air—my resolve is confirmed. I must be disciplined and expect that there will be no rescue.

While enjoying the heat from the stove, I sense something staring down at me. Turning my head east, I look up at the heights of the rocky crest of Olancha Peak. It's inviting me to its challenge. The snowcapped 12,123-foot peak towers over the valley with authority. I will need to sleep before attempting a climb I estimate will take eighteen to twenty hours.

With the sun soon mating with the peaks to the west, warm and fully dressed I make one more attempt to break into the main cabin. Again expending lots of energy only to barely splinter the thick wooden window, I begin searching for other shelter.

I pull the tarp covering the firewood clear off the pile. Looking for the best place to set it up, I hike to the rear of the cabins and to my surprise I find two outhouses. The smaller one especially draws my attention because I think it may be easier for my body to heat a smaller compartment. Returning to the tarp, I drag the heavy black blanket across the snow. With the tarp folded in half and the outhouse door open, I slide it across the wooden floor, spreading it out at the base of the uncovered crapper throne.

Before bedding down for the night, I limp over to some bushes to urinate. The orangish yellow color and the putrid smell tell me that I'm reaching my last reserves of strength. As I picture the helicopter flying away earlier, I ask myself, Am I destined to die after eleven days in the wild?

With one last extended salute to the valley's guardian peak I shut the outhouse door behind me. Sliding between the folded halves of the tarp, I position myself so that I can see outside through the long, narrow gap between the door and the jamb, waiting to see the change in the darkness.

Since my last stay in a cabin, when I was rolled up in the carpet, I have had only catnaps during sunlight hours. This five-star outhouse, combined with the warm cozy tarp, makes me so warm and comfortable that my only concern is that I will sleep too late tomorrow morning.

Making final adjustments, I pull the tarp over my head to trap all my body heat. After breathing inside the tarp envelope long enough to heat it, I slightly raise the top half that covers my face. That allows me to breathe the fresh frozen-excrement outhouse air. Contentment is where you find it.

All day Rocco has hunted for signs of the Maule. He has positioned himself high up on ravines, cliffs, and peaks, giving him a broader and clearer view of the terrain and treetops below. Using this approach, he hoped to spot human tracks in the snow, aircraft parts still dangling from the trees, or signs of freshly cut treetops that were clipped by the Maule when it passed.

Using the light of the quarter moon, Rocco returns frustrated and empty-handed to his frozen iron horse still leaning against the tree. He unloads the pistol and stuffs it back into his backpack. With the backpack and snowshoes secured to the rear seat of the motorcycle, he starts dragging the cycle free from the icy tree.

He pops the choke, then presses the ignition switch. Coughing, she comes to life. Rocco lets her idle while he zippers and tucks his clothes tight, sealing any openings, preparing to ride exposed into the frozen wind.

Exiting the backcountry mountain road with his headlight leading the way, he travels down a two-lane highway. His wet clothes from today's strenuous hike begin freezing as he cruises at 50 mph. Shivering as he climbs a mountain pass, he rides directly into a local sleet and snowstorm. The ice and snow quickly stick to his helmet shield, killing his visibility. To keep from crashing he quickly flips the helmet visor up so that he can see, allowing the subfreezing air and snow and ice to prick his bare face.

Trying to pass through the storm's footprint, he hits an icy patch on the road, sending the bike into a series of out-of-control fishtails. Rocco veers into the left lane, into the headlights of an eighteen-wheeler. Without time to think, Rocco's instincts tell him that even if the road were dry on a sunny afternoon the two vehicles would collide. As the eighteen-wheeler sounds its air horns, preparing for a head-on crash, Rocco keeps his nerve, inching the bike toward the double-yellow line. Deafened by the air horns and blinded by the snow, wind, and ice, Rocco grazes the eighteen-wheeler, slipping and sliding into the right-hand lane.

He spots a collection of bright lights a quarter of a mile up the road and coasts to a stop at a motel. In the office, he rings the bell and an old man comes to the window. His body shivering and his teeth chattering, Rocco says, "I need a room with hot water fast! A phone! And do you have some place where I can dry my wet clothes?" The old man glances out through the windows at the snowstorm, then back at Rocco, who is still shivering and wearing his motorcycle helmet, and asks, "What brings you up this way on a bike this time of year?" Rocco responds, "My brother crashed his plane in the mountains and I'm trying to find him." With a look of amazement, the old man says, "Yes, we can help you!"

Shivering and shaking, Rocco hurries to the motel room. Still dressed and wearing the helmet, he immediately starts running hot water in the shower then races to get his wet clothes off, throwing them to the floor. Jumping into the steaming water, he thinks of my predicament: stranded in the high Sierras during the winter, most likely hurt, with no food, no communications, and no expedition gear.

After thoroughly warming his body, he phones my house. Denise answers the phone: "How did you make out? See anything?"

"I snowshoed around Sherman Peak and saw nothing. I'm at a motel. I ran into a storm."

"How are you doing? You OK?"

Rocco, not wanting Denise to panic, says, "It's a little chilly, but I'm fine. I'll call you tomorrow morning. Wait! Do you have any new leads?"

"Not really, no. What time will you be back tomorrow?"

"If it's clear in the morning, I'll head back."

Fourteen
The Boulder Field

December 7–8

In my thirty-three years of trying to live healthily and happily, sleeping in houses with central heating and beds decorated with colorful, thick, warm comforters and electric blankets, their kitchen cabinets filled with foods and spices, and refrigerators packed with fresh meats, vegetables, and cheeses, I never thought that I would find such tranquillity in a smelly, old mountain outhouse.

However, the serenity does not lead to a night of uninterrupted sleep. Each time I begin to settle into suspended consciousness, my eyes spring open and my muscles contract, almost popping me off the outhouse floor. From somewhere within my gut I mutter deeply, "You sleep and you die!"

Desperately needing sleep with Olancha Peak awaiting me, I start doing the reps solely to calm myself, a motion that has become an involuntary nightly ritual of survival. Dozing for one-hour intervals, I awake and peek through the gap in the door, checking the darkness before returning to sleep.

After the fourth session of sleep, I sense the change in the darkness. Smoldered with pain and exhaustion, I try to evade my internal alarm clock by pulling the tarp over my head, secluding myself from the outside world. Seconds pass. Still covered by the tarp, I begin laughing. I can't believe I'm so lazy. It's just like when

I'm at home. I love to stay up all night, then sleep late into the morning.

Unable to rest peacefully, knowing that the snow is frozen, making this the ideal time to hike, I leave my warm sewage-smelling quarters behind. Marching on top of the starlit frozen base, I head toward the silhouetted heights of Olancha Peak. Although the wind is pelting me with loose ice particles and bending thick branches in the overhanging trees, I focus on the peak. "I'm coming for ya!" I mutter.

With each struggling gimp closer to the high windy peak, I yearn for the warmth and security of the tarp, but it was too bulky and heavy to carry along with me.

After crossing several runoff streams, passing through a few tiny snow-covered fields filled with deer, and crawling up and down several icy ravines, I reach the base of the mountain. The distance between the cabin outhouse and where I now stand was rugged terrain, draining me of all my energy. The wind has settled. In the clear blue sky the sun is shining brightly at a 10:30 position. It's a great day for flying.

Trying to plot my 4000-foot mountain ascent, I study the lines of the terrain, choosing the chute between Olancha and the mountain to its south. Still an hour's hike away, this steep incline is a collection of massive boulders and trees that have tumbled down from higher elevations, forming a boulder field almost a half mile long. I consider splitting the peak's conquest into a two-day hike.

I'll have to settle that issue later. I continue to crawl forward, the pain in all my fractures temporarily numbed. In some strange way I seem to be gaining mental momentum as I advance closer to civilization. I softly say to myself, "I'm alive and I've got a chance. I can make it." Wave's and Lloyd's faces appear in my mind. They're depending on me to bring back help, I remind myself. "I've got to make it. I've got to. What if they weren't rescued?"

Aiding each limp with my walking stick, I'm forced to wade through waist-deep snow again. The warmth and security of the outhouse is centermost in my mind. Breaking out in laughter, I

think, I'm getting closer to the desert and I hit even deeper snow.
It's one thing after another.

The terrain is so physically demanding that it dictates my path.
Although I'm adjusted to the pain in my broken ribs, I'm laboring
to breathe. With my short, choppy, erratic breathing, my lungs
never have a chance to fully inhale, forcing me to suck in air immediately after I exhale.

As I pick my way through the wilderness, I follow a mule deer
trail to a dead end. The bushes and prickers are so thickly over-
grown that a mule deer could barely pass through. I decide to
alter my hiking line to where the two mountains meet. Yet at this
V-shaped location I discover a winter runoff stream of snow and
ice. Boulders and ice make this path impassable too. I have spent
thirty minutes altering my hiking line, wasting precious energy
and time.

Following the trail, I return to the prickers. As I stare at the
large thick sharp thorns, I think, If the deer can do it, so can I. As
I climb under the thorns on my belly, they knife through my clothing, shredding my skin. Thorns are anchored in my body from all
angles. I stop moving completely. I can see the mule deer trail, but
when I try to move an inch in any direction, the spiky thorns pull
on my flesh. I finally accept the fact that if I'm going to exit this
briar patch I have to let the prickers shred me a little. I make sure
to protect my face, especially my eyes, and in a blast of skin-
tearing pain I bull the rest of the way through.

Standing on the far side of the steep, slippery mule deer trail, I
rest while I remove the thorns from my body and clothing. With
the daylight hours dwindling rapidly, I decide to climb a little farther to where I can see some pine trees, hoping to find some materials to construct a fort should I decide to make the peak's
summit a two-day hike.

The pine trees offer no shelter, so I advance through to an almost vertical section where the snow is only a foot deep and the
terrain is open with a few mixed rocks the size of a fat raccoon.
Between the rocks and snow I have plenty of traction, but I lack
sufficient air, and soon I am lying on my side with my feet locked

against some rocks while I choke, cough, and spit trying to catch my breath.

When my breathing becomes calm, I look up the incline, and to my surprise the bottom of the boulder field is just ten feet away. From my angle it looks like it stretches on forever, disappearing into the sky. Separating me from it is the densest wiry brush I have ever seen. It's so thick that not even a rabbit could get through.

Instead of crawling on the ground, I go for the direct approach, right over the top. A few prickers pierce my skin, but I squirm over them, ripping my skin free from the thorns until I reach the snow on the other side, putting me at the edge of the boulder field, where the real climb to the peak starts.

Like other kids, I loved to climb and play on boulders. Now I have a long steep field of them. The boulder field is clear from any obstructions, and facing slightly south, it is exposed to the intense sun rays.

There is no runoff water for me to drink, so as I hike and crawl over the rocks I chew on icicles that have formed in the shadows between them. My thirst proves to be stronger than the icicles can satisfy, though. On the tops of some of the boulders are large indentations that are filled with water. Some of them are not frozen solid, allowing me to break the ice, then suck the remaining water from the pocket. After each pocket drink, I spit out the dirt and pebbles. As I continue my slow, grinding climb, I sometimes pass by melting ice. Stopping at these oases, I slurp and suck the area dry.

Urinating for the first time today, I see a tint that I have never seen before. During these twelve days of starvation in the wild, my body has been feeding on its tissue. My fat supply was already lean when I started this expedition. I weighed 158 pounds. From the looseness of my clothes and the look of my arms and legs, I estimate my weight at 120 pounds.

As I climb up the boulder field, I quickly realize that hopping from rock to rock is much more mentally and physically demanding than hiking on solid ground. If I misstep, I may fall fifteen to twenty feet, deep into a cold, shadowy crevasse. The leaping quickly wears me down and I start to feel light-headed, almost blacking out.

Hoping the dizziness will pass, I rest for several minutes. I try to stand, but immediately experience severe dizziness and nearly fall between two boulders. Afraid that I will black out while standing on a rock, I now stay close to each rock's surface, attacking the boulder field at a crawl.

When this expedition began eleven days ago, I knew the elements would weaken me, eventually undermining my ability to think logically. I tried to prolong this attack by drinking lots of water during daylight hours, avoiding direct sun exposure, keeping my clothes dry, and pacing the journey. Until this moment I believed that daylight hours offered refuge. It's the freezing nights that I dreaded.

Now, as I bend my legs constantly to navigate the rocks, the dizzy spells come hard and fast, blurring my immediate surroundings. As my vision comes back into focus, I spot a large boulder about fifty feet away that looks like it offers cover from the sun. Knowing I need a respite from the intensity of the sun, I slowly prop myself up on my feet against a rock. As the earth spins beneath me, I wait for the blurry state to pass. With my head still in a fog, I start advancing toward the rock. On my third short step my foggy head fades to black, my knees weaken, leaving me with my face resting against the cold rock.

Several minutes pass. I focus only on breathing. I say softly, "How can I overcome this? There must be a way. What is causing me to black out? Is it a certain muscle group? A certain movement?"

Some fifty yards up the field on the left I can see some pine trees. From my angle it looks like a perfect spot to rest and possibly hold for the night. Light-headed, I advance up through the boulders. When the dizzy spells begin to surge, I stop until they pass. Then I push on, securing myself safely at each step.

I notice that when I attempt to extend my legs from an almost fully bent position, straining the muscles, the blackout surges come hard and fast. By restricting my leg movements to about a 20 or 30 degree bend, I'm able to navigate the field without any more dizziness attacks.

With the combination of the sun beating down on me from a 2:00 position and my body's complete lack of nutrition, my energy now comes in short, low-level bursts. Dripping with sweat and laboring to breathe, I sprawl out on a boulder with the left side of my face resting on its cold abrasive surface. Relaxed, I shut both eyes to enjoy the daylight hours of warmth and listen to the rhythmic calming sound of the light breeze gently swooping up the boulder field. The wind flows like waves on the ocean. The gusts are steady, but at times a stronger wave of air passes over the boulders, creating a deeper moan.

I'm lying almost in a dream state. Images of my life with my mom, dad, brother, and sister reel through my mind like pictures in a crowded, confusing montage. As the flickering mental photos slow down to a point where I can see and identify each picture and its related experience, the photos of Wave and Lloyd slowly begin to click through.

The image brings me back to 8:30 a.m., Sunday, November 27, the day we crashed. Two hours before we went down, we had landed on a dried-up lake bed just north of California City Airport. The three of us were filled with excitement as we talked and walked around the Maule on the lake bed. I can see Lloyd lowering his head as he walked under the wing, snapping photos.

The dream images shift and I'm now back at the crash site with Wave and Lloyd. Wave is staring into my eyes asking me, "If you go, can you make it?" I see myself slowly nodding my head while I reply yes. As I wallow in my semitorpor, I try to identify an unusual noise. I begin to incorporate the steadily increasing sound into my dream, almost building my dream around the noise. At the same exact moment that my dream state converts the sound to an image of an airplane, my eyes suddenly explode wide open. A burst of energy hits me as I spot the plane in the distance coming right at me.

Because my coat was tied around my waist while I climbed the boulders, I'm able to quickly remove it so I can wave the red jacket into the air when the plane gets closer. My present position makes it tough to be spotted from the air so I decide to hike to the biggest boulder in the area. If I can get on top of that boulder, even a blind man could see me.

The plane is coming from the southwest. As the noise gets louder, I struggle to get into position to wave it down, but I can't. Running out of time, I start waving my jacket like the checkered flag at the Indy 500. Just a ladder's height away, the single-engine Cessna buzzes above me, heading up the boulder field. Without enough altitude to clear the peak, he banks his left wing, setting up for a left-handed turn to the northwest.

Still waving my coat, I scream at the pilot. I can see that he is wearing sunglasses and headphones. As he banks the plane even more to complete the left turn, I can see that they are David Clark headphones, which have a chrome bracket connecting the earphones. The sound from the engine and propeller is so deafening that I cringe while still waving my coat. Wow! He spotted me! He dips the wings back and forth as if he is trying to communicate with me.

This is the third day in a row I've seen aircraft and now, at last, I've been spotted! Viewing the tail end of the aircraft as he levels his wings, completing his turn, I say thankfully, "Wave, you made it. You guys directed the rescue team this way, thank you. I'm saved! This madness is over."

A warm sensation tingles throughout my body as I anticipate reuniting with Wave and possibly Lloyd. Yet my contentment turns to confusion as the plane continues north along the ridgeline. He should be flying circles around me, keeping me at his wing tip while we wait for the rescue helicopter. Soon he is three miles to the north, circling another valley for the second time. As he completes the circle, he levels his wings heading to the west.

Pissed off, I accept the fact that he never saw me, and I continue climbing toward the big rock. If he returns, I will then be in a better position to flag him down. Thirty minutes pass. I sit on top of the rock with my jacket in hand listening for the Cessna.

Waiting to be rescued in the sun on this rock is a risky move. In order to survive the night at a high, windy elevation, I must follow my strict schedule and begin building shelter. As I get ready to search for shelter, I faintly hear the plane to the west and slightly south. A few minutes pass and I spot him moving fast, wings level, flying straight at me about five miles away, next to Monache Mountain. As I stand up, I can see that he is at the same elevation as I am. As I start waving my jacket, I hear a slight change in the sound of the engine. I say, "Oh no, he's climbing."

Still holding his course, he zooms past the cabins and outhouse at the base of the mountain. Seconds pass. The Cessna flies directly overhead. The engine and prop thunder throughout the boulder field, radiating vibrations into my cheeks, lips, and clothes. Before I can let out a scream, the plane disappears over the ridgeline, the noise fades, and the air is still.

I gape into the clear sky. "What the hell was that!" If that was a CAP search plane it was one of fifteen aircraft that CAP launched today.

I gambled and I lost. I wanted to be rescued. If I were rescued and Lloyd and Wave were still at the crash site, a rescue helicopter would be en route for them right now. In my physical condition minutes can be the difference between life and death, but I elected to expend a lot of time and energy climbing the boulders so that I could be in position to wave down the plane. It did not pay off, and the sun is now settling below the peaks to the west. I'm at a high, windy elevation and it's below freezing. My clothes are wet. I have no shelter and I'm surrounded by cold rocks.

Understanding that I'm on my last sprint for life, I scan up the mountain and spot a tree lying on its side. Hoping to construct a fort from the downed tree, I resume a slow hike up the boulder field.

Although now I'm more physically exhausted than I was during peak daylight hours, the blackouts and dizzy spells have stopped. The blackouts must have been a combination of intense sun exposure at elevation, depletion of nutrition, and complete exhaustion.

With each step toward the gusty peak, I feel the increase in wind shear. Reaching the downed tree two hours later in the darkness, I find the frozen area offers no shelter.

Using just the light reflecting off the snow, I scan the area trying to identify the dark objects in the forest, searching for anything that will help insulate me from the cold. In the distance I spot a clump of large dark figures. As I remain focused on the objects, one of them looks like a tent and one is a tree. Visually drawn to the tentlike object in the darkness, I stare at it thinking, Am I seeing things? I can't hike from object to object based on wishful thinking. I must be sure before I commit the last of my energy.

Since I'm unable to spot any other shelter, I resume the night climb, stumbling in the darkness as I head toward the tentlike object. Stopping to catch my breath, I can feel that the air is thinner. To get enough oxygen I'm forced to suck the cold air harder and faster.

After I conquer the last stretch of the boulder field, I collapse to my knees from fatigue. I roll over onto my left side, focusing on inhaling as much oxygen as I can. While lying on the frozen windy surface, my body shivers while I pant loudly. Slowly I start to recover from the lack of oxygen, giving me the strength to wiggle my frostbitten feet and hands, checking to see if they're still alive.

Using my walking stick, I push myself to my feet, then finish the five-minute hike to the tentlike object. The "tent" turns out to be a live pine tree lying on its side. There are also a couple of dead fallen trees that offer no shelter, so I try digging under their trunks, hoping to make a cavity big enough for me to escape the cold. After a few minutes of digging with my walking stick, I realize the ground is too frozen.

With the dark, freezing wind pelting my face with ice, I have no choice but to lower my head and raise my arms to protect my eyes as I climb higher up the peak in hopes of finding shelter. The wind is so strong that if my feet are not solidly planted into the white crust, the gusts blows me off balance, nearly sending me tumbling down the steep mountain terrain.

Leaning my body weight into the wind, I stabilize myself with my walking stick. I cover my exposed face with my jacket collar. With only my eyes exposed I look to the west. I can see the nighttime silhouette of Monache Mountain and the length of the Monache Meadows. I can faintly see some mountaintops farther west of Monache Mountain that I passed over on my journey thus far. As I continue to stare, I'm filled with pride. With the sight of all the ground I've gained, I feel renewed strength and hope.

Scanning farther up the mountain, I set my eyes on another small wiry tree. Limping toward my goal, I'm soon leaning against the tree. This area is similar to the spot I just came from. A few trees are lying on their sides, but the snow is deep and the ground is frozen. The only difference is I'm closer to the top of the peak, where the winds are fiercer and the temperatures are lower.

Strangely, I'm not unhappy. The wind gusts are so strong, my body sways from side to side. I begin laughing as I say, "All this way, and now I'm going to freeze. Man, this is too much. I can't believe this is happening." I have to push on. Whatever happens, I can't give up. I cannot go to sleep. This is going to be the worst night of my life.

The steep, tricky, icy terrain is nearly impossible to navigate in the dark. My depth perception and my ability to find safe footing is seriously compromised. Although it's night, the snowy surface is not frozen thick enough for me to glide across the top, so I sit down on one of the downed snowy trees. Since I started this trek the waterproof boot repellent has faded, and for the last couple of days water has been seeping into my boots. While I sit, I quickly remove one boot and remove the liner. When I turn the boot upside down, water pours out. Next I wring out the boot liner. Then I do the same to the other boot.

With both boots ready, I head to another tree farther up the peak.

Even though the climb is strenuous, making my body work hard, which generates heat, I'm shivering from the abusive wind and subfreezing temperatures. I can remember skiing Killington, Vermont, when I was a boy. The windchill was reported to be -40° F. Until now, I have never been in nastier winds or been so cold.

As I'm just steps from the lonely tree, I can see the area offers no shelter nor materials to construct shelter. I need a windproof tent, a winter sleeping bag, and dry clothes to change into. Unable to remain standing any longer, I sit down on one of the snow-covered trees. My uncontrollable shivers quickly turn into convulsions, sending me on my back in the snow.

Fighting the involuntary contractions, I tell myself I have to move. It's the only way to keep from freezing to death. But closer to the peak, where tree cover is scarce, where the wind gusts explode over 100 mph, I lie in the dark curled up in the fetal position, shaking as my body temperature lowers.

My body is seized by violent convulsions. Desperately I say, "Get up before it's too late!" Responding, I say, "OK, give me a minute. I'll be all right." Minutes pass and all I do is repeat the dialogue over and over.

As my body shakes wildly in the snow, I slowly move a couple of feet until I'm cuddling the base of the tree, once again in the fetal position. My body continues the steady convulsive outbreaks as I get on all fours, then lean my head against the tree just above its snow line.

Using the trunk for support, I slowly slither up until I'm standing. Still shivering, I lean my left shoulder and my head against the tree for support while I slowly begin walking counterclockwise around the tree, an inch at a time, keeping my body moving, trying to generate body heat. I can feel more pain than ever from my fractures and the amplified tightness from my torn ligaments and tendons.

Circling the tree, completing the first lap, I say, "Peter, don't stop walking around this tree. Walk all night. You must stay moving or you will die. You can do it."

I continue to inch around the tree in the dark, expending the last of my energy, falling and slipping to my knees at times. The wind shows no mercy, hurling loose ice and snow. With a cold, stuttering angry voice I scream into the freezing mountain wind, "This sucks so bad. Hey, Wave, I hope you and Lloyd got rescued. Things aren't looking good for me."

Fifteen
Final Descent

December 8–9

Over and over play the distressful thoughts of nearly being spotted twice today by what I believe is a search plane. I find myself motionless, sagging against the tree. I've circled it so many times that I loathe it. With only the fumes of a fight left in me, I'm unable to stop my frozen body from sliding down the tree, resting in the snow. Using the same self-coaching techniques that I have used for the last twelve days, I say desperately, "You're cheating. Get up. You get out of it what you put into it. You must keep moving. Come on, come on. There are people in this world worse off than you."

Planted in the grave of snow, unable to move, I stare up at the thick broken cloud layer. The dense blanket looks to be about 1500 to 2000 feet above the peak and covers the mountain range as far as I can see. I stare into the polar skies waiting to spot a break in the clouds so that I can find my stars, ensuring my easterly heading. As the clouds pass overhead, I can occasionally see the dim light coming from the quarter moon located to the east at a 10:30 position.

Able to confirm my eastward line at last, I focus on the moonlight reflecting off the snow. If the cloud layer remains broken, I may have just enough light to trek to the summit.

A climb at night is risky, but I have no energy to spare. Instead of walking circles around the tree all night, I could burn the same calories conquering more ground to the east. Plus, if this is the last mountain pass that I have to crest, I may reach civilization tomorrow afternoon instead of the next day.

Unlike the daytime hikes, I focus my climbing line through open snowy terrain, staying clear from trees and rocks. With my eyes adjusting to the moonlit darkness I'm able to carve my way through the lonely black thicket. Because the freezing temperatures have put a thin frozen crust on the snow's surface, and also since I've lost so much weight, I sink less than six inches into the snow.

I reach the top of a knoll. As I hike down the high mound, the skag brush under the snow compresses, cushioning my shattered ankle as I limp across the soft spongy terrain. Only an occasional raggedy tree fern extrudes from the white blanket.

Although the winds have died to a slow steady breeze, the knifing cold continues to plague me. The burning sensation in my feet has passed; they no longer have any feeling. My fingertips too are numb.

As I reach the crest of another knoll, I stop so that I can wiggle my feet and hands. While I try to increase the blood circulation, I face southwest, which gives me an aerial view of Monache Meadows. The moonlight enhances a panoramic picture of the snow-covered meadow below. As I remain fixed on the spectacle, a feeling of contentment begins to percolate from within my center core.

Mentally preparing to shove off, I take a few deep breaths, then say, "Don't worry. Just a couple of more days until you reach civilization. You can do it."

After limping only a few steps, I stop. While resting on my walking stick, I look down at my frostbitten feet wondering, If I make it out of here, will my feet be amputated? How many toes will have to be cut off?

Headed to the bottom of another knoll, I keep my head down, concentrating on only the immediate three or four feet directly in front of me. Reaching the base of the mound, I stop to rest, using my walking stick to support me. As I begin to trek up the next slope, I see the heavenly picture of the silhouetted mountain ridge against the backdrop of a quarter-moon-lit sky.

With my face pointed down, I study the terrain while pressing eastward. Nearly at another knoll's apex, my body halts, refusing my mental commands to continue moving. Wanting and needing to be nourished by the same warm, calm, content feelings that passed through me as I stood and stared at the Monache Meadows, I slowly raise my head, expecting a soft gentle breeze of tranquillity to fill the mountain air. Suddenly I spot a fixed bright light just beyond the dark rugged ridge profile. From where I stand I can't tell if the light is located on the eastern side of the Sierras, where the snowcapped mountains slope down to meet the desert floor at the western side of Owens Valley, or if the light is shining from the Inyo Mountains, which border the eastern side of the Owens Valley, over ten miles from the eastern slope of the Sierras.

After not being spotted by two search planes and one helicopter; being unable to break into two cabins that showed good prospects for food, communications, and materials to start a fire; and having been pounded by a two-day blizzard that dumped over five feet of snow in some areas, I try to refrain from any excitement that the light radiates, in fear that the shine will kill my scarce reserve of the will to live.

This star could be the top light of the aviator lights that are mounted to a radio tower. Like other radio and wireless towers, the lights allow pilots to see the tower at night, preventing a collision. Pilots also use the towers for reference points, aiding them with navigation.

Although I can't identify the beacon's location with certainty, its presence calms me and unnerves me at the same time. It's something different. It is something I have not seen in twelve days: fixed man-made light.

Another possibility is that the light could just be a light beacon located on a mountainside, signaling the top of the mountains to low-flying aircraft at night. That would be no help to me.

Temporarily breaking my visual connection with the beacon, I scan the frozen wilderness 360 degrees, hoping to spot candlelight coming from an old log cabin, but my faithful walking stick and I are accompanied only by the guardian peak and the fixed light.

Avoiding the emotional draw of the light, I lower my head to focus on the immediate terrain and advance east. Fighting the boiling excitement of seeing the light, I try to keep my head down, but my eyes give in to the pressure, rolling upward in their sockets, straining my forehead, trying to catch a ray from the light. Battling the light lock, I keep my head down, protecting myself from more disappointment as I trek up another moderate incline.

As I reach the next incline, I slowly and humbly raise my head preparing for the glitter. Sighing with relief my eyes go blurry. I cry, "I've made it." The light is accompanied by a second light farther down the tower, signifying it's an aviator-light tower on the eastern slope of the mountain range, located in the Owens Valley, three or four miles south of the town of Olancha.

Energized by the lights, I push on toward the peak, scaling a steep rocky section. As I labor to the top, pulling my head up over the last of the peak's jagged rocks, nearly cresting 12,000 feet, I can see about twelve miles to the southeast the intense lights of the Naval Air Warfare Center Weapons Division, China Lake, illuminating a footprint of the vast southern mouth of the Owens Valley. This live ordnance and explosive test facility sits at an elevation of 2283 feet and has three major runways, including one 9991 feet long. Sitting on top of the world on a cold rock ledge with a sheer drop-off of 600 feet, all nervous emotions extinguish as I hawk at the 1700 square miles of restricted military space. While I repeatedly scan the dark valley from south to north, trying to orient myself with the low lights of the tiny towns spread along Highway 395, the steady icy wind whistles over the peak. It's a calming sound, similar to what a conch shell makes when you hold it to your ear.

I continue to gaze at the dull lights coming from scattered houses and ranches located in the valley. Headlights travel northbound and southbound on 395, but as soon as they get close to my perpendicular line to the highway the lights disappear from sight.

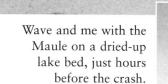

Wave and me with the Maule on a dried-up lake bed, just hours before the crash.

Lloyd with the Maule.

Maule N5629-Juliet as it looked when rescuers arrived. We were lucky to survive the crash.

A fallen tree can provide good shelter if there is room to crawl underneath.

This is what I saw day after day: deep snow and steep mountainsides.

I constructed very
effective shelters from
evergreen boughs and
needles.

The Jordan Hot Springs. I don't know what would have happened if I hadn't stumbled across these hot springs. Notice how little snow there is.

Every day I would hang out clothing to dry in my struggle to fight hypothermia.

Olancha Peak, my last major obstacle, but still a two-day hike away.

The boulder field, where I nearly died.

Civil Air Patrol plane at Lone Pine Airport. Two CAP pilots; my sister, Denise; me; and Captain Kennedy.

Colonel Sydney J. Wolfe of CAP and me. CAP made a tremendous effort to find us.

When I saw this sign, I knew I was going to make it.

The Ranch House Café.

My sister, Denise, never gave up hope, and she helped me recover from my injuries.

My dad, Rocco, was always in my thoughts as I fought to survive.

Wet, cold, and starving, I think about a hot shower and all the food that I'm going to cook. I'm going to make waffles, covering them with fruit cocktail. I'm going to eat all kinds of fruits. I'm going to heat pineapple rings in the microwave and eat them on the warm couch in front of the TV. I'm going to take my dad to an all-you-can-eat Italian buffet, then stick him with the tab, laughing with him all the way home.

The high-altitude mountain cliffs that I am standing upon can't be navigated without climbing gear. I have to find a route to the south where I can descend gradually before dropping down a chute. With my walking stick gripped tightly in my left hand, firmly planted in the snow, I smile, then begin laughing with a new hope and strength. While listening to my laughter echo over the sparsely habited valley floor, I gimp atop the ridgeline in the moonlight.

I find myself savoring the hours that are left in my kinship with one of the last frontiers in the west. For the last twelve days as I labored to breathe, the mountains breathed in unison with me. When I cried, the icy streams wept with me. When I fell over in the snow from exhaustion, the swaying branches on the tall trees comforted me like the embracing arms of my family. At night the land shared its needles and bark, allowing me to cover myself. As close as I've been to nature in the past, my spiritual connection with the endless wild land will never again be so clear, so warm, so true as it has been for these past twelve days.

Moving along the ridgeline, I search for chutes with timber. The trees will keep the snow layers locked together, preventing an avalanche as I hike down the steep narrow terrain. The trees will also offer support, letting me use low-hanging branches as a rope, lowering myself downward one limb at a time. But so far the only chutes that I've spotted are nearly vertical rocky alleys that lead to the desert floor the fast way, straight down.

I'm able to lose some altitude quickly by climbing down a rocky staircase. The snowy landing offers another captivating view of the Owens Valley. My adrenaline flows at the sight. If I don't find a chute that I can climb down, I will follow this slow-tapering ridgeline south all the way to where it flows into the high desert just before the Tehachapi Mountains.

Soon I'm forced to maneuver around some house-size boulders that block my view of the Owens Valley. As I complete the circuit, the valley reappears, and I discover that I'm now standing atop a 25-foot-wide chute. Bordered on its left side by a sheer rock cliff, the steep chute slowly arcs to the left. At 150 feet down I can see the tips of the trees. The right side is bordered by a wall of rock that almost reaches the treeline below. I stand atop the chute, debating whether to go for it. It's steep, but if I make it, I can save a lot of time, so I say yes.

Picking my line of descent, I search for an area where the temperature most likely remains constant throughout the day, where the snow and ice layers fuse together so that there is less chance of an avalanche. The problem is that the high-elevation chute faces directly east with nothing obstructing the sunlight. This means that the snow and ice on the chute melt and freeze on a regular cycle, which is conducive to avalanches.

Still, if I'm going to take the chute down, now is the time because in a few short hours the sun will start beating on the valley, weakening the snow and ice layers. Staying clear of the cliff and its endless drop-off, I cautiously begin heading down the chute on the right side, almost rubbing my right shoulder against the rocky wall.

As I descend, I lose my footing and tumble a short distance down the chute before I'm able to lock myself in the depths of the waist-deep snow. With my wind violently knocked out of me, I lie in the snow coughing and gagging, trying to catch my breath.

Recovering from the chute's bite, I stand, then begin brushing the snow off my jacket and from around my collar. I stare back up, realizing that I was lured into the chute's palm, and I'm now at a point of no return.

With my wet frozen clothes covering my shivering body, all I can think about is dropping a couple of thousand feet to where the temperatures are above freezing. Also in just a few hours the sun will be rising, heating the desert floor, creating warm thermals that will rise along the ridgeline.

I aim for the treeline, hoping to use the trees to block my fall in case the snow chute gives way. At neck deep, the powder is too high to hike through, forcing me to intentionally fall and roll down the hill. The pain is so physically exacting that I'm forced to stop rolling so that I can catch my breath.

Each rest that I take between these agonizing rolls, I brush the snow off my head and face and from around my neck. Then I pick another vertical section to roll through, angling to the right to avoid the cliff I can see in the moonlight while still staying clear from the sharp rocks on the right.

Recovering from another tumble, I rise to my feet, then collapse. I'm completely spent. I've been hiking for twenty-four hours. I just want to sleep. I say aloud, "I'll wait until tomorrow to trek on."

But before I can even steal a wink of shut-eye, the strong guardian force that has picked me up by my belt loops for the last twelve days says, Where the hell are you going to stay? Up here in the cold wet snow? You can see the lights! Hike to the lights! Get a rescue team for Wave and Lloyd today! Get up, and get moving!

The vertical chute now forms an elbow to the left. As I make the transition into the curve I notice that it's darker. There is less snow-covered area for the moonlight to shine on. With my walking stick in my left hand, I slowly feel my way. Suddenly, without warning the snow base gives out, sending me sliding toward the edge of the 500-foot drop-off.

As I slide on my back feetfirst, I can see the snow in front of me disappearing over the cliff's edge. Desperately I kick my heels into the moving shelf, hoping to anchor onto a rock or stump under the sliding white mass. It's no use. The momentum of the moving snow is too great. I'm riding a snow sled to my death. The force causes my body to roll over, so I'm sliding on my stomach. Placing both hands above my head, I scratch at the snow, trying to slow down, while I jam both feet into the ground.

As I approach the cliff's edge I can feel the energy from the white wave coming to a halt. Suddenly I feel my feet going over the cliff's edge, kicking in the air. My knees drag against the cliff's edge as they slide over the ledge, then my waist, then my chest. I finally manage to stop, dangling over the cliff with my entire body weight supported by only my left forearm, which is resting on a six-inch outcrop of rock.

Afraid to twitch a single muscle, thinking that my forearm will slide off the tiny slippery shelf, I remain motionless with my left cheek and nose gripping the outside edge, trying to reduce the pressure from my unsccurc forcarm hold. As I stare into the dark depths 500 feet below I can faintly see long spear-headed rocks. Weaker by the second, I strain to hold my forearm and body still while fighting off wild panic.

Forced to cough at the exact wrong time, my torso shudders slightly, causing my forearm hold to slip another inch. I concentrate on not moving the frostbitten fingers on my left hand so that the forearm muscles will not expand or contract, changing the angle on which my forearm grips the tiny rock outcrop.

The shelf is slightly angled downward, causing me to fractionally slip a hair at a time. Gently I search for toeholds on the rock wall. But my toes just slide against the slippery wall in the darkness.

Because the snow above broke loose, sliding off the cliff, the remaining white layer is shallow. At an extended arm's distance away to my right, I spot a dark knob protruding from the thin snowy base. With my left forearm continuing to lose traction, my only chance for survival is to use my broken right shoulder to pull me to safety.

Unable to raise my right hand above my head, I place it against the rock wall with my fingers spread apart, then begin walking them up the wall like legs on a spider. As my right hand inches above my head, spikes of pain in my mangled shoulder quickly surge through my body. I can hear and feel the fractured bones crunching and grinding underneath the skin. As my eyes water from the screeching pain, I try to keep my body perfectly still.

Whimpering like an animal caught in a jagged-tooth trap, I fully extend my right arm until the tips of my gloves just touch the bottom of the dark knob. Unable to reach farther, I poke my fingers in the snow searching for another handhold, but find nothing to grip. Pieces of snow fall from my fingertips, disappearing down the dark abyss. Trying to gain a few inches, I gently lean to the right while slowly pushing with my left shoulder on my left forearm. As it starts to slide, I push against the rock with my face, allowing my right hand to grab the knob. It's the root to a bush. Not secured but balancing with my left forearm, face, and right handhold, I test the strength of the root, slightly tugging on it, making sure it won't pull out of the wall like a dried-up cork on an old bottle.

Although I'm nearly slipping from my catlike position, I'm afraid to trust the root's strength. While gently pulling on the knob and pushing with my face, I'm able to reduce the pressure on my left forearm, allowing me to slide my left forearm back against the outcrop's wall. Now secured by my left forearm, face, and my right hand, I rest my muscles, allowing the pain shrieking in my shoulder to subside while my strength builds.

I've babied my right arm and right shoulder for twelve days, thinking to preserve the broken shoulder for an emergency. Understanding that it will supply me with only a few seconds of full power, I prepare for a burst of nightmarish pain by panting steadily against the rock wall. With one motion I push with my left forearm and pull with my right arm. Screaming with agony, I pull myself up a few inches, then reposition my left hand so that I'm now pushing on the outcrop with it. Fighting the pain, I lift my left knee up high enough to rest on the ledge.

With my left knee gaining a purchase, I ask my right shoulder for one more effort. Again I pull myself another six inches up the wall. My right shoulder pops, crunches, and grinds, causing levels of pain that I didn't know existed. Panting and shaking, I lock my stomach against the knob while positioning my shattered left ankle on the tiny rocky shelf, supporting my body weight. Afraid to rest, thinking that my shoulder will shut down, I grab another bush with my left hand and press my stomach, waist, and knees against the dark knob for traction. Slowly I maneuver back on the chute until I'm sitting in the snow. I dig both heels into the thin white layer, anchoring my body firmly. Like a wounded animal, I gently place my left hand against my ripped shoulder, comforting it while moaning with pain into the cold silent darkness.

After convulsing with pain for more than twenty minutes, I rise to my feet jittering from the near death experience. Staying clear of the dark hole, I sidle slowly to the left of the cliff, where the terrain changes to a boulder field that leads downward. Feeling my way, I use a combination of footholds and handholds to climb down the rock declivity. Reaching the bottom of the cliff, I can't believe how steep and high that rock wall is. As I scan the cliff's base, I shudder at the tips of the sharp jagged pillars that I would have fallen on.

Carrying through the lonely mountain air is the dripping sound of water. I've lost enough altitude that water trickles through the icy rocks. The area I'm now in is a waterfall during the snow-melting season. It is too difficult to hike through because of the steep drop-offs and the thick vegetation that borders the water channel. I have to find a more moderate descent.

Still high above the valley floor, the terrain changes into desert skag brush, with short cactus growth sprinkled in with light sporadic snow patches. Cutting across the unstable soil, my featherlight footsteps break it loose. As the disturbed dirt flows down the steep incline, the rocks pick up speed, violently tumbling down the mountain, disappearing into the darkness, giving off smashing and cracking sounds below as they slam into other rocks.

I slide fifteen or twenty feet down the mountain at a stretch on my buttocks. The episodes come so often I develop and hone butt-sliding skills like a child learning to sled. Keeping my body low to the ground, anticipating the terrain breaking loose, I wait for the slide to start as I continue cutting across the mountain. I balance my body by holding my left hand out against the ground as the sledding starts. To steer I use my right foot like a rudder on a boat. By keeping my right leg fully bent with my foot flat on the ground against my buttocks and my toes curled up, I'm able to glide over the sharp stationary rocks without jamming my foot or toes. Also my right foot against my buttocks creates a longer sliding surface and allows me to raise and lower my buttocks with the natural spring in my ankle and knee. My left leg is nearly fully extended with my shattered ankle one or two inches above the ground, leading the ride. Every time it makes contact with the ground or jams against a planted rock, it explodes with pain.

On each sledding run the dirt, rocks, brush, and cactus shred my snow bibs on my buttocks area. When possible, I stop the fast out-of-control rides by using my right foot to veer off onto the dry, wiry skag brush, but sometimes I'm forced to jam my right foot into a large rock, stopping me abruptly.

As I set closer to the bottom, I can hear water gushing. I'd like to hike along this snow-runoff creek, but the boulders and the thick vegetation make that impossible.

After drinking from the creek, I regain enough altitude to have a panoramic low view of the valley. While resting on a rock, I watch the darkness lift and the scattered lights that decorated the valley floor fade. Buildings of different sizes and shapes now sprinkle the distant landscape. Looking straight through a canyon, I can see matchboxlike cars traveling along Highway 395. In an ugly reminder of civilization, thick black smoke bellows out from the Owens Valley about two miles south. From the looks of the ominous cloud, it appears somebody is illegally burning large quantities of rubber.

I spy a dirt road in the distance that cuts across the desert from the highway and leads to the mouth of the canyon. Keeping the dirt track in view, I lie calmly on the mountain incline with my feet locked into the rocks. Although the sun is not visible yet, I can feel the warm air rising off the valley floor. It's the warmest weather I've been exposed to in thirteen days.

I push on. I need to reach the dirt road before the sun is fully up. Glancing at the lower elevation, I spot what looks like a mule deer trail running along the creek, exiting the canyon, and leading to the dirt road. Thirsty and curious about the trail, I slide down to the creek. The cold water flows steadily in the shadow of large bushes and trees. Thin ice covers the creek's banks, and the ground is carpeted with a thin layer of snow because of the lack of sunlight.

The trail offers me sections of clear terrain, but at times I'm forced to abandon it, hiking around steep inclines and thick brush. As I labor to follow this trail, I marvel at how strong and tough the animals must be to spend their whole lives walking up and down these canyon walls.

As the trail levels out and I can limp along the creek, I'm startled to come eye to eye with a black and white cow wearing a cowbell. As the frightened animal jumps up his bell rings out. The beast quickly disappears into the brush and the bell fades. I laugh at the thought that a 400-pound cow fled because of my starved dirty whiskered face, hungry for a juicy steak.

I continue trekking down the gradual slope through the canyon, hoping to spot the rancher who owns the cow. Along the path I reach an area where there is a short drop-off. Soon after climbing and sliding down it, I am forced to stop at a chest-high, rusty cattle fence. Searching for a way to get around it, I look across the creek and to my surprise see a snow-covered dirt road. Finding a series of spaced rocks that protrude from the water, I hop across the two-feet-deep stream. Passing through a break in the fence, I limp down the road, leaving footprints in the shallow virgin snow.

Because I'm moving at a slow pace and snow is muting my steps, I'm alerted by a deep rumbling from twenty feet ahead. My limp changes to a stalker's gait as I move closer to the sound, which is coming from under some tall brush. I spot a mountain lion poised to attack some unsuspecting game birds. I stop and stare. Wanting to get closer, I cautiously inch forward. The large predator is so focused on its prey that it doesn't even notice me. Suddenly the birds explode into flight. As they try to escape the thick cover of the tall brush their wings and bodies entangle with each other, slowing them. Coming up empty, the lion turns in my direction, locking his eyes on me. The sneering cat shows no signs of fear as it measures my worth. Then it dissolves into the brush.

As I approach the kill zone, my mouth dries. I scan all around, hoping the lion didn't double back to attack me from above. Passing through the belt, I spot fresh deer tracks. From the tilled snow, dirt, and leaves, it looks like a buck was scraping the ground with his antlers, searching for food.

As I exit the jaws of the canyon, the snow-covered road changes into dusty dirt and cuts across dense wiry vegetation. But before I can continue with my journey, I must bid farewell to the mountains. Turning around I stare at the snowcapped peaks. The clear blue sky is resting on the jagged ridgeline that I descended throughout the night. As I stutter good-bye, tears roll down my cheeks. I stand on the valley floor at an elevation of 3700 feet, just four miles away from the busy highway. I have made it. I don't want my relationship with the mountains to end, but it must. I want to take them home and show them to my family and friends. I want them to see the mountains through my eyes and hear the wind through my ears and feel the cold crisp air like I did. But I do not want them to experience the brutal torture that I have endured. I know a part of me will remain forever in these mountains. The mountains took a part of me and gave me life in return. As I stand here leaning on my walking stick, I look at the mountain range with a panoramic view feeling as if I'm saying good-bye to my best friend, whom I will never see again. As I try to give them the respect they deserve, I thank them for the safe passage.

Sixteen
Ranch House Café

December 9

Putting the Sierra Nevadas to my back, I hobble down the sloped dirt road, inching my way toward civilization. As Owens Valley opens up, the sun bakes the desert valley floor. The creek flows fifty yards to the left, easily spotted because of the dense colorful vegetation growing along its banks.

The black clouds to the south are being fed by a blaze that burns like an out-of-control oil-refinery fire. Thinking that there must be people feeding the fire, I consider heading toward the smoke to get help. But before I start hiking that way I reconsider. Those people won't help me contact the sheriff because they'd be afraid of going to jail. As I complete my thought, a white truck races down the dirt road out of the fire area. Although I lose visual contact with the truck, I'm able to follow its movements by the dust whirl that engulfs the vehicle as it speeds away, escaping to Highway 395.

The sad truth is that many times when I went dirt-bike riding in the desert with my buddies or flew low over desolate desert country with the Maule, I saw massive amounts of garbage dumped or left to burn in the middle of nowhere. Then people abandon the eyesore, desecrating the land and breaking the law. As I stare at the black pollution pumping into the blue skies over the pristine Sierra canyon, the complexities of modern life, which I was forced to leave for twelve days, greet me on my return.

Feeling the heat from the desert sun, I remove my jacket, then tie the sleeves around my waist. I push on, staring at the cars in the distance and thinking, Man, I look like shit. I'm dirty and smelly. I have a grimy beard, dried-up scabs on my face, oily matted-down hair. I must look like a vagrant. My gums and teeth are coated with bug and bark residue. How do I present myself to people? Do I keep my sweatshirt hood over my head or let people see my desperate face?

Since I'm still above the valley, I can spot Haiwee Reservoir, which is located a couple of miles south of Olancha. Wave and I used the long, thin reservoir for ground reference and navigation on our flights with the Maule up and down the valley. I had learned that the reservoir was constructed in 1913 by the Los Angeles Department of Water and Power as a part of the Los Angeles Aqueduct system. There are actually two reservoirs, North Haiwee Reservoir and South Haiwee Reservoir.

Because it is long and narrow, it is an ideal reservoir for natural purification. The water flows slowly through Haiwee, allowing sediment to settle and exposing the water to air and sunlight. Historically more than 70 percent of Los Angeles's water has passed through Haiwee. Once the water leaves Haiwee, it flows through conduit, tunnel, and pipe, never seeing open air and light, all the way to Los Angeles.

Stopping to rest, I drop to my knees, then sprawl out on the lumpy warm dirt and squint into the fiery rays of the sun. In the distance, power lines are strung through the valley like Christmas lights. The relaxing warm rays from the sun and the dry soil bed comfort me as I close my eyes, nearly falling asleep.

By not staring at the distant highway while hiking across the scrub flats, but instead keeping my eyes focused right in front of me, I feel more like Highway 395 is within my grasp. All I have to do is keep putting one foot in front of the other.

Information leaks to the DeLeo camp that CAP believes that survival for thirteen days in the wilderness with blizzard conditions after a severe mountain crash is impossible. CAP is now making arrangements for a full mission stop after this upcoming weekend. Rocco, Denise, and my father quickly begin organizing the funds to rent helicopters to comb the Sierras once CAP cancels its search mission.

Desperate, they even act on information supplied by a psychic. Although Denise is not a pilot, she rents an aircraft and hires a fellow Long Beach pilot named Stephen to overfly some open desert target areas. As he completes the preflight checklist on the Cessna 172, Denise kicks one of the tires on the main landing gear, fighting the tears rolling down her face, and says, "Dear God, let today be the day. It's been thirteen days. I can't take much more. Whatever will be, will be. I'm ready to accept the outcome."

Nervous, Denise climbs into the backseat, then buckles her safety belt tight. To her surprise a short, fat, dirty young man with thick glasses named Josh takes the copilot seat. Lifting off from Long Beach at ten o'clock, the aircraft heads to General Fox Field, where the CAP search mission headquarters is. Once Stephen brings the taxiing plane to a stop, Denise gets out and marches inside the airport buildings looking for the top brass.

Suddenly she is so shocked she nearly vomits. Large photos of Wave, Lloyd, and me are pinned to a bulletin board with the words "Today's Mission" written above.

Face-to-face, Denise informs CAP that the DeLeo camp has rented a plane to perform aerial searches over the dry country of Bakersfield, the Mojave Desert, and along the Los Angeles Aqueduct system. Feeling the pressure from Denise and knowing that they already made plans to pull the plug on the search, CAP thanks her for informing them of her flight plans and her intended search areas. CAP agrees that her aircraft should remain in constant radio communication with them so that it can coordinate with other searching aircraft.

While monitoring CAP's radio frequency, the tiny Cessna rolls down Fox airstrip, heading to Bakersfield. In the meantime, peppering the skies today fifty-one CAP personnel launch fifteen aircraft that fly forty-one sorties. The aircraft log a total flight time of 67.3 hours, with 21.9 hours in grid searches.

At home my brother and my father review my flight records, maps, and the notes acquired since the search began, hoping to turn up a fresh lead. After searching the house for clues they decide that Rocco should go back to Long Beach Airport to talk with other pilots and aircraft owners. Little do they know that I've already emerged from the mountains.

After keeping my head down for a long hiking stint, I see the power-line towers in my peripheral vision. I shout, "I have made it to the power lines! All right! You see, the head-down-while-you-walk trick works." Then as I look toward Highway 395 I groan. "Oh God! All this time and I've only hiked halfway."

The dirt road intersects with another dirt road, which runs north and south, parallel to the highway. Since I need to head east, I cut a trail straight through the skag brush in a direct line to the highway. The buildings along it are now just a stone's throw away. Tasting the end of the fight, I march forward when suddenly I hit a nine-foot wire fence capped off with barbed wire. Feeling, seeing, and hearing the traveling cars on Highway 395, I waste no time climbing over the paltry obstacle. But I'm forced to stop when I reach the cement edge of the Los Angeles Aqueduct.

The twenty-foot-wide concrete channel directs the mountain water south, parallel to Highway 395 until the aqueduct crosses the highway and flows into the Haiwee Reservoir. Stopped in my tracks at the raging water's edge I scream with frustration. The artificial river is about eight to ten feet wide. Kneeling down, I take a closer look at the water's depth while thinking aloud, "If I jump, can I swim across to the other side in this strong current?" Since the concrete is a smooth finish, it offers no traction, no climbing aid to get out of the channel on the other side. Plus, it's very difficult to climb when your clothes are three times heavier than normal because they're soaking wet. I have not eaten in twelve days, I'm much too weak to fight the current if the water depth is over my head, and what happens if the current takes me south a quarter mile? Does the channel go underground?

Wow! I can't believe I am contemplating trying to swim across the aqueduct. I tell myself, "Relax! Don't do anything stupid now."

While I hike south, searching for a long board or anything that will help me cross the channel, the gushing of the water is muted by a low-flying plane. Thinking it's a search plane, I quickly untie my jacket sleeves from around my waist and start waving my red jacket. The plane is flying south 800 feet overhead. As with the other planes before, though, it doesn't see me.

Catching my eye in the distance is an interruption in the fence. Homing in on the wiry blemish, I find a tear in the fence that leads to a cement slab that runs under the water channel. I crawl on my left hand and knees through the cold smelly concrete tunnel, trying to avoid broken glass, beer cans, discarded condoms, and other assorted garbage.

Reaching the end of the tunnel, I poke my head over the concrete ledge, finding a long drop-off to the ground. Luckily, old tires are stacked up there like a rubber ladder.

On the other side of the aqueduct I'm faced with my last obstacle before reaching the highway. There is another fence and a concrete structure that helps channel the water during flash floods. Again I find a tear in the fence and the other side is a dirt ravine. As I climb up, I find myself in the backyard of a hotel.

Quickly walking around the building, I find the office abandoned and the parking lot deserted. Hoping someone lives in the hotel year-round, I bang on the door with so much force that I nearly shatter the windowpanes. Looking through the ghostly windows with despair, I see no phone; the office is military clean, showing no signs of life. It must be the off-season. If the phones are turned off, I have no reason to break a window to get in.

Limping across the hotel entrance ramp from Highway 395, I have to decide how to present myself to the passing cars. Do I go with the starving-vagrant look, hiding my face, keeping my sweatshirt hood up, or do I lay the chips on the line and leave my hood down? It's Friday, and a lot of these cars traveling north are coming from Los Angeles, a city of homicides and carjackings.

As I place my foot on the highway's asphalt, I close my eyes and cry with relief. I toss away my faithful walking stick, reducing my threat to the passing cars. The sun is almost at its zenith. At present the highway is clear, but in the distance I can see some cars coming from the south. I wave my left hand in desperation to flag them down. The drivers of the first three cars respond by beeping their horns aggressively as they nearly clip me with their right front fenders.

While waiting a few minutes for another wave of cars to pass, I lower my sweatshirt hood, trying not to look like a fleeing fugitive. A few stragglers are coming from the north, and although I need to go north, I wave at them, too. Again the cars race by, not even giving me a second look, treating me like I'm a crazy deranged beggar. As a fast-moving train of cars from the south approaches, I wave and pray for a driver to pull over, but the vehicles zoom past, kicking up pebbles that pelt me in the face.

Frustrated that the speeding vehicles just keep beeping their horns, and tormented by the thought that Wave and Lloyd desperately need to be rescued, I start limping fast on the dirt shoulder. Soon I spot a road sign that reads "Ranch House Café 2 Miles Ahead." With the long lonely journey now reduced to a two-mile hike up the desert highway, I summon up a last reserve of energy. Understanding that the traffic is light because it's a weekday afternoon, I decide to keep walking toward the café. When cars approach, I will put out my thumb.

Hearing another wave of cars rumbling from the south, I continue walking until the cars break over the crest, coming into visual contact. Determined to stop a car at all cost, I walk into the center of the road with my feet and hands spread apart, waving my hands. The cars leading the pack show no signs of slowing down or avoiding me. At the last second the first car swerves sharply to his right, sparing my life. The remaining cars hit their brakes, screeching their tires. Knowing I've gotten help at last, I wait for the cars to pull over. To my dismay the people in the cars start pointing their fingers at me like I'm a circus freak. All the cars slowly navigate around me while the people continue pointing their fingers and laughing. I stand in the center of the highway shouting, "Call the sheriff."

Finally a car comes to a stop thirty feet up the road. I start limping toward it as the passengers roll down their windows. As I draw closer, one of them shouts at me, "Get a job, you bum!" Someone else screams out, "Loser." The driver steps on the gas and leaves me limping alone on the barren desert highway.

Though disgusted, I understand their decision not to give me a ride. I probably scared them, leaving them to think that I'm a crazed desert walker wandering the highway aimlessly. A hundred yards to the north, on the left side of the highway, a trailer park appears. Exploding with hope as I spot a late model truck parked there, I increase my limping pace, advancing toward the dark, shiny truck. Now fifty yards away, I think, It was just washed. It shows no signs of desert rash. It's the only vehicle in the area. This truck must belong to the person who lives here and maintains the trailer grounds.

Just then a commercial truck traveling southbound pulls over a quarter mile down the road onto the northbound shoulder. The driver's door swings open, and a man climbs down. Keeping one eye on the quiet trailer park, I curiously study the truck driver's movements. Why did he pull over in the opposite lane and leave his truck facing against traffic on the shoulder?

As the driver walks to the rear of his truck, he slides on a pair of gloves. He has to fix his trailer, or make some type of adjustments, possibly giving me enough time to get to him before he heads down the road. The dark-haired man bends down near the center of the truck's bed and begins shuffling some large thin objects. As the man stands up straight, I utter, "Hey. Help. Help." Either unable to hear me or ignoring the vagrant hobbling toward him, the man starts loading what looks like street signs that are stacked in a pile on the side of the highway, waiting to be picked up.

I draw up to him at last. Pointing to the snowcapped mountains, I say, "I look like shit and I smell like shit, but please listen to me. Two weeks ago on Sunday I was in a plane crash in the mountains and there are still survivors. I hiked out to bring back help. Will you please help me?" His jaw drops open. Knowing that I caught him off guard, I give him a few seconds to respond. As I labor to breathe, I try to fight my built-up emotions when suddenly both eyes become blurry as the tears roll down my cheeks.

The man responds, "What do you want me to do?"

Pointing to the sign, I say, "Take me to the Ranch House Café to use the phone so that I can call the sheriff!"

The man pauses, then says, "It's against company policy to take someone for a ride in the truck that is not an employee of the company."

"There are people that could be dying. Unless we get a rescue team together now, they will die!"

Reading the man's reluctance, I pull out my wallet and plead for help. "Hey, man, look at my driver's license. I'm a clean-cut guy when I have not been in a plane crash and forced to survive in the wilderness for thirteen days."

Sensing the man needs further convincing, I reach into my jacket pocket, pulling out the money I grabbed from the plane. "I have two hundred ninety or ninety-five dollars. It's yours for just two miles up the road to that café. Please help me."

Now, realizing that I'm telling the truth, he responds with compassion. "OK! What do you want me to do?"

"Just give me a ride to the Ranch House Café so that I can use a phone to call the sheriff. From there I can take care of it."

The man opens the heavy passenger cab door, then tries to help me into the truck by holding and pushing on my fractured body. Afraid he's going to injure me further, I softly utter, "I can get in by myself. Thanks for the help." I climb up and sit on the padded seat inches from a complete stranger while holding my grateful emotions in check.

After we roll into the café's parking lot, I climb down off the truck, then limp over to a phone booth. I grab the receiver and then draw a blank, unable to recall my calling card numbers. Trying to jog my memory, I rapidly tap the number keys, but no digits come to mind. Staring at the keys, I try to recall my house's phone number or my office number, but I can't remember any of them. Embarrassed that I can't use a phone, I say to the driver, "I can't remember my calling card number. I cannot use this phone."

Quickly he responds, "Let's go inside and use their phone."

At the café's front door a father, mother, and three beautiful little girls are staring at my unkempt appearance. Following the family of five, the driver holds the door open as we enter the chatter-filled café. Leading the way, the driver approaches the bar stool counter, then says to the two waitresses working behind the counter, "He has been in an accident and needs to get ahold of the sheriff."

Quickly one of the waitresses dials the police, then hands me the ringing receiver as I sit down at the counter. The sheriff answers. I say, "My name is Pete DeLeo. I was in a plane crash twelve days ago. The tail number to the aircraft is N5629-Juliet."

The jabbering in the small desert café slowly comes to a halt. He responds, "Juliet?"

"Yes, Juliet for J. J means Juliet. It's the tail number to an aircraft. N5629-Juliet, J. You may have already rescued the passengers. You may just be looking for me. I spotted some planes in the area. You may have already rescued the passengers."

As I hear him sigh, I realize that he probably thinks this is a crank phone call. I say, "The description of my plane is white and red with a black stripe. The wings are white on the top and on the bottom. The top of the fuselage is white, the bottom of the fuselage is red. The sides of the fuselage are red and white with a black stripe in the center. Have you found the aircraft?"

His voice sounds more urgent. "No, but we have been looking for you."

"The plane went down northeast of the Kern County airport and crashed at high altitude in a heavy wooded area. What we need is a helicopter or plane to go back in for my friends. Can you get a helicopter to the café to pick me up so we can go back in for my friends?"

"No, but I can have a sheriff there in twenty minutes with a squad car."

As I hand the phone to the white-faced waitress, I notice all the customers' eyes in the immediate area are fixed upon me. My gaze quickly roams to a clock, which reads 12:15.

With compassion the waitress asks, "Can I get you something to eat or drink?"

"I just need a glass of some type of juice."

She replies, "Orange juice, apple juice, grapefruit juice, tea, coffee, milk?"

Having a shrunken stomach from starving for twelve days, I remember when I was a youngster and my mother told me that apple juice was good on an empty stomach because of the low citric acid. "Apple juice please."

The soft-spoken waitress then offers to make me a sandwich, burger, or soup. Avoiding heavy food intake for fear of vomiting, I order a bowl of New England clam chowder and two slices of bread.

As I alternate between slowly sipping the juice and hot soup, I break into tears. I lower my head in my arms, allowing my emotions to bleed into the privacy of my arms and the café's smooth countertop. Finding strength, I think about the phone call with the sheriff and Wave's and Lloyd's life-and-death rescue ahead.

I'm blowing on a spoon full of chowder when I'm interrupted by the ringing phone on the wall. Knowing it's the officer calling back to verify my information, I wait for the waitress to answer the phone. She quickly passes me the receiver. "Yes, this is Peter DeLeo."

The officer asks, "What's your name again?"

"Peter DeLeo."

"And you say you were flying in an aircraft that crashed?"

"Yes. A Maule. It's a bush plane. Tail number N5629-Juliet, J for Juliet."

"And this crash happened when?"

"Two weeks ago on Sunday I was forced to crash-land my plane in the center of the Sierra Nevada mountains."

"And you say you hiked out of the mountains alone?"

Losing my patience, I respond, "Yes."

All around the café, gaping faces are looking at me. Trying not to make a scene, I ask the officer, "When will the sheriff be here? I just talked to you five to seven minutes ago and you said he was on his way."

"He will be there in ten to fifteen minutes."

I've now become the lunchtime spectacle. As I resume sipping my juice and slurping my soup, the other waitress approaches me. "Would you like to sit in another area?" Taking my juice and soup, she escorts me to a more private section that is chained off, used only when the café is busy or for private parties. After putting down my juice and soup, she takes a seat across from me in the booth.

With my body still suffering from hypothermia, I focus on slurping the hot soup, trying to warm my inners while fighting occasional urges to cry.

The woman asks, "You were in a plane crash?"

"Yes. Twelve days ago we crashed in the center of the mountains. My two friends are alive and still back at the wreckage site. I need to get a rescue team back for them now."

"You survived in the mountains for twelve days?"

"Yes."

"What kept you going?"

I look her in the eye. "I needed to stay alive to get help for my two friends." But before I even finish, I can see the woman is fighting an outbreak of tears.

Breaking free of her emotions, she asks, "Can I get you more juice or soup?"

"Some more apple juice, please, and yes, another bowl of soup."

Returning to the table with another serving, the waitress keeps me company while I steadily eat and drink. The phone rings again. The other waitress nods her head to me and after I limp to the counter, she hands me the receiver.

The officer asks, "Your name is Peter DeLeo?"

"Yes, Peter DeLeo."

"You were piloting an airplane that crashed?"

Irritated, I respond, "Yes. A Maule. It's a bush plane. Tail number N5629-Juliet, J for Juliet."

"And this crash happened when?"

I'm on the verge of exploding, "Like I told you two times already! Two weeks ago on Sunday I was forced to crash-land my plane in the center of the Sierra Nevada mountains. My friends are still at the wreckage site. When will you have a helicopter ready to launch a rescue?"

"We're working on that now. You say you hiked out of the mountains alone?"

Pushed to my limit of frustration, I tell the officer, "Listen, just get your sheriff here now! OK?"

The sheriff responds, "OK," then hangs up.

Returning to the booth, I've barely picked up the spoon when the phone rings again. Limping back to the counter, I take the receiver. When the officer starts asking me the same exact questions for the fourth straight time, I interrupt him. "What are you doing? You keep calling me every five minutes asking me the same exact questions. What are you doing? Just get a sheriff here now!"

With every customer and employee in the desert oasis now staring at me like I'm a crazed wild animal, I ask the waitress to move my soup and juice to the front counter near the phone in case the officer calls back in another two minutes. Sitting on the bar stool, with everyone's eyes fixed upon me, I focus on putting as many nutrients in my body as I can before the rescue begins.

Seventeen
The Rescue

December 9

As I wait for the sheriff to arrive, minutes pass like long nervous hours. While slurping the hot chowder, I stare at the second hand on the clock, watching daylight slip away from me. Launching a rescue today will soon be out of the question.

A man approaches me from behind saying, "Hey!" I immediately recognize him as the father of the three girls who came in at the same time I did.

"Yes."

"I don't mean to listen in to what you're saying, or eavesdrop, but I understand that you were in a plane crash and you need a rescue team for your friends and that the sheriff department may be giving you a hard time."

"Yes."

"The reason why I'm telling you this is because I'm very tight with China Lake, and I can have two helicopters ready to go in thirty minutes."

"Great! Don't go anywhere. You sit here. If the sheriff department gives me a hard time, then we will get in those helicopters and we're out of here."

Returning to my chowder, I picture Wave sitting next to a campfire inside a fort that he constructed from parts of the Maule. Trying to anticipate Lloyd's physical condition, I draw a blank. The only images I can draw up are of Lloyd at the pool hall and his last words to me at the crash site while he sat trapped in the copilot seat of the Maule. Suddenly, breaking my daydream, one of the waitresses says, "The sheriff is here!"

A middle-aged sheriff walks directly to me and takes out his investigator's pad. With a pen in one hand he flips open the pad to a blank page. Before he has a chance to say a word, I ask, "What are you going to do, take a report?"

"A few short questions."

"How long are you going to be?"

"Just a few minutes."

"OK."

As the sheriff starts asking me the same questions that the other officer asked earlier, I refrain from lashing out. I need his help to rescue Wave and Lloyd. Afraid he will think I'm in shock, or want to haul me to a hospital, I slide my driver's license over to him. "You can ask any question you want, but ask it once."

As the sheriff writes down my license information, I add, "Hey listen, your friend on the phone just got done asking me all these questions."

The sheriff says, "I'm ready to go. You're the one eating."

I instantly push my food away. "Hey, listen, I'm not eating."

I ask the waitress, "How much do I owe you?"

"Nothing," she says.

I say, "I can't let you buy this food for me. Please, tell me how much."

"No, no, please take it."

I lead the way, dragging my shattered left ankle through the front door of the café while moaning from pain. The sheriff, noticing my physical condition, says, "How about we just sit on this bench for a minute and talk in private, OK?"

When I'm seated on the bench outside the café, he continues. "I really need to take you to the hospital. Tell me where the plane is and we can send somebody up to locate it while you and I go to the hospital. You need medical treatment now."

"If I tell you where the plane is, which I will gladly do, you still will not be able to find it. It's in a heavily wooded area. The wings are white, so they blend in with the snow. Plus for the last two weeks it's done nothing but snow. The plane is probably buried in the snow. If you have not found it by now, you're not going to find it unless I take you there. Listen, the fastest way to rescue my two friends is for me to take you there, so let's go."

"I have to get you medical treatment. You're in shock. I'm sure you have multiple injuries that you're not even aware of. Tell me where the plane is, OK?"

"OK. It's about thirty minutes northeast of Kern Airport, at about an elevation of 8500 feet." Looking him in the eye, I say, "Listen, if I'm not dead now, I'm not going to die. I have no internal injuries that are going to kill me. I have been monitoring my urine, spit, and examining my rectum for blood for thirteen days. If I had a head injury, I would not know it; this is true. But I don't think I'm at a point where I'm going to die, OK? When I crested over several high windy peaks I was at elevation, where the air is thinner. I was still able to breathe. So I believe I'm OK."

Knowing the best chance for Lloyd and Wave is for me to lead the rescue, I say, "I agree with you. My body is in shock, but my mind is not. I'm fully coherent. I need your help to put together a rescue team for my friends. When they're safe, then I will go with you to the hospital. If you cannot help me, it's OK because there is a man in the café that said he can have two China Lake choppers ready to go in thirty minutes."

The sheriff replies, "Let's get in the car, OK?"

As we approach the car I'm very hesitant about getting in. Still, as the sheriff opens the passenger door, I get in. Quickly walking around the patrol car, he opens his door, then hops in. Deep in thought he leans forward with his chest resting against the steering wheel and his head hanging over the dash, almost touching the windshield.

Breaking the silence, he says, "Here's my problem. I don't know what county the plane crashed in, so I don't know who to call and who to involve in the search. That's the reason we're having a problem right now."

"OK. Whatever we have to do, let's do it." Trying to force his hand, I add, "If you are at all concerned with saving and protecting life, then you will have me in a plane or helicopter immediately to show you where that plane is. That is what we need to do. I know it and you know it."

From the shocked expression on the sheriff's face, I can tell that he realizes I am being sincere. "OK, but wait a minute. I need to make a phone call."

Using the same pay phone that I tried to use when I first arrived at the café, the sheriff makes a quick call, then returns to the car. "I'm going to take you to Lone Pine Airport. It's a thirty-minute ride. There will be a sheriff's plane ready to go when we get there."

"What kind?"

"A Cessna 182."

Speeding northbound on 395 at 100 mph we race against the remaining daylight on our way to Lone Pine Airport. As we drive through the town of Lone Pine, the sheriff sounds the siren and flashes the lights, navigating through the small-town traffic until we reach the airport. As we enter the airport office, Bill Woodward, the Lone Pine Airport operator, says, "I'm glad to see you. How did you make it? Did you have any food with you?"

"I left it behind with Lloyd and Wave."

Again Bill asks, "How did you make it?"

While experiencing a sharp flash of pain, I answer Bill with a low animal growl, "Sheer determination."

"Susan, your girlfriend, has been calling me every day to see if we found you."

I ask, "Where is the sheriff's plane?"

Bill responds, "It will be here in thirty minutes."

I walk over to the heating vent and put my frostbitten feet up close to the hot air, and remove my wet jacket and drape it near the vent.

Eyeing the clock as it hits 1:20, I say, "Bill, can I get some water?"

He replies, "Yes. Drink the bottled water."

While I swig some down, my eyes lock on the candy bars at the counter. I should load my system with sugar. It's fast energy. "Bill, can I eat some of these candy bars?"

"Sure."

Grabbing four candy bars, I stuff two in my jacket pocket, then peel back the wrapper on one bar, letting the sweet sugary chocolate melt in my mouth. As I finish my second bar, I become impatient. "We're losing daylight. Where is the sheriff's plane?"

Bill says, "We're waiting on Deputy Dog."

Another officer and Bill spread some maps out on the office table. "Where did the plane go down?"

"Do you know where the waterfall is north of Kern Valley Airport?"

Bill and the two deputies respond, "No."

"Do you know where the hot springs are? There are several buildings there. A tree has fallen over and crushed a cabin at the hot springs. Do you know the place?"

"No."

I ask, "Do you know the set of cabins just on the other side of Olancha Peak?"

"NO."

Frustrated, I ask, "Why don't we contact the forestry service? They should know these places that I'm describing to you. They for sure will know where the hot springs are located. From there we can use that as a reference point to help locate the crash site."

After talking to the forestry department, though, the deputy says, "They don't know the hot springs or the buildings that you described, or the waterfall. They can't help us."

Deputy Dog walks in, filling the entire office door. "How are you doing?"

Responding to the bearlike man, I say, "OK."

He looks at the map. "Using this map, can you show us the general location of the crash site?"

"Do you know the hot springs where there are a bunch of cabins, with one cabin destroyed by a giant tree that fell on top of it? Do you know the cabins on the other side of Olancha Peak on the eastern end of the valley?"

Deputy Dog shakes his head. "No."

We're still waiting for the overdue sheriff's plane to arrive. The time is 1:55 p.m.; it's been an hour and forty-five minutes and I'm still on the ground. Firing at Bill and Deputy Dog, I say, "We need to get in the air. We're losing daylight."

Bill responds, "The kid's right! We're losing daylight. We need to get up in the air now!"

Since the sheriff's plane never showed up, Deputy Dog says to Bill, "How fast can you be ready to go with your plane?"

"I'll be ready to go in five minutes."

At the same time, Denise is flying over a section of the California Aqueduct system searching for signs of Wave, Lloyd, and me when her plane receives a radio transmission from CAP mission headquarters saying, "Return to the search base now!"

Since Denise privately rented the aircraft and paid Stephen to pilot it, she has no obligation to CAP, and because they refuse to explain why they're ordering her plane back to the airfield, she tells the pilot to radio back, "No. We're going to continue searching."

CAP continues to request their return to base. Still not understanding why, Denise instructs Stephen to radio the CAP and decline their order again. Stephen triggers the radio switch, then says, "No, we're going to keep on searching. We will not land."

"Land immediately!"

"No!"

CAP asks the pilot, "Is Denise aboard the plane?"

"Yes."

"Land immediately at Fox Field."

The tiny Cessna 172 cockpit falls silent. It dawns on Denise and Stephen that CAP has information on Maule N5629J, but fears that the media may be scanning the radio channels, trying to break the story.

■ ■ ■

While Maule N5629J's sister is rolled out of the hangar, Deputy Dog, Bill, and I try to find the hot springs, the Kern River, the cabins, or the waterfall north of Lake Isabella on the map. Because we're only able to locate the Kern River, I say, "Just take me to the waterfall. From there I can re-create my flight and bring us to the wreckage area."

Bill says, "I don't know where the waterfall is."

"I do. It's just north of Kern Valley Airport, north of a bridge."

The deputy says, "OK, Bill, we're taking your plane."

Exiting the airport office, Bill asks me, "Do you want to call somebody before we go?" When I answer yes, he shows me to the phone.

Knowing my dad will not answer my business or house phone, I dial the X-ALLOY business, betting that Kevin or Rick will be in the office making sales calls. After two long frustrating rings I leave a voice-mail message: "This is Pete, your partner. I was in a plane crash. I hiked out. I'll be here until we rescue my two friends."

Needing to contact somebody, I phone Susan at work: "Susan, this is Pete."

She replies with a scream: "Who is this? This is a cruel joke! Who is this? Is this Peter's brother, Rocco?"

She breaks into sobs as I say, "Susan, this is Peter, OK? It's me. I was in a plane crash. I have to go. I'm going back in for Wave and Lloyd. Bye."

Wasting no time, Susan phones my house, but the call is forwarded into voice-mail. Determined to spread the news, she phones Jack's Aircraft, asking, "Is Rocco DeLeo there?"

When he gets the phone, she shouts, "Your brother is alive! Peter just called me. This is Susan. That's all I know."

"OK. Thanks. I'm heading to the house right now to tell my father."

I watch Bill finish his preflight check as his helpers finish topping off the main fuel tanks. Boarding the Maule at 2:20 p.m., I sit in the center of the rear seat, then buckle up tightly. The deputy is flying shotgun, and he and Bill fill the front compartment of the Maule with heads, hands, arms, and broad shoulders, making me feel like a sardine.

Heading south, flying over the Owens Valley, we climb to the elevation needed to enter the Sierra Nevadas from the eastern slope when the deputy asks me, "Where did you come over these mountains?"

I point to the high snowcapped peak below. "I came down that one at night."

"What do you think happened? Why did you crash?"

"I think it was wind shear."

As we fly over the white-blanketed Monache Meadows, I spot the dark bear stool on the snow that I saw back on Wednesday. Using the stool as a reference point, I look out the window on my right. I soon spot the cabins on the eastern side of the valley. "Those are the cabins I was talking about. That's the outhouse that I spent the night in. There's the boulder field."

The deputy points to the south, at an area known as Kennedy Meadows, but says nothing.

Bill says, "Let's try to spot your footprints in the snow and follow them back to the plane."

That is impossible for several reasons. Since it's snowed nearly every night, my tracks would be covered. Second, from the air it is impossible to track prints in the snow when they disappear into densely wooded areas. Finally, we would run out of gas or run out of daylight because we would be circling and circling, trying to spot my tracks after we lost them.

"Hey, listen," I say, "the only way to do this is fly directly to the waterfall, then head north and follow the river. Where it forks go right."

"Does anything look familiar?" Bill asks.

"From the air it all looks totally different. Let's go to the waterfall and retrace my flight."

Bill turns his weathered face so he is looking me eye to eye. "I have complete confidence that you can take us to the plane. I know you can do it."

■ ■ ■

As Denise and Stephen taxi off General Fox's runway, she spots two CAP members standing at the airport flagpole. Fearful of devastating news, she notes the time at 2:40 p.m. as she fights to keep from sprinting to the two uniformed men. She walks with a calm, rhythmic stride, holding her head up high.

She tries to read their facial expressions, but they stand stiffly at attention until one of them says, "Your brother is alive!"

Denise begins to cry. "What about Wave and Lloyd?"

A long pause fills the desert air. Then one of the CAP men says, "We're not allowed to comment about them."

Crying, Denise asks, "I want to know where my brother is. What is his medical condition?"

"Your brother is currently up in a plane leading a rescue team back for Wave and Lloyd. We're hopeful for them, but we're not sure."

Unable to stop crying, Denise walks into the airport office, passing CAP's photos of Wave, Lloyd, and me. As Denise enters the operations area, she asks the two men again, "Where is my brother? Can I talk to him? What kind of condition is he in?"

"He has refused all medical attention and is leading a rescue team to Wave and Lloyd as we speak."

"I want my pilot to take me where he is."

"Your brother is up in a plane. Go to Long Beach. You need to be with your father."

Emotionally spent, Denise repeats, "Please take me to him," but they don't reply.

	2200	2/4	FM CA CAP (Capt. BRENNER) PILOT HAS WALKED OUT. BELEIVES
			ONE OF THE OTHER OBJECTIVE IS DEAD & THE OTHER IS INJURED
			BUT ALIVE. INYO CO. SHERIFF HAS THE PILOT. CAP WANTS TO
			TAKE THE PILOT UP, TO FIGURE OUT WHERE THE CRASH SITE IS.
			ONLY A FEW HOURS OF LIGHT LEFT. BELEIVES A HELO
			FM FT IRWIN CAN ASSIST. SHERIFF AGREES. NOT A LOT
			OF INFO @ THIS TIME. WILL ALLOW HIM TO GATHER
			MORE INFO WHILE I TRY TO FIND A HELO.

Denise phones Susan. "Peter is alive! They launched a rescue for Wave and Lloyd."

"I know! Peter called me and Kevin. I called your father and your brother, Rocco."

Needing a few minutes alone, Denise enters a small storage room located near CAP's operational area, where she sits down on the edge of a large cardboard box and begins crying in peace. After ten long minutes, she regroups. She exits the storage room and asks Stephen to fly her back to Long Beach Airport, where she can share the news with her father and brother and they can pray as a family for the rescue of Wave and Lloyd.

After flying west for thirty-five minutes, we spot the bridge over the Kern River just north of Kern Valley Airport. Retracing Maule N5629-Juliet's final route, we make a shallow bank to the right, flying north over the white water of the Kern River. Reaching the river's fork, we follow to the right, to the general vicinity of Wave and Lloyd.

Recognizing the surrounding snowcapped peaks, I talk into the plane's intercom system. "We're in the area."

The deputy asks, "Which canyon do you think it's in?"

"It is in one of these two canyons here."

"OK, good."

I look out the tiny bush plane window. "Look down there. That's the hot springs and there's the cabins." I'm filled with hope that we will be able to spot the Maule before sunset. I press my face against the window, desperately searching for a smoke signal from Wave's fire.

The deputy asks, "Are you sure we're in the right area?"

"It's either up this canyon or the one to the left."

Bill lowers the flaps a notch, climbing up the canyon. Reaching the mountain peak, we make a 180 degree bank turn to the left, then fly back down the canyon. We see only heavily wooded, snow-covered terrain. After making two sweeps, Bill says, "Let's try the canyon on the left, OK?"

Lowering the flaps, we fly up the other canyon. Reaching the top, we bank turn to the left, then slowly fly back down the canyon, but again we spot nothing. With the sun starting to set, Bill says, "Let's try it again, OK?"

Quickly I respond, "Yes, we still have time."

Lowering the flaps, we climb back up the canyon. As we complete our turn at the top, Bill says, "I'm going to fly low and slow, OK?"

While Bill puts the plane into a slow slip maneuver, flying her down the canyon just above the treetops, all three of us try to spot the wreckage. I'm looking out the left rear window when suddenly, before I can form the words, Bill says, "There it is!" My plane is leaning on its left wing and its tail is sticking straight out of the snow. Shocked by the sight of my destroyed plane in the vast snow-covered mountains, it takes me several seconds to register the picture in my mind before I respond with a sad "Yes, I see it."

Since our radio communications are obstructed by the mountain peaks, Bill is unable to contact the China Lake helicopter that is en route to our location. Instead he radios a CAP plane that is a couple of thousand feet overhead, relaying to them that we spotted the wreckage site. The CAP plane directs the rescue helicopter into the area as we continue circling the site searching for signs of Wave and Lloyd.

Anticipating Wave running to a small snow-covered clearing to flag us down, I desperately stare through the rear window of the bush plane. I'm overtaken by a cold empty sensation throughout my entire body. I think, Wave! Where the hell are you? Why aren't you trying to contact us?

With the sun now below the distant mountain peaks, we continue circling, trying to spot Wave in the shadowy mountain terrain. The China Lake rescue helicopter arrives, flying just above the treetops over the wreck, then stops over a small flat clearing to the north. The helicopter hovers while the crew checks the winds and the clearance between the rotor blades and the tree branches before attempting to land. With just enough clearance

between the helicopter's rotating blades and the surrounding pil-
lar-size trees, the pilot lowers the chopper onto the tiny mountain
clearing. With little daylight to spare, the rescuers jump out into
the waist-deep snow while the helicopter hovers a couple of feet
above the snow.

The rescuers—strong, athletic, and with plenty of endurance—
begin hiking toward the wreckage. Hoping to find someone alive
in the destroyed aircraft, they search the Maule. They find Lloyd
fully dressed, frozen solid, slumped forward in the copilot seat.
An autopsy performed later by the Tulare County coroner indicates that Lloyd died from cardiorespiratory arrest that was
caused by blunt trauma to his chest, which broke his ribs and
chest plate, filling both sides of his chest cavity with air, a condition known as pneumothorax.

With Wave nowhere in sight, the ground rescue team radios
Bill: "We found Lloyd, but we can't find Wave."

The chopper rests with its skids in the snow. The rescuers
search in the murky light reflected off the snow. The deputy,
thinking that I might have some information to help the ground
rescue team, asks, "Where would Wave go?"

"He might have taken the survival equipment with him and
headed to a south peak, where it's warmer. He might be trying to
find a better location, someplace where he can be seen. Wave and
I agreed he would remain at the aircraft and I would hike out, but
two weeks is a long time. He might have figured I didn't make it,
and started to hike out. He would probably hike south and pick
up the Kern River like he and I discussed."

Just as I finish, the ground team radios Bill, saying, "We found
him."

The deputy relays to me, "They found him."

"Is he OK?"

Giving a deep sigh, the deputy turns around in the copilot seat
to face me, then says in a low tone, "They found him about thirty
feet from the plane lying in the snow. He didn't make it."

Wave's body is lying on the open snow, evidence that he survived the two-day blizzard because his body is not buried. The

ground rescue team carries my friend to the helicopter. By now darkness has fallen and because the rescue team does not have the extrication tools needed to cut Lloyd free, he will have to spend another cold lonely night in the Maule's destroyed cockpit.

As Bill completes the last flying circle over Wave's and Lloyd's resting area, he levels the wings so we're headed toward Lone Pine Airport. Silence fills the cabin as we fly east, by chance retracing my thirteen-day trek. In the backseat of the tiny bush plane, I shiver inside, loathing my lonely, hollow victory. Refusing to accept the deaths of my two companions, I keep closing my eyes, then shaking my head, hoping the agony will pass.

Sensing my emotional struggle, the deputy turns around. "Hypothermia is not a painful way to die. It's supposed to be a nice, calming, relaxing way to die, and that is probably what Wave died from." An autopsy revealed Wave's cause of death was cardiorespiratory arrest due to hypothermia, caused by exposure.

Although I appreciate the deputy's comment, I am distraught. I just hiked for thirteen days trying to rescue my two friends, but lost them both. Lloyd did not have a chance, but Wave did. It was not his time to go. The pain from my two friends aboard my plane dying begins penetrating my soul, making me angry. As I think of my two companions perishing alone in the cold, Bill and the deputy seem so far away. My eyes see no color. My ears hear no sounds. My skin has no sensation. I feel nonexistent. I feel as if I don't belong.

Eighteen
Media Madness

With the failed rescue flight nearing an end, Bill aligns the bush plane with Lone Pine's runway lights. At the short final approach Bill turns on the landing lights on the wings, and negotiates a textbook Maule landing. We taxi over to the airport office and exit the plane.

While Bill and the deputy march ahead through the darkness, I limp behind. Several uniformed men are waiting at the office door under an outside floodlight. They approach, introducing themselves as the CAP. "We're sorry about Lloyd and Wave."

As I enter the tiny airport office I'm deafened by the blaring TV and astonished by the crowd gathered around the tube. Eyes turn toward me and someone says, "The media is going to start airing your story now!" Not processing what the man is saying, I think, What story? What the hell is this guy talking about?

After being isolated from the outside world for thirteen days, I'm unable to understand the strong interest around the television. Suddenly, somebody slams the office door, startling me. My attention is captured as I hear the newscaster shouting my name and displaying my photo on national TV. Saddened by the ringing words "Peter DeLeo the sole survivor!" I lower my head, mourning the loss of my two companions.

I take refuge in the office bathroom, sensing eyes are upon me. The chatter is now silent. I can hear the newscaster's voice as he rambles on. "The sole survivor of a plane crash hiked out of the freezing snow-covered mountains today." I close the door behind me, sit down on the toilet seat, then lean forward with my face in my hands. The office chatter resumes, but I cannot make out what they're saying nor do I want to.

My nerves are eased as the newscaster completes my story and moves onto another headline. Craving more news on the survivor, the office crowd changes the channel to CNN, where the misery is repeated, cutting me to the bone. The newscaster says, "Peter DeLeo, the lone survivor of an airplane that crashed two weeks ago in the high Sierra Nevada mountains, hiked out of the wilderness today. DeLeo reportedly led a rescue team back for his two companions, Lloyd Matsumoto and Waverly Hatch, but they were dead when rescuers reached them."

Crying in the privacy of the bathroom, I think, Wave and Lloyd were good people. Focusing my thoughts on the day we crashed, I think, Lloyd was so strong. During all that pain he was experiencing he never asked for help. And Wave—we put together a survival plan. How clearheaded he seemed. He showed no fear. What the hell happened when I left?

Fifteen long minutes pass before someone speaks softly through the bathroom door. "Peter, are you OK?"

In a saddened cry I say, "Yes, I need to be alone."

"OK. If you need something let us know."

"Yes. Thank you."

Five minutes pass before I hear footsteps approach the door again. The soft knocks make me think that someone needs to use the restroom, so I reply, "I'm coming out right now."

As I swing the door open, the CAP is standing at the doorway. "You need to go to a hospital now. How about if we take you to a hospital in this area?"

"I know I need to go to a hospital. I have a lot of broken bones. I have frostbite pretty bad and serious malnutrition. But I want to go to a hospital in Long Beach, where I live, because they are going to be my doctors throughout this entire process. I don't want to go to a doctor here, then when I get home start all over with a whole new team of doctors, OK?"

"OK."

Sighing with pain, I ask, "Is there any place around here where I can rent a car?"

Surprised, the CAP says, "Why?"

Physically and emotionally drained, I say, "I want to go home. It's a long ways from here. I need to rent a car so I can drive myself home."

Interrupting me, the CAP responds, "No, no, no. We're going to transport you closer to Long Beach in a CAP aircraft. Normally we do not transport people, but we will transport you in this case if you feel up for flying."

"Yes, thank you very much. Where are you going to transport me to?"

"Fox Field, in Lancaster. Somebody from your family will meet you there."

Confused, I reply, "Who? I have no family in California. Only my father and he can't meet me in Lancaster, he's handicapped!" I am unaware that my brother and my sister are both here in California.

"Maybe your business partner can meet you there?"

"Maybe?"

"While you're en route to Lancaster we will make the arrangements."

Too tired and too sad to argue, I agree, thinking that in Lancaster I should be able to rent a car.

After thanking Bill and the deputy for their courageous help in locating Wave and Lloyd, I board the CAP's single-engine Cessna. As we lift off the end of the runway heading south, I sit alone in the darkness in the backseat while the two CAP members pilot the aircraft. Once we're at cruising altitude the copilot turns to me: "It's a pleasure and an honor to transport you." Surprised and unable to respond, I remain silent as he continues, "It's very rare that we get the chance to be part of a search where there are survivors, and this opportunity to transport you makes all our hard work and our many hours of training worth it. If in our CAP careers we only find just one person alive, then our hard work was worth it. I know we did not find or rescue you, but being a part of this search, somebody living through it, makes it all worthwhile."

Nearly choking with emotion, I'm overwhelmed. I want to thank him and the entire CAP, but I know words cannot repay all of their life-risking missions that they perform for fellow flyers. As I look at the copilot, holding the aviation chart, I see a hero. In the pilot seat I see another hero. They are a team and they fly proud. The men and women who make up CAP risk their lives, performing search-and-rescue missions in the slight chance of preserving the life of a person they don't even know.

As we near General Fox's airspace, the pilot radios the airport tower for permission to land. The tower gives the pilot the OK but informs him that a media circus has formed. Local and national news stations are arriving in helicopters and vans, and media crews are setting up their cameras and microphones. Ending his transmission, he says, "It's a real mess down here."

As the pilot radios back Fox tower, telling him he needs a quick second to think, the news channels listen in to the radio transmission. Not wanting to throw me to the wolves, the pilot and copilot quickly discuss our options and then request permission to fly through Fox's airspace to another airport. The tower grants permission, but the CAP brass along with the media waits to hear where our final destination will be. Since CAP rules require the pilot and copilot to report our destination, the pilot radios the CAP brass, then begins talking in a personal code, knowing that the media helicopters and media vans will begin racing to our destination as soon as they crack the code. After a series of back-and-forth radio dialogues, the pilot and the CAP brass chuckle.

After flying over Fox Field, the pilot turns to me and yells over the engine noise, "We're going to Van Nuys Airport. I think we have the jump on the media. The people that were going to meet you at Fox will be at Van Nuys, but it won't be long before the media catches on. They will probably think we're taking you straight to Long Beach. They will saturate Long Beach Airport, then fan out to the surrounding airports."

Saddened from the loss of my two companions as I sit in the dark in the backseat of the small Cessna, I think, The media. What do they want with me?

After landing at Van Nuys Airport, the two CAP members exit the aircraft, then ask with compassion, "Can you walk? Do you want us to help you?"

"I'll be OK, thanks."

Van Nuys is a good-size airport with a large collection of hangars, buildings, and offices. As we enter the main building a woman greets us saying, "Hi, can I help you?"

The CAP responds, "Is there a room or a conference room that we can wait in? We are waiting for someone to meet us here to transport this gentleman home, OK?"

The woman glances at me, and I can tell she recognizes me from the TV. She asks us to follow her and leads us to a plush conference room furnished with a TV, tables, comfortable chairs, and a small couch.

Out of natural instinct I limp over to the far wall, from where I can see the entire room and the door. As I sit down, the woman smiles at me and leaves the room. All three of us remain silent as I watch the two CAP members check their watches every two minutes as if they're waiting for a bomb to go off. Fifteen minutes pass. There is a soft knock at the door. By their reluctant faces, I can tell the officers fear it's the media. One of them slowly opens the door and finds it's the woman who showed us to the conference room earlier. As she smiles she says, "I baked you some cookies and made some hot chocolate. The cookies aren't as good as I make at home. I just threw them together."

As the woman walks over to me carrying a tray of cookies, she hands me a large cup of hot chocolate, "Would you like some chocolate chip cookies? They're still hot."

Almost falling in love with her kindness, I say, "Yes, please," and take a warm cookie from the plate.

The woman, seeing how hungry I am, places the plate of

freshly baked cookies on the table in front of me and exits the room. Starving, my body craving sugar, I continue eating the cookies one after another until the plate is nearly clean and my stomach aches. While trying to sip the hot chocolate I think, This is the best hot chocolate I ever had, but it's so hot I can't drink it to wash down the cookies. But before I finish my thought, the woman returns smiling with water and juice. "Here you go. In case the hot chocolate is too hot, you can use this to wash down those cookies."

It's now close to 8:30 p.m., and I haven't slept since the outhouse two nights ago. The sugar rush from the chocolate cookies has passed and my eyes begin closing. Suddenly the door crashes open, nearly jolting me out of my chair. My brother, Rocco, comes in smiling.

"What are you doing here?"

Fighting back his tears, he quickly walks to me. "I've been snowshoeing and searching the Sierra Nevada mountains for you since last Saturday."

As I stand on my feet, my brother puts his arms around me and hugs me tightly. With my broken bones crunching from my brother's strong embrace, I whisper to him, "Easy, I have a lot of broken bones." Nodding, he lessens the pressure. I can see he is still in tears.

Breaking the intense emotional moment, I offer him some cookies and ask him if he wants to share my hot chocolate. As he eats and sips the hot chocolate, I greet the two men, Stephen and Phil, who flew him from Long Beach.

Phil, a fellow flyer, an acquaintance of Wave, and a Maule owner, says, "How ya doing?"

In a sad voice I say, "Wave didn't make it. Thanks for flying up to get me."

"I know."

Stephen says, "I was searching for you earlier today in an airplane with your sister when CAP notified us that you hiked out of the mountains. Your sister is home with your father. I piloted the aircraft here with Phil and your brother."

"Thanks for helping, Stephen."

My short hospitable stay at Van Nuys Airport has come to an end. After sincerely thanking the two CAP members for their help I say good-bye as Stephen, Phil, Rocco, and I head toward the Cessna 172. As we walk across the tarmac, Phil notices my slow painful limp and asks, "Do you want us to wheel the plane over to you so you don't have to walk as far?"

With my brother at my side ready to catch me if I fall, I continue at a snail's pace. "No."

Rocco offers, "Can I carry you?"

After fighting to survive for thirteen days in the frozen wilderness, I respond to the warm supportive company of my brother with a heartfelt sigh. "No. I'm in too much pain to have someone touch me. Do you know what I mean?"

Rocco, no stranger to injury, says, "Yes, I understand. You did good. You did real good. I'm proud of you."

Tears drip down my cheeks. "I took too long to hike out. Wave and Lloyd are now dead."

"I was in the mountains looking for you. The terrain is rugged and unforgiving. You did the best you could. You survived! You made it out!"

Mournfully I reply, "Lloyd was hurt bad; he did not have a chance. I thought Wave would be alive for sure. I don't know what happened to him."

Rocco stays at my side with his arms around me, protecting me in case I fall. "It's time to go home."

As Phil and Stephen wheel the plane over to us, Rocco says, "Let's stop and wait for them to get here with the plane, OK?"

After fighting the elements for the last two weeks, I'm unable to shut down. "I can't. I have to keep moving."

Almost in a whisper, Rocco says, "I understand."

Just as we finish boarding the tiny Cessna, news helicopters swarm in, landing at our side. From inside the plane the four of us watch the media crews exit the choppers, running with their heavy cameras, tripods, and microphones in their hands toward the airport office.

While Stephen pilots the aircraft, Phil flies copilot, and Rocco and I sit behind. As we enter the Los Angeles basin, I think about my road-racing days and say to Rocco, "I'm going back into racing motorcycles."

Laughing, he asks, "Why is that?"

"Because if you crash, there is an ambulance right there at the track. They can have you in the hospital immediately; none of this thirteen-day survival bullshit!"

But I don't want to be taken to the hospital. I want to go home.

As we approach Long Beach Airport, Stephen radios the tower for permission to land. Giving the tower fake tail numbers, he asks to taxi to a fixed base operator that is not associated with the rental of the aircraft. The plane is untraceable as we taxi down the lit runway. Since I've rented this tiny Cessna many times, I know the plane's tail numbers and I'm aware that Stephen just slid the aircraft under the tower's logs, but I'm not sure why. As the plane comes to a rolling stop in the darkness near some hangars east of where the Cessna is normally tied down, Stephen kills the engine. Phil says, "Get out quick!"

At the same time I exit the aircraft, I ask Phil, "What is going on? What are you guys doing? How am I going to get to my house?"

Phil responds, "I have it all worked out. My cousin is waiting in a truck right over there." He points at an idling vehicle about twenty-five yards away. As the truck rolls up in the darkness with its headlights out, I think, How did he get his truck on the tarmac? You need permission to enter the airport with a vehicle. Man, I love these guys.

Phil says, "The media is swarming Jack's Aircraft. We can't go there. We have it all planned out so that the media can't attack you."

With us inside, the truck slowly exits the fenced gate, coasting past the media army waiting for the Cessna 172 to taxi up to Jack's Aircraft. As we inch down the media-populated dead-end road, we're forced to stop several times as newscasters and film crews cross the street, heading to Jack's.

Once we are driving down my quiet residential street, we're forced to stop three hundred yards from my house because of a media traffic jam. The street, usually barren at 10:00 p.m., is crammed with media satellite trucks, vans, and motor homes. With a news truck on our rear bumper, we wait like sitting ducks inside the truck's cab as media personnel move their vehicles into driveways, onto sidewalks, and across lawns, clearing a path, allowing us to pass. Horns beeping and headlights and flashers flashing, in a stop-and-go, inch-by-inch rhythm we finally reach the front of my house. My house and my neighbors' houses are lit up brighter than the sunniest day in southern California but I can't see my front door because of the dense crowd. Some camera crews have taken a position atop their trucks while others have set up scaffolding. Sounds of generators buzz in the peaceful night. We stare at the trucks from ABC, CBS, NBC, Fox, and others that I have never heard of. Over the mass confusion and steady plugging sound of the generators, someone inside the cab says, "Did they make us?"

Rocco replies, "No, if they made us, they would be attacking the truck. They would leave the vans and trucks in the way so we could not pass, forcing us to walk to the house so they can jam cameras and microphone in his face."

An army of people is holding coffee, notepads, cameras, lights, and microphones, anticipating my return. Preparing for a long haul, the crews break out chairs and tables, setting them up on the sidewalks and lawns, like a Fourth of July party.

As we gape at the spectacle, Phil asks, "How can we come in through the back door?"

I respond, "Bring the truck down the back alley. But let's go up a couple of blocks so that we're out of sight first. Then we can enter the alley a couple of blocks north and cruise down the alley with the lights off."

After inching a block and a half farther, we make a right, then an immediate right down the alley. As we slowly roll down the dark alley, using only the outside floodlights on the alley garages, we wait for reporters to spring out from behind a Dumpster, garage, or parked car, holding their cameras and microphones, demanding an interview. Surprised that the media left the back alley clear, Phil whispers, "Wait here. I'll check the route to the back door of the house."

Returning in a minute, Phil says, "It's clear, but probably not for long. Someone's going to hear us or spot this truck any second."

Rocco helps me limp around the garage toward the back door. As I limp up the back stairs, some media folks spot me entering the house. But I make it inside first. With the back door locked and secured behind me, I drag my shattered ankle across my kitchen of four years with a sense of unfamiliarity. I head into the living room expecting to see only my dad and my sister, but the place is crowded wall to wall. I see Rick, Kevin and his girlfriend Judy, my friends Greg and Linda Hauser, Susan, Denise, and many of my sister's friends. I quickly scan the crowd for my father and find him sitting quietly at the dining room table. As I limp over to my father, I spot several people in the crowd raising their cameras to their face getting ready to shoot a picture of me. Putting my good hand on his shoulder, in a burst of a cry I shout, "It's good to see you!"

Nodding his head, he begins to cry with relief. With my hand still comforting my father, I raise my head to look at the crowd. "It's OK if you counted me for dead."

Before I even finish the sentence, my living room is filled with sighs from my family and friends. Without one shutter clicking the cameras are lowered. With my body still engulfed in hypothermia, I say, "I need to take a warm bath. I need to bring my body up to operating temperature."

As I limp back to my bathroom I hear the voices chattering in the living room. "We need to take him to a hospital right now. He doesn't look good!"

Rocco enters the bathroom as I struggle to unzip my jacket. Wanting to help, he says, "Do you want me to lift you into the tub?"

In a tired, almost dead voice, I say, "No, I have too many broken bones. I know what hurts and how to move in order to keep the pain as minimal as possible."

"OK."

I ask, "Can you remove the doors from the shower so that I can get into the tub easier?"

After Rocco places the doors against the wall, Susan and my sister come in and begin trying to remove my clothes. As they tug on my tattered smelly garments, my broken bones howl in pain, and I hiss like a wild animal, "Don't touch me. Don't touch me!"

Denise quickly exits the bathroom while Susan asks, "How can I help you?"

"I have to do it myself. If you touch me you will hurt me."

With her eyes wide she says, "OK."

In a more conciliatory voice I say, "Susan, fill the tub up with lukewarm water. It cannot be hot. It must be lukewarm or it will burn my skin."

When I'm stripped down to my underwear, Susan and Denise stare at my emaciated body. I've lost over forty pounds in thirteen days, I learn later. With the tub full of lukewarm water, I slide into it, thinking of the celestial waters at the hot springs.

It's 11:00 p.m. As I lay submerged, someone bangs violently on the front door. Greg, my best friend, six-foot-five, 265 pounds, ex-military, opens the door. "Yes, can we help you?"

A reporter asks, "Can we get a statement?"

Holding the reporter at bay, Greg says, "Give me a minute and I'll get right back to you."

"Thanks."

Unknown to me, Denise, Rocco, and Greg exit the house and walk up to a podium. Denise makes a national public statement on behalf of the DeLeo camp.

The besieging media, still hungry for a survival story, remain in my front yard and all along the street, their blinding lights shining and their powerful noisy generators running. Even after this, a reporter hammers on the back door and asks to interview me. Denise sighs in anger as she answers the door, saying, "Please, it's midnight. We need to get some rest."

The reporter, wanting an exclusive, says, "I would like to talk with your brother Peter so that I can do a story."

Holding herself back, Denise says, "Not now, it's late!"

Embarrassed, the reporter says, "Oh, oh, OK, I'll contact you tomorrow."

Susan continues to drape warm wet towels over those parts of my skin that are exposed to the cool air. She changes the murky, slimy water five times during a 4½-hour bath. Feeling semi-thawed-out, I prepare for excruciating pain as I get out of the tub. Staying one step ahead of me, Rocco comes in and helps me out.

Draped in a towel I limp into my bedroom and slide in between clean fresh sheets. Treating me like a baby, being careful not to disturb my broken bones, Susan pulls the blankets gently up to my neck. Finally, after thirteen days of hell, I'm relaxing in my bed when Denise and Greg enter my bedroom. Denise announces, "You have to go to the hospital right now."

Knowing I have very little wiggle room, I utter, "I'm sleeping in my own warm bed tonight and into the late morning in comfort. Tomorrow at noon I will go to the hospital."

Before Denise has time to respond, Greg says, "That's good, get some rest. I'll come back tomorrow and give you a ride."

As I lie in bed, my feet and hands begin stinging and burning from the frostbite. Soon the pain escalates to a throb and I wonder how many of my fingers and toes will be amputated. Trying to increase the circulation, I continue my nightly ritual of survival reps, wiggling my toes and moving my fingers as I doze off in the security of my family and friends.

I'm in a light sleep alongside Susan, when suddenly I wake up to find my feet jammed into the bottom of the wooden bed frame like it's a fallen log preventing me from tumbling down the mountainside while dozing off during the arctic nights. Without realizing I'm in the safety of my house, I quickly sit up and begin doing the survival reps. I search the ceiling for stars while saying in a pumped-up adrenaline tone, "You sleep and you die!"

Jumping from under the bedcovers in shock, Susan says, "What's wrong? Are you OK?"

"Where's the sun? The sun? The stars?" At last, I realize where I am.

After letting my eyes adjust to the darkness, I lay my head back down on my pillow. I stare at the four confining walls of my bedroom, yearning for the open wilderness. Needing to make a connection with the outdoors, while remaining in bed I pull the blinds off my bedroom window with my right foot. Susan, disturbed by the clanging window blinds, says, "What are you doing?"

"I need to see the sun when it comes up."

Susan, unaware of my connection with the wilderness, sleepily responds, "OK."

While Susan dozes back to sleep, I stare out, waiting patiently for the minuscule change in the darkness that I've learned to sense and love. Although the change in the darkness arrives, the city still sleeps. Soon, the early morning birds begin chirping, relaxing me, comforting me, putting me to sleep.

After dozing off for a few hours I awake to chatter in my living room. Susan remains sleeping next to me while I listen to Denise say, "He has to go to the hospital now."

Rocco responds, "Let's wake him when Greg gets here."

Denise knocks at the door. "Are you sleeping?"

"No, come in."

As she enters the room Susan awakes. Denise asks, "Are you hungry?"

"Yes, but all I want to eat is Daddy's applesauce, OK?"

While I'm eating the applesauce and sipping some apple juice in the comfort of my warm bed with Susan lying beside me, the relentless media decide it's time for an interview. We hear knocks simultaneously at the front door and rear door. When Denise answers the front door, a representative from Connie Chung, anchor for the CBS news program *Eye to Eye,* hands her a large fruit basket while scribbling a contact name and number on a piece of paper ripped from a notepad. After setting the fruit basket down, Denise races to answer the repeated banging at the back door. Before she can say a word, an excited reporter asks, "Can we get an interview with your brother Peter?"

Playing it cool, Denise says, "He's still sleeping, but give me your name and what paper or what news station you're with and I will pass it on to him."

Shortly after that, Rocco comes in my room. "How do you feel?"

"I'm OK."

"I wish I could stay, but now that you're home, I have to return to Connecticut."

Wanting his company, I plead with him, "Stay for a couple of days. I'll be up and walking in two, maybe three days."

Smiling, he says, "Buddy, you need to take it easy for a long time. It's going to take probably three to four months' time to heal those injuries. Get used to the idea now. You're alive. Take the time you need to heal properly."

Stubbornly I respond, "I'll be up and walking about in a couple of days."

With a growling laugh I know so well, he says "Sure! Man, you look like you've been through a war. Wait until you get X-rayed. Then we will see how many broken bones you have."

"Well, I really don't want you to go. I know you're right. Hey, Rock, thanks, thanks for coming out here to search for us."

"No problem. I'll be back out when you get better. Then we can go rock climbing."

Rocco gives me a brotherly hug. We shake hands as I say, "OK, I'll see you later."

Thinking ahead, Denise phones the Community Hospital of Long Beach. "Shortly I will be bringing my brother to your ER room. There may be a media circus because he is the man who hiked out of the mountains yesterday after surviving a plane crash in the Sierra Nevada mountains two weeks ago. We're going to try to shake the media on our way to the hospital. Can you keep his presence at the hospital low-key?"

Meanwhile, the sheriff's helicopter flies back to the crash site to extract Lloyd from the wreck. Despite having a known Global Positioning System location, they are unable to find the downed Maule because of the heavily wooded terrain. After tiring from the search, the sheriff's department contacts Bill Woodward to help locate the wreck. Finally able to set the chopper down near the wreck site, the extraction team cuts the seat rails and some mangled metal before removing Lloyd's frozen body from the plane.

Greg, punctual as usual, walks in the back door at noon sharp to transport me to the hospital. Thinking we can avoid the media in the front yard, Greg helps me slip out the back door into his Suburban parked in the back alley. After making a series of quick lefts and rights, Greg says, "We're not being tailed." At the hospital, Denise, Susan, and Greg walk with me as I limp toward the ER, then stop abruptly. I see a news box with my photo plastered on the front page of the *Press-Telegram*. Greg puts in some coins and pulls out several copies. "Since no one has your story yet, let's see what they have to say."

PILOT SURVIVES 12 DAYS IN WILD

The pilot of the small plane missing for nearly two weeks on a flight from Long Beach to Lake Isabella walked out of a rugged mountainous area in Inyo County Friday afternoon, wounded but coherent, and then returned to the wilderness with a helicopter rescue team in a heroic but futile attempt to save his two passengers.

Peter DeLeo, 33, a Long Beach resident described by friends and relatives as a survivalist, walked nine days in the Sierra Nevada before emerging on the eastern slope. . . .

I weigh in at 115 pounds. The X rays and MRI reveal seven broken ribs on my right side, five separate breaks to the left ankle, four breaks to the right shoulder, a torn right rotator cuff, a torn anterior cruciate ligament in the right knee, frostbite, malnutrition, and deep lacerations over my entire body. After setting a walking cast on my left ankle and putting my right arm in a sling the doctor releases me, saying, "I don't think a hospital bed is going to help you. I think what you need is to be in your own bed near your family."

Expecting me to be hospitalized, Denise replies, "That's great. The guy was in a plane crash and has sixteen broken bones with serious frostbite, and you're sending him home?"

"If he didn't die by now, he's not going to."

In frustration Denise gives in, "All right, thanks, but this makes no sense."

Arriving back at the house, we're besieged by cameras and microphones as Greg and Susan help me limp up the back porch with my left ankle in a cast and my right arm in a sling. We go in the house without saying a single word to the media. They pound on the back and front doors, demanding a quote.

Denise, trying to appease them, answers the front door and is greeted by a representative from Diane Sawyer and Sam Donaldson, the co-anchors for the ABC News program *PrimeTime Live*. The representative hands Denise a large fruit basket, a large colorful flower arrangement, and a typed letter from ABC News.

As soon as Denise shuts the door, the banging starts again. Thinking that the *PrimeTime* representative forgot something, she opens the door. Now it's a representative for Katie Couric and Bryant Gumbel, the co-anchors of *Today*. Denise is weighted down with more fruit and flower baskets and another typed letter. "Katie and Bryant would like to request a live interview with your brother for Monday morning, December 12."

Taken by surprise, Denise responds, "Thank you for the fruit and flowers, but right now we're just trying to heal as a family. I'll give the letter to my brother."

Soon we have over ten jumbo-size fruit and flower baskets, enough fruit to last six months. I decide to keep only the ones sent by friends and family, and ask Denise and Rocco to give the rest to less fortunate families in Long Beach.

Unable to find peace in my own home because of the media steadily banging on the doors, both phone lines ringing nonstop, and people coming and going from my home as if it were a city bus terminal, I long to return to the serenity of the wilderness.

Greg's warmhearted wife, Linda, arrives with a pot roast with mashed potatoes and carrots. The colors and savory aroma nearly make me foam at the mouth. I want to tear into the food, but I say, "Linda, thanks so much! My stomach is still shrunken. I can only eat things like applesauce, oatmeal, pudding, and Jell-O, but please leave that food right here so I can nibble on it as my stomach expands."

With a happy laugh Linda says, "You're so welcome. I'll put it in the refrigerator and you can microwave it when you're ready to eat it."

At midday Sunday, I leave my warm bed, crawling on both knees and my left hand toward the bathroom, when I spot the Sunday edition of the *Los Angeles Times* and the *Long Beach Press-Telegram* spread across the living room coffee table. Craving a survival story, they both feature prominent articles on me.

That night the pain from my frostbitten feet and hands is too much for me to bear. I decide this time to go to Long Beach Memorial Hospital. Concerned that doctors in sunny southern California don't have much experience treating severe frostbite, before we leave I ask Susan to phone several hospitals near ski resorts for information on treatments. That way we'll be educated before we talk to the doctors at Memorial.

I'm taken in and re-X-rayed, then I meet a team of doctors who will monitor my progress daily at my house.

By Monday, December 12, my body's ability to move is gone. I now need help to move from my bed or the couch to the bathroom. Late that evening I'm lying on the couch watching TV with my father. He stops at one of our favorites, *The Tonight Show with Jay Leno*. I'm chuckling at his opening monologue when suddenly Leno begins telling my survival story, using me and it as a joke to knock Denny's restaurants. My father laughs, "Even Leno wanted a piece of you."

A long week has passed, and still five media trucks are parked in front of my house, one from each major news network. Cars continue to pull into my driveway daily, then someone knocks at the door. Hollywood and the literary world find their way to my small home, offering to purchase the film and book rights to my story. I refuse all interviews and deals as I mourn the loss of Wave and Lloyd.

After several failed attempts at getting my story, the TV tabloid *American Journal* calls on the tenth day. "We have to do a story on you. Give us the exclusive interview and we will make you a national hero. But if you don't give us the story, then we're going to destroy you."

Upset, Susan phones me to say, "*American Journal* just offered me $15,000 to do an interview, but I declined."

Still unable to get any rest at my house because of the media madness, I make plans to spend a relaxing night at Susan's house, but the plans go south when *American Journal* phones Susan's house again and leaves a message on her answering machine. "Susan, this is *American Journal*. It's very important that we talk to you. We will be airing our story on Peter DeLeo very soon, possibly tonight. It will be a negative story unless we have information. We need to talk to you."

That same night when Denise takes out the garbage, she finds the trash cans in the alley are dumped all over the ground. Someone has searched through their contents, paper by paper.

With the media hounding me, sadly and reluctantly I decide not to pay my last respects at Lloyd's and Wave's memorial services for fear that they will be turned into a disrespectful media frenzy. More than four hundred relatives and friends attend Lloyd's service. Denise attends both services accompanied by a media deflector, my attorney, Patrick Bailey.

Another round of large flower arrangements, jumbo fruit baskets, and large canned hams is sent to the house along with letters requesting interviews with all the big names in the media business. My face is still being flashed across the TV channels nightly. Reporters find people to interview who claim to be close friends of mine, but in truth they aren't even passing acquaintances.

Finally, at the end of the third week, the last of the media trucks leaves my neighborhood. Yet my neighbors phone me at 11:30 at night to warn me of a prowler who is peeking through my windows, looking inside my mailbox, walking up and down my driveway, and trying to get into my vehicles. Angered by the prowler's complete lack of respect for my home and privacy, Susan flicks on the outside floodlight as she quickly opens the front door. The journalist, David Roberts, surprised and scared, ducks behind my vehicles trying to stay out of sight, then starts crawling like a mouse down my driveway in the dark toward the street. Once beyond my property line he rises to his feet, then starts a stupid-looking guilty walk, acting like he was on the sidewalk the entire time. Susan yells at him, "What do you want?"

He stutters, "My name is David Roberts. I'm a writer for *Men's Journal.* You're Denise DeLeo, Peter's sister?"

Cutting Roberts off as he continues to babble on, "No, I'm not. What are you doing on this property? Get off or I will have you arrested!"

"I tried to call you but no one ever returns my call, so I flew out here."

In a stern voice Susan says, "That is no excuse for you to be looking in the windows of our home and trying to break into our vehicles. It's 11:30 at night, and people are trying to sleep. Plus you're trespassing!"

"Can I get an interview with Peter?"

Amazed at the man's audacity, Susan says, "I don't think so. You show no respect for anybody."

Hearing all the racket from my bedroom and unable to walk, I crawl out into the living room and say to Susan, "Come inside. Let him be."

Through all this time people from Long Beach and around the country send warm letters and colorful cards of support. Children of my friends and neighbors draw colorful pictures for me that I hang throughout my house.

I read warmhearted thoughts from my friends and from people I don't even know who are supporting me through this difficult time. Every time I read a card or letter, I cry from their sincerity.

Their loving thoughts and prayers help me weather the storm. Opposite is one of those moving letters, reprinted with permission from the writer.

Without ever talking to me or anyone I know, *American Journal* airs its story about me several times over the course of three months. And *Men's Journal* releases David Roberts's ten-page, tabloidlike article that claims to know my survival story. Throughout this three-month period, reporters from around the world continue to call.

It's clear to me now that I will never again enjoy my privacy until I agree to do an interview. The question now is when and with whom.

A producer from the ABC News television program *20/20* named Rob Wallace calls, asking whether I would consider doing an interview with Barbara Walters. Knowing *20/20* is one of the most respected news shows in the world, I tell Rob that I have declined all interviews to date, but that if I decide to do an interview, the correspondent must be willing to hike back into the Sierra Nevadas to retrace my journey. And we would have to rent a helicopter so that we can fly around the Sierras. Rob agrees and asks if he can stay in touch with me. He phones me regularly over the next few weeks, slowly building my trust. He suggests that Tom Jarriel be the correspondent because of his extensive experience and his award-winning stories from backcountry mountains and the third world.

By April 1995 my broken ribs feel mended, but I still have knifing pain from my torn ligaments, torn tendons, torn rotator cuff, and shattered left ankle when I walk and sleep. Still physically weak and limping, weighing 138 pounds, I return to the Sierra Nevadas with *20/20* for a five-day shoot (their story, "The Survivor," airs in April 1996).

Dear Mr. DeDeo

I know you are exausted after your ordeal and I hope this note isn't a bother to you. I am a nurse in the E.D. I wanted to talk with you but also wanted to respect your privacy so I'll express my thoughts through this note. (You can throw it out if you desire)

This morning as I was sitting in church I heard a very moving sermon about having passion for those who are lost. The reason this sermon was so moving to me was because my pastor told us of your story. With tears in his eyes, he spoke of the nobility of your actions. He told of your passion to rescue the others before you ate or received care. This illustration, your story, will forever be etched in my mind. Because, my story is one of the opposite. I, in the spiritual sense, was rescued, but for years have been content to sit and drink hot chocolate so to speak. Your story, this sermon, has been an awakening for me. Your actions are far reaching. More than you know.

You are in my prayers.

Sincerly
Cheri Aardema.

PS. My church is Rosewood Christian Reformed Church in Bellflower on Woodruff & Rose St. My pastor is Dan Brink. And I'm sure I can speak for him by saying, thanks for your life changing events. Please call either my self or Dan Brink if we can give back to you any part of what you have given us.

Nineteen
My New Path

As my thirty-fourth birthday approaches on January 22, 1995, I find myself questioning daily why I lived after the crash and Wave and Lloyd did not. I continue to play our flight over and over in my mind, asking, Could I have seen it coming? What could I have done differently? How do you make sense out of forty-nine- and fifty-seven-year-old men dying when they're in perfect health?

Wrestling with these confusing thoughts, I start thinking about cutting out all the things in my life that are dangerous. Before putting my motorcycles up for sale, though, I want to ride one of them one more time.

I call Brad Hazen, the friend with whom I was going to bike to Canada, at his mom's house in Santa Paula, California. I ask him to come over. My right arm is still in a sling while the four fractures to the right shoulder heal. Whenever I breathe deeply, my chest still explodes with pain from the seven broken ribs. The left ankle is still in a cast. At least the swelling in the right knee has decreased, and I'm now able to see clearly out of both eyes.

When Brad arrives, we limp out to the garage, then I ask him, "Help me get my street bike out of the garage and pointed down the driveway toward the street."

Laughing, he says, "What for?"

"I want to ride it, but I can't roll it. It's too heavy."

"OK, but why do you want to ride it?"

"I want to see if I still like riding bikes. If I don't, I'm going to sell all my bikes and give up riding."

"OK."

As Brad rolls the machine out of the garage, Denise pokes her head out of the back door. "You're not going to ride that, are you? You still have a cast on your left foot and your arm is in a sling. If the doctors find out that you were riding a motorcycle you will be in big trouble."

I say, "No, we're just letting it run to charge the battery and circulate the oil."

"Bullshit!" she cries, then slams the door.

After Brad helps me sit on the bike, I click it into gear. After hitting the main street with the 130 horses underneath me, I enter the freeway for one exit, cracking the throttle open, feeling the blasting power band, smiling all the way. But because the ride causes intense pain, I quickly return to the house. I'm now certain that my passion for bikes lives on.

At the end of January, the dark color in my frostbitten hands and feet begins to fade. The tissue will survive. The doctors inform me that I will need several corrective surgeries on my ankle, shoulder, and knee to function normally again, but first I need to gain weight and to allow my body to heal as much as it can before undergoing the knife.

At about this time I get some bad news about X-ALLOY's business and by July, I withdraw my interest and financial backing from the company. My other business, HyperSoft Integration Systems, continues to thrive but the workload is too much for me in my present condition, leaving my business affairs in a vulnerable state. With my days filled with physical rehab, I can support only HyperSoft's current clients, producing no new sales.

My once productive workdays now consist of eating breakfast, loosening my joints with a long hot shower, then exercising on a mountain bike. Then I stretch and do a short session of light

weight training, followed by another hot shower and sleep. After
the nap, I eat lunch, stretch again, bike, lift weights, then take yet
another hot shower, then back to sleep. After dinner, I walk, work
out, shower, and then taper off my regimen with laughter by
watching Jay Leno before crashing for the night.

In the summer, my broken bones now mended, I take a trip to
the desert with some old buddies to ride dirt bikes across the vast
terrain. Although I am forced to stop after only a short spurt of
riding because of the severe pain in my left ankle, right shoulder,
and right knee, I rate the trip a ten out of ten because I rekindled
the red-hot passion for desert riding I had felt before the plane
crash.

Several months later, I decide to test my ankle and knee on the
Sierra ski slopes. As I head north on Highway 395 to Mammoth
Mountain, I yearn to see Olancha Peak. As it comes into sight I
slow down in my truck and stare at the snow-covered chute I descended on the twelfth night of my journey. Soon comes the sign
"Ranch House Café 2 Miles Ahead." As I pass the café, I smile
and cheer, "Yeah, I lived! I made it."

I take the ski lift to the top of Mammoth. Alone on the chair
lift taking in the sight of the endless waves of snowcapped peaks,
I am suddenly overpowered by the fear of being trapped in the
freezing Sierra Nevadas. When the chair lets me off at the top, I
quickly make my way over to some other skiers and return
downhill. While driving my truck home, I'm attacked by another
wave of fear. If I crash and go off the mountain road, how long
will I be there freezing at the bottom of the canyon before someone finds me?

In March 1996 my ankle is cut open so the orthopedic surgeon
can screw together an unhealed hairline fracture. Then in May,
while I'm still in a cast, my right rotator cuff, tendons, and ligaments are repaired. In July the anterior cruciate ligament in my
right knee is replaced with a cadaver's Achilles tendon. In October
the metal hardware is removed from my left ankle.

In the midst of the surgeries and physical rehab, I fall behind in new software development, leaving me unable to support my existing client base, and HyperSoft folds.

After almost two years of physical rehab, and still mourning the losses of Wave and Lloyd, I decide a long trip will do me good. As the spring of 1996 approaches I discuss with Brad that trip across Canada and into Alaska on trail bikes, but we needed the Maule to make that trip. Since I am still healing from the frostbite, I lean toward warmer climates.

When I was going through the surgeries and rehab, I pinned two maps of the world on my wall, then dreamed about where I could go. Catching my interest were the untamed regions of Central and South America. I am challenged by the idea of riding a Baja motorcycle from the California/Mexico border to Panama and then south into Colombia. I'm eager to become strong, healthy, and whole.

In the early summer of 1996, I purchase a Honda XR600 dirt bike, the perfect Central and South American adventure machine. Every day I look in at my partner in the garage, which helps me stay focused on the upcoming trip.

On January 17, 1997, still limping from the knee surgery, I cross the border into Tecate, Mexico, with Brad Hazen and two other friends. On the fifth day of the trip, in a tiny Mexican village, I celebrate my thirty-sixth birthday. Since my friends have limited time to travel, and I am in no rush, we decide to split up, going our separate ways midafternoon on the tenth day. After several months of traveling through Central America, I reach the southern tip of Panama, the Darien Gap.

While high up in the Colombian Andes, alone on a desolate, snow-covered dirt road, I remember the star on my thirteen-day journey through the Sierras.

In a flash I understand what it meant. My mother had been with me. She saw what was happening and gave me a well of strength and hope spiritually. I was granted a chance to live, a slim chance. If I chose life, I would have to fight for it.

I am filled with a sense of clarity and a weight lifts from my shoulders. While sitting on my iron horse, viewing the surrounding Andes Mountains some twenty kilometers from the Ecuadorian border, I decide that when my South American adventure is over, I will return to the United States to write about my experience in the high Sierras.

Eighteen months later, I return to my roots in Connecticut, feeling blessed to be granted a fresh outlook on life. Using the minicassette recorder that Greg Hauser gave me on December 10, 1994, the day after hiking out of the wilderness, to record my journey, I begin playing the twenty hours of my recorded Sierra adventure for the first time.

As I begin writing the first chapter, I sense the Sierras calling me. With the completion of each page the unexplainable feeling to return to the mountains grows. Once I've written five chapters, it becomes clear that in order for me to lay my story before you, I must return to the Sierra Nevadas during the winter to retrace my journey, recapturing my thirteen-day ordeal.

I fill a winter pack with an eight-day supply of freeze-dried foods, hot chocolate mix, instant hot soup, two 35-mm cameras, tripod, an 8-mm movie camera, ten rolls of 35-mm slide film, six batteries for the movie camera, five extra batteries for the 35-mm cameras, a sleeping bag, a tent, one spare set of interior clothes wrapped in a waterproof sack, a nine-inch survival knife, a loaded pistol with eighteen extra rounds, snowshoes, sixteen ounces of fuel to start campfires, and other odds and ends, but no compass or map. My friends Glenn and Carmen Kerns take me by snowmobile thirty miles into the mountains and reluctantly drop me off at Blackrock Mountain. Using the same navigational techniques, I retrace my path, snapping off pictures as I snowshoe across the wilderness. At times I think aloud, sharing my feelings with the mountains and wondering if Lloyd and Wave can hear me, too.

Reaching the top of cloud-covered, windy Olancha Peak on the eighth day, I am saddened by the thought that my reunion with the mountains will be over the following day. At daybreak on the last day, I descend the east side of Olancha Peak onto the desert floor. I have conquered my fears. I have relived the harrowing trek out of the mountains. I have reminded myself that the human spirit is resilient even when faced with overwhelming obstacles. As I hike down the dirt road toward Highway 395, putting the snowcapped Sierras to my back, my old dream of flying a single-engine bush plane around the world begins to percolate.